T0184208

Bitext Alignment

Synthesis Lectures on Human Language Technologies

Editor
Graeme Hirst, *University of Toronto*

The series consists of 50- to 150-page monographs on topics relating to natural language processing, computational linguistics, information retrieval, and spoken language understanding. Emphasis is on important new techniques, on new applications, and on topics that combine two or more HLT subfields.

© Springer Nature Switzerland AG 2022
Reprint of original edition © Morgan & Claypool 2011

All rights reserved. No part of this publication may be reproduced, stored in a retrieval system, or transmitted in any form or by any means—electronic, mechanical, photocopy, recording, or any other except for brief quotations in printed reviews, without the prior permission of the publisher.

Bitext Alignment

Jörg Tiedemann

ISBN: 978-3-031-01014-9   paperback
ISBN: 978-3-031-02142-8   ebook

DOI 10.1007/978-3-031-02142-8

A Publication in the Springer series
SYNTHESIS LECTURES ON HUMAN LANGUAGE TECHNOLOGIES

Lecture #14
Series Editor: Graeme Hirst, *University of Toronto*
Series ISSN
Synthesis Lectures on Human Language Technologies
Print 1947-4040   Electronic 1947-4059

Bitext Alignment

Jörg Tiedemann
Uppsala University

SYNTHESIS LECTURES ON HUMAN LANGUAGE TECHNOLOGIES #14

ABSTRACT

This book provides an overview of various techniques for the alignment of bitexts. It describes general concepts and strategies that can be applied to map corresponding parts in parallel documents on various levels of granularity. Bitexts are valuable linguistic resources for many different research fields and practical applications. The most predominant application is machine translation, in particular, statistical machine translation. However, there are various other threads that can be followed which may be supported by the rich linguistic knowledge implicitly stored in parallel resources. Bitexts have been explored in lexicography, word sense disambiguation, terminology extraction, computer-aided language learning and translation studies to name just a few.

The book covers the essential tasks that have to be carried out when building parallel corpora starting from the collection of translated documents up to sub-sentential alignments. In particular, it describes various approaches to document alignment, sentence alignment, word alignment and tree structure alignment. It also includes a list of resources and a comprehensive review of the literature on alignment techniques.

KEYWORDS

alignment, bitexts, parallel corpora, sentence alignment, word alignment, tree alignment, statistical machine translation, transduction grammars, text mining, lexicon induction

Contents

Preface

Bitexts are valuable linguistic resources for cross-linguistic research and practical applications in natural language processing. The most predominant application is machine translation, in particular, statistical machine translation. However, there are various other threads that can be followed which may be supported by the rich linguistic knowledge implicitly stored in parallel resources. Bitexts have been explored in multilingual (and monolingual) lexicography, word sense disambiguation, terminology extraction, computer-aided language learning and translation studies to name just a few.

Central to the work with bitexts is the task of alignment – the process of linking corresponding parts with each other. The aim of this book is to provide a detailed review of common techniques and approaches to alignment at various segmentation levels. The book covers the essential tasks that have to be carried out when building parallel resources, starting from the collection of translated documents up to sub-sentential alignments. Traditional methods and recent developments will be presented including references to existing tools and resources.

The intended audience of this book includes graduate students and researchers in computer science, linguistics and computational linguistics. The presentation is rather self-contained and requires only a minimum of prior knowledge in probability theory and basic statistics. It might be helpful to be familiar with basic concepts in computational linguistics and computer science as well as machine learning approaches.

Enjoy!

Jörg Tiedemann
May 2011

Acknowledgments

This book would never have been possible without all the work carried out by my fellow researchers in the field of computational linguistics. I need to acknowledge all the scientific results and algorithms explained and presented in a large number of publications all around the world. I would also like to thank my reviewers for their constructive comments and many valuable suggestions. But especially thanks to my little family for all their patience with me and my long working hours, during evenings and weekends. Thanks, girls — Kajsa, Tove, and Therese!

Jörg Tiedemann
May 2011

CHAPTER 1

Introduction

Bitext and alignment are two concepts which are strongly connected with each other. The term **bitext** was originally coined by Harris [1988] in order to refer to documents along with their translations into other languages to be used in translation studies. Since then, bitexts have attracted a lot of interest in a larger community with many other applications in mind. Therefore, it is now common to let the term bitext refer to a wider range of parallel resources, not only original documents and their direct translations. Such resources may include various translations of a common source, sometimes even involving other intermediate languages that have been used to produce the final translations. Furthermore, two alternative translations into the same language from a common source may also be considered to be a bitext in this broader sense of the term. Figure 1.1 tries to illustrate such a setup.

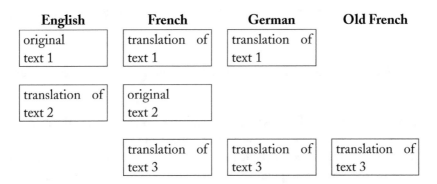

Figure 1.1: A parallel corpus consisting of several bitexts

An important characteristics of a bitext is the property that there is some kind of correspondence between the two texts coupled together, for example, translational equivalence. **Alignment** is the task of making this correspondence explicit, which makes it a central task in processing bitexts.

In computational linguistics, the term **parallel text** is often used synonymously with the term bitext. Unfortunately, this creates a confusion with the research on translation theory and terminology as already pointed out by Véronis [2000]. In translation studies, the term *parallel text* usually refers to a pair of text collections from the same *domain* but not necessarily including translations of the same documents. In computational linguistics, however, such corpora are usually referred to as (bilingual) **comparable corpora** instead [Rapp, 1995]. After several decades of research on bitexts in computational linguistics, the term **parallel corpus** has now been established to refer to collections of bitexts, and we will use this term in that sense throughout this book.

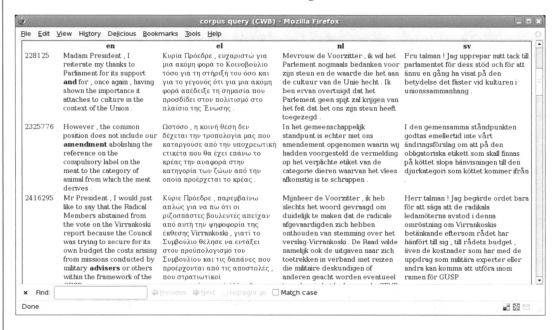

Figure 1.2: A multilingual corpus aligned at the sentence level. This example is taken from Europarl [Koehn, 2005] using the search interface of OPUS [Tiedemann, 2009a].

Figure 1.1 illustrates, in fact, a parallel corpus in that sense. It consists of several documents that can be coupled in various ways. The first task in creating parallel corpora is to establish alignments between documents which essentially creates bitexts that can be processed further. In Figure 1.1, the mapping is shown in terms of rows with corresponding documents where each pair of documents in a row is part of a document-aligned bitext. Note that we have a very liberal view on parallel corpora in the sense that they may include various types of correspondence relations (varying translation directions, alternative translations with unknown translation history coupled together, etc.) and that the corpus does not have to be complete in all parts. This is a very common scenario in some established parallel corpora, for example, in the well-known collection of proceedings from the European Parliament Europarl [Koehn, 2005] or the parallel corpora in OPUS [Tiedemann, 2009a]. To make a distinction with stricter settings we will call parallel corpora **translation corpora** if they only contain direct translations into one language coupled with the original source in another language from which they are translated from. Other properties can also be used to classify parallel corpora in the same way monolingual corpora are described. They can be domain-specific or balanced, static or dynamically growing. Essentially, the characteristics of the corpus will be up to the designer of the collection, and most corpora are created with some specific purpose in mind.

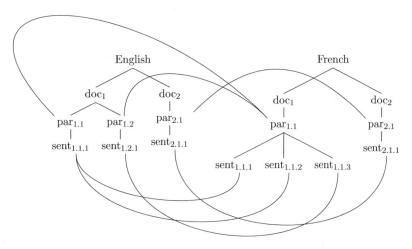

Figure 1.3: Hierarchical alignment on various levels of segmentation granularity.

Alignments between smaller textual units are necessary for many applications. Figure 1.3 illustrates, for example, the alignment of paragraphs and sentences within linked documents. Automatic alignment approaches for those tasks will be the focus of this book. It is a common strategy to run a top-down hierarchical refinement procedure starting with the alignment at a very coarse level of segmentation (for example documents) and then to proceed with alignments of more fine-grained segmentations. The main reason for this procedure is to reduce the search space for fine-grained alignment algorithms by restricting it to already aligned regions at some higher level. This is very effective if coarse-grained segmentation is straightforward and alignments at that level can be established with high reliability. More details about the interaction between segmentation and alignment will be discussed in Chapter 2. A strict top-down refinement strategy is, however, not required and in several cases, interactions between mappings on various levels can be used to improve the alignment. For example, in Chapter 4.2 we will discuss sentence alignment algorithms that make use of word-level mappings.

Note that Figure 1.3 illustrates alignments in terms of links that may refer to only partial relations in some cases. For example, the French sentence $sent_{1.1.2}$ partially corresponds to the English counterpart $sent_{1.1.1}$. The correspondence relation is complete when adding the link to the French sentence $sent_{1.1.1}$. Figure 1.4 illustrates how individual links can be mapped to aligned segments.

So far, we have only considered **monotonic alignments**. This corresponds to the original meaning of the term alignment (as it is also used in other fields such as signal processing and genetics) which can also be seen as the task of segmenting both sides of a bitext in such a way that the nth segment on one side corresponds to the nth segment on the other side of the bitext [Simard and Plamondon, 1996]. Therefore, alignment is also sometimes referred to as parallel segmentation or bisegmentation [García Varea et al., 2005, Wu, 2010]. While this is true for some types of alignment techniques in computational linguistics, the term of alignment has been used in a broader sense as well. Since

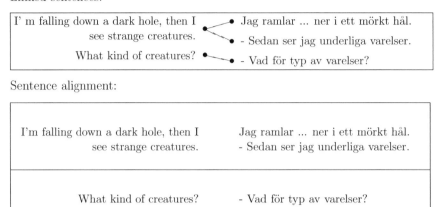

Linked sentences:

I' m falling down a dark hole, then I see strange creatures.	Jag ramlar ... ner i ett mörkt hål.
	- Sedan ser jag underliga varelser.
What kind of creatures?	- Vad för typ av varelser?

Sentence alignment:

| I'm falling down a dark hole, then I see strange creatures. | Jag ramlar ... ner i ett mörkt hål. - Sedan ser jag underliga varelser. |
| What kind of creatures? | - Vad för typ av varelser? |

Figure 1.4: A small aligned bitext of English and Swedish subtitles from the movie *Alice in Wonderland*.

the late eighties and especially since the work on statistical machine translation [Brown et al., 1988], the term alignment also refers to mappings with crossing links, for example, among words and phrases. This "misuse" of the original term is now so much established that we will not argue about it and simply include the possibility of crossing links in general which makes it possible to establish alignments between words as shown in Figure 1.5).

(a)
koffie •   • I
vind •   • like
ik •   • coffee
lekker •

(b)
ik ↔ I
vind lekker ↔ like
koffie ↔ coffee

Figure 1.5: Crossing links in word alignment and corresponding segment mappings for a Dutch-English sentence pair.

In defense of the term word alignment, we can think of a complex permutation operation that moves tokens around such that monotonic mappings can be established as shown in Figure 1.5 (b).

In the following, let us first have a look at some motivating examples to explain the use of parallel corpora in various fields and for various applications before defining basic concepts and terminology in Chapter 2. In Chapter 3, we will then discuss aspects of obtaining parallel data and how they need to be pre-processed. After that, in Chapter 4, we will focus on techniques for the alignment of sentences, and Chapter 5 describes essential word alignment techniques. In Chapter 6, we will consider other types of sub-sentential alignment emphasizing the alignment of hierarchical structures. Finally, we will conclude the book with some final remarks and an appendix with links to existing tools and resources.

1.1   APPLICATIONS

All bitext alignment approaches are driven by two questions:

1. *What are the assumptions we can make about the input?*
   For example, it is important to know how closely related the two bitext halves are that we try to align. Are the translations complete? Is A a (direct) translation of B, or are A and B translations of another text? Can we assume that all information is presented in the same order? How accurate is a translation and how much variation can we expect (due to translator's freedom or other reasons)? How, with what constraints and for which purpose was the bitext produced? Translation? Localization? Simplification? Are both versions meant for the same kind of audience?

2. *What is the purpose of the alignment?*
   What do we want to do with the aligned bitexts? What do we expect from the alignment quality? Who else could be interested using the (aligned) bitext?

Collecting bitexts and aligning them is not a well-defined task in itself but completely depends on the application one has in mind. Some applications require large amounts of possibly noisy parallel data[1] automatically aligned on a fine-grained level where others require precise mappings of well-structured data from a small sub-domain.

As we have said earlier, the first mentioning of the term bitext was in connection with translation studies. Obviously, for purposes of those investigations, a bitext has to be clean and well-defined (with known translation directions and other important meta information) and alignments need to be very accurate. However, the main application of parallel corpora today is data-driven machine translation. Especially, the intense research on statistical machine translation (SMT) has created a huge interest in automatic alignment techniques and many algorithms discussed here have their origins in this field. Furthermore, bitexts and alignment play an important role in other practical applications including computer-aided translation (CAT), lexicography (monolingual and bilingual), word-sense disambiguation, extraction of lexico-semantic information and computer-aided language learning (CALL). Figure 1.6 gives an overview over some typical application areas and their connections to bitexts and alignment.

More exotic applications include investigations on alternative translations of a common source. They have been used for applications such as detection of semantic similarity [Marsi and Krahmer, 2010] (which can be useful for paraphrase extraction, sentence fusion in summarization and textual entailment), censorship detection [Fernandez, 2003] or studies of language change [Dura and Gawronska, 2009].

---

[1]*Noisy* means here that there are substantial missing or incomplete parts on either side or weakly corresponding parts in the parallel data.

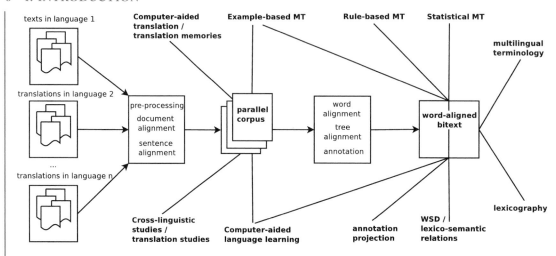

Figure 1.6: Application areas of aligned parallel corpora.

1.2   FURTHER READINGS

There are many publications of particular uses of parallel corpora in various application areas. Melamed [2001], Merkel [1999], Véronis [2000] consider a number of topics including lexicography, machine translation and terminology extraction. Many researchers have developed techniques for the automatic extraction of bilingual lexical information from parallel corpora. See, for example, [Ahrenberg et al., 1998, Melamed, 1996b, Smadja et al., 1996, Tufiş, 2002]. Macken et al. [2007] present the use of parallel corpora for supporting translators. The use of parallel corpora for the extraction of monolingual lexico-semantic information has also been shown in a number of publications. For example, Dagan [1991], Diab and Resnik [2002], Tufiş et al. [2004] show that translations are a valuable source for lexical disambiguation. Dyvik [2002] extracts WordNet-like relations, van der Plas and Tiedemann [2006] extract synonyms and Villada Moirón and Tiedemann [2006] identify idiomatic expressions using evidence from word aligned parallel corpora. Bannard and Callison-Burch [2005], Callison-Burch [2008] propose methods for finding monolingual paraphrases from parallel corpora. TransSearch [E. et al., 2000] is an example CAT tool that exploits bitexts.

The list of references could be continued, but we leave this section with this rather arbitrary selection of publications. Let us now look at some basic concepts and terminology before introducing specific alignment algorithms.

CHAPTER 2

Basic Concepts and Terminology

Several alignment techniques have been presented in numerous publications using a variety of notations and terminology. Bitext alignment at different levels of granularity is often treated and also described very differently. However, the general idea is always the same: Alignment aims at coupling corresponding segments together in a given bitext. The principal difference is the type of segments considered and how they are connected with each other in a global structure. Properties of alignments and how they can be found can of course vary substantially. Let us now look at some basic concepts in order to define a common terminology to discuss similarities and differences of alignment approaches on various levels.

2.1 BITEXT AND ALIGNMENT

A bitext $B = (B_{src}, B_{trg})$ is a pair of texts B_{src} and B_{trg} that correspond to each other in one way or another. Correspondence can, for example, be *translational equivalence* in the case of bilingual bitexts. Even though the indexes src and trg commonly refer to *source language* and *target language*, respectively, we usually do not require that one half of the bitext is the original source text and the other half is the target text that has been produced on the basis of that source text. However, it is often convenient to think of source and target texts when talking about bitexts. Correspondence between the texts is treated as a symmetric relation between both halves of a bitext.

A text can be seen as a sequence of **text elements** which together form a string. For bitexts, there are two such sequences, $B_{src} = (s_1, ..., s_N)$ and $B_{trg} = (t_1, .., t_M)$. It is sometimes convenient to add empty elements in order to allow *empty alignments* corresponding to deletions/insertions. **Bisegments** (sometimes called bitext segments) are aligned pairs of segments **p** and **r** that contain elements from the source and the target half of the bitext, respectively. We will use the following notation for bisegments: $(\mathbf{p}\|\mathbf{r}) = (s_{x_1}, .., s_{x_I})\|(t_{y_1}, .., t_{y_J})$ with $1 \leq x_i \leq N$ for all $i = 1..I$ and $1 \leq y_j \leq M$ for all $j = 1..J$. An **alignment** $\mathcal{A}$ is then the set of bisegments for the entire bitext.

In general, an alignment reflects the correspondences between bitext halves and should, therefore, be seen as a **symmetric relation** between segments. Ideally, there should be a bijective correspondence relation, meaning that there is a one-to-one mapping between all segments in B_{src} and B_{trg}. However, this is in most cases not achievable, and the general aim is to find a partial bijective map allowing some segments unaligned. In any case, an alignment always refers to the entire structure and not to individual items linked together. It is common to abuse the term alignment to refer to non-one-to-one mappings between text elements from the source and the target. In this way, an alignment is described by **links** between individual elements that may refer to partial correspondence relations between them. In order to make this distinction, we also define the set of **bitext links** $\mathcal{L} = l_1, .., l_K$ which describe such mappings between elements s_x and s_y: $l_k = (x, y)$ with $1 \le x \le N$ and $1 \le y \le M$ for all $k = 1..K$. The set of links can also be referred to as a **bitext map** that aligns bitext positions with each other. Such a bitext map can then be used to induce an alignment $\mathcal{A}$ in the original sense as described above which contains bisegments composed of linked elements. Look at the example in Figure 2.1.

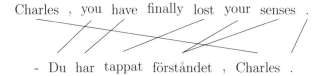

Figure 2.1: Word alignment represented as links between individual tokens. The example is again taken from the subtitles of the movie *Alice in Wonderland*.

Extracting bisegments from this bitext map can be seen as the task of merging text elements in such a way that the resulting segments can be mapped one-to-one without violating any connection. In this sense, the final alignment is guided (or constrained) by the existing links that have been established between tokens in the bitext. This is a common strategy in various alignment approaches. The reader should be warned that the majority of the literature treats the procedure of linking text elements as the essential alignment process. Bisegmentations are not always explicitly produced. However, in many cases the mapping between link structures and bisegments is quite straightforward. Alignment types are therefore often described as possible many-to-many mappings referring to the number of basic text elements included in the coupled segments. For example, the bisegment (your senses)‖(förståndet) in Figure 2.1 would be classified as a two-to-one alignment. This is essentially the same for the example of sentence alignment in Figure 1.4 in Chapter 1 in which the first bisegment consists of one source sentence and two target sentences. The basic difference here is that a text element now refers to the entire sentence instead of individual word tokens.

Considering the difference between bisegments and link structures leads to two general approaches to automatic alignment:

Text linking: Find all connections between text elements from the source and the target text according to some constraints and conditions which together describe the correspondence relation of the two texts. The link structure is called a bitext map and may be used to extract bisegments.

Bisegmentation: Find source and target text segmentations such that there is a one-to-one mapping between corresponding segments.

In both cases, segmentation plays a crucial role as we will discuss in the next section. Both approaches depend on the definition of a text element as the basic unit that may appear in alignable segments and how they can be properly identified. Bisegmentation explicitly leads to two additional monolingual segmentations whereas text linking strategies do this implicitly.

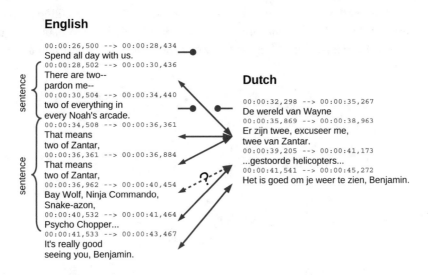

Figure 2.2: Sentence (fragment) alignment for movie subtitles (taken from "Waynes world" in English and Dutch which is part of the multilingual subtitle corpus in OPUS [Tiedemann, 2007]).

2.2   ALIGNMENT AND SEGMENTATION

The type of segmentation of a text into basic text elements determines the type of alignment that can be established. In the examples given so far, we have already seen different kinds of segmentations, for example, a division into sentences (**sentence boundary detection**) and a division into word tokens (**tokenization**). Many other types are possible, for instance, paragraphs, N-grams, syntactic constituents, morphemes or characters. Depending on this segmentation we will talk about document alignment (base elements=documents), sentence alignment (base elements=sentences), word alignment (base elements=words) and so forth.

The importance of segmentation is often ignored in the literature on text alignment. However, it plays a crucial role in the success of the algorithm. Consider, for example, the bitext in Figure 2.2. Several important segmentation decisions have to be made before running any alignment algorithm on such example texts. For example, one has to decide whether to consider sentence fragments shown within a time frame or whether to extract proper sentences as much as this is possible. For the latter, we need to support sentences to run over several adjacent time frames which creates difficult alignment problems as depicted in Figure 2.2. Certain parts have been left out, merged or split in the corresponding translation which makes it difficult to find a proper match. In this example, it seems to be wiser to stick to time frames which give an alignment algorithm more freedom when deciding what to align. However, many other time frames contain more than one sentence, or even running sentences from previous time frames may stop in the middle of a time frame and a new one starts immediately thereafter. A segmentation based on time frames is doomed to stick to that division and cannot handle cases where this does not match with corresponding segments in the target text. Furthermore, a division into time frames most certainly leads to many bisegments that do not form proper sentences. Depending on the application, this might be a serious problem.

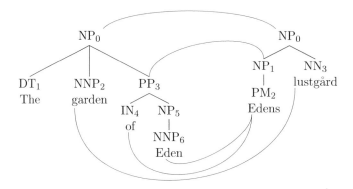

Figure   2.3: Example   tree   alignment   from   the   parallel   treebank   SMULTRON [Gustafson-Čapková et al., 2007] (taken from Sophie's World, English-Swedish).

Another important influence on the alignment algorithm comes from the structural relations between segments. In the cases we have discussed so far, we assumed simple **flat segmentations**. The main property of such segmentation schemes is that all segments are disjoint, meaning that they do not overlap in any way. Another restriction that is common is to consider contiguous segments only. Together with the requirement of disjoint segments, this gives us the typical setup of, for example, sentence alignment which deals with flat contiguous units only. However, segments to be aligned may be related in hierarchical structures which turns the alignment problem into a **tree alignment** problem. Figure 2.3 illustrates an example for a tree alignment of syntactic constituents.

It is common to consider nested structures only, and, in fact, hierarchical refinement approaches to alignment can be seen as an instance of tree alignment because of the nested structure of segmentation levels (see Figure 2.4 and Figure 1.3 in Chapter 1).
Note that structural dependencies between alignable segments can either be given or can be created as a bi-product of the alignment process. Approaching alignment in terms of a bisegmentation problem, we can constrain the algorithm to consider certain types of segmentations only. This is usually necessary to restrict the search space as we will discuss later, and these constraints determine the type of alignment that can be produced. For example, we may require bisegments to be contiguous and compositional in order to allow arbitrary nested tree structures as the ones illustrated above. Further restrictions may apply to reduce the search space even more. We may also require segments to be disjoint but allow discontinuous elements to obtain flat alignments like the ones shown in 1.5 in Chapter 1 which includes the discontinuous segment "vind ... lekker". Another common constraint for flat alignments is to focus on the smallest possible alignable units. Taking the example from

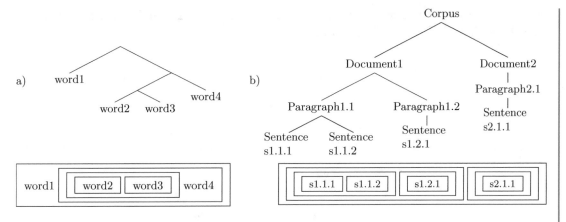

Figure 2.4: Nested segmentations and their tree representations.

Figure 2.1, we would, in that case, prefer the bisegments (you)‖(Du) and (have)‖(har) over the larger bisegment (you have)‖(Du har).

To sum up this general discussion, proper segmentation is essential for the performance of automatic alignment processes, and segmentation decisions determine the type of alignment that can be produced.

2.3   ALIGNMENT SPACES AND CONSTRAINTS

So far we were concerned with the definition of the concept *alignment* as the final result of an alignment process. It is now important to discuss issues that are related to automatic alignment algorithms. An alignment program basically takes a bitext as its input, which needs to be segmented in one way or another as discussed above. The output will be a bitext map in terms of links between individual text elements (for example, word tokens) or a bisegmentation or both. The task of the algorithm is to optimize this mapping according to some correspondence function. Internally, this is often implemented as the search for an alignment with a minimal overall alignment cost measured by some designated cost function $Cost(\mathcal{A})$. For the optimization procedure, we need to define the **search space** that includes all possible alignment alternatives, and we also need to instruct the program how to search through this space.

Usually an unrestricted alignment search space is huge and restrictions need to be applied. Let us take, as an example, the search space of aligning individual tokens in a word alignment task. This space can be visualized as a two-dimensional matrix having the source text on one axis and the target text on the other. Marked positions in the matrix correspond to *activated* links (see Figure 2.5). As the bitext map refers to the entire alignment structure, this leads to a total of 2^{n*m} possible mappings assuming that we have n tokens on the source side and m tokens on the target side. It is clear that it will not be feasible to search such dimensions in an exhaustive brute-force manner even for reasonably small bitexts. Note that in this example we already include the restriction that we only consider an already aligned sentence pair.

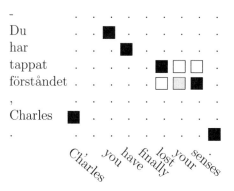

Figure 2.5: A word alignment matrix for the example sentence from *Alice in Wonderland*. Filled boxes can be interpreted as *sure* links whereas empty boxes can be seen as *fuzzy* or *possible* links.

The following two questions have to be addressed in this setup:

1. How do we compute appropriate costs for alignment hypotheses in a given bitext?

2. How can we perform an efficient search through the alignment space?

These questions are basically answered by the **alignment model** that is chosen for a particular task. Alignment costs are often derived from distributional features, correlations and interactions between individual links. Alignment spaces are usually restricted in various ways using **alignment constraints** (see below). Additional search bias and greedy local decisions can be introduced to make the alignment search more efficient.

Alignment constraints can effectively be used to reduce the alignment space substantially. [Wu, 2010] lists several common constraints that have been applied in a large variety of alignment algorithms:

Bijectivity constraint: Restricting an alignment to one-to-one mappings substantially reduces the size of the alignment space. In this space, each text element may appear in at most one link. Cherry and Lin [2006a] call the space created by such a constraint the **permutation space** as the number of possible alignments is reduced to $\min(n, m)!$ candidates (ignoring NULL links). This one-to-one constraint is actually often used in word alignment even though bijectivity is usually not possible on that level (at least not for a complete mapping). Algorithms that make use of one-to-one constraints are, for example, competitive linking [Melamed, 2000] and weighted bipartite matching [Taskar et al., 2005]. The black boxes in Figure 2.5 illustrate such a partial one-to-one alignment whereas the empty and the gray boxes are not possible in permutation space. It is easy to see that any one-to-one alignment for a bitext with non-identical number of elements ($n \neq m$) will be partial (and, therefore, not strictly bijective). It is possible to introduce artificial *empty* units (usually called NULL) to make the mapping complete. This is necessary for some alignment algorithms in which complete mappings are required.

Functional constraint: In this setting, it is required that every source element is linked to *exactly one* target element. The binary relation expressed by the alignment becomes a **partial function** (also called right-unique) that allows many-to-one mappings (several source elements can be linked to the same target element) but not one-to-many (one source element cannot be mapped to more than one target element). Naturally, this constraint leads to asymmetric models in which alignment direction is important. Looking at Figure 2.5, the black boxes together with the gray box can be described by such an alignment function (which is not bijective due to the two-to-one mapping between "your senses" and "förståndet"). However, the additional empty boxes cannot be explained by such a model. The functional constraint is often combined with a requirement to be **left-total** to force the model to assign links to every source element. Adding special NULL tokens on the target side is then again a solution to allow unaligned elements. The alignment space is still of the order of the permutation space as above and alignments can conveniently be described as a mapping function $a : n \rightarrow m$ that maps positions in the source text to positions in the target text. Prototypical models that apply such a functional constraint are the IBM word alignment models [Brown et al., 1993], which will be discussed in Chapter 5.

Monotonicity constraint: Another common constraint is the restriction to non-crossing links. In other words, linked elements appear in the same order in both halves of the bitext. This constraint is usually enforced for paragraph and sentence alignment (see Figure 1.4) and also reduces the search space substantially (pushing alignments to the region around the diagonal of the alignment space). Monotonicity can also be used as a soft constraint, meaning that the model includes a preference for monotonic alignments but does not enforce them. For example, some word alignment algorithms implement a strong preference for monotone alignments but still allow some **distortion**.

Segmentation constraints: The size of the alignment space also depends very much on the segmentations on both sides as we have discussed earlier. Common restrictions are disjoint segmentations for flat alignment or nested segmentations for hierarchical alignments. Essentially, any segmentation performed before an alignment constrains the search space as we have discussed in section 2.2.

Segment size constraints: Another possible restriction is to limit the size of many-to-many mappings. For example, in sentence alignment, it is common to define a number of possible mappings with a specific maximum size for each segment to be mapped. Together with monotonicity, this type of constraint enables the use of efficient dynamic programming solutions to perform an exhaustive search in the alignment space.

Anchor constraints: Certain alignment points are known and can be considered to be hard constraints for the search algorithm. Anchor points can be either already aligned segments or aligned segment boundaries. Most alignment algorithms use at least the origin and the end of the bitext as anchor points assuming that both bitext halves completely correspond to each other. Further anchor points can be inferred by various methods, for example, from the bitext structure or previous alignments on coarser segments. It is also possible to use anchor point candidates as soft constraints biasing the alignment algorithm in certain search directions.

Syntactic constraints: Modeling aligned bitexts as the result of a generative process makes it possible to enforce additional constraints on the alignment space. For example, alignments have to meet the generative capacity of the underlying grammar formalism when certain types of transduction grammars are used. We will discuss examples in Chapter 6.2.

Distortion limits: It is also possible to restrict the distortion of aligned elements, i.e., the maximum distance of aligned elements with respect to their positions within each bitext half.

Constraints can be seen as prior knowledge that biases the alignment search according to the known properties of the bitext and its implicit correspondence structure. The purpose of implying constraints is twofold: (i) Alignment quality can be improved; otherwise, it may suffer from insufficient cues and correlations. (ii) Efficiency can greatly be improved by reducing the alignment space.

Naturally, several constraints can be combined in order to optimize an alignment algorithm. For example, anchor constraints are often combined with monotonicity constraints which allow dividing the alignment space into smaller sub-regions defining independent sub-problems. Figure 2.6 illustrates a case where anchor constraints are marked in bitext space according to corresponding paragraph boundaries (top left figure). Assuming monotonic one-to-one mappings between paragraphs, we can now divide the alignment space into smaller regions between adjacent anchor points (right-top figure). Sentence alignment within these regions can then efficiently be performed and may then produce a mapping such as depicted in the lower-left part of Figure 2.6. Note that we now have one two-to-one alignment between sentence $s5$ on the source side and sentences $s5$, $s6$ on the target side. Committing ourselves to these mappings, we can then reduce the search space for subsequent word alignments to the regions of aligned sentences (see the illustration at the bottom-right of Figure 2.6). This **hierarchical iterative refinement strategy** is very common in bitext alignment approaches that try to map segments on various levels of granularity. It can be seen as an instance of a *divide and conquer* strategy in which complex problems are solved by a multi-branched recursion algorithm. However, in our case sub-problems may require different models and algorithms than their ancestors. Many alignment strategies actually require a coarse-grained mapping of corresponding segments in order to compute appropriate statistics and to extract alignment features necessary for the link operations on a lower level (see, for example, statistical word alignment described in Chapter 5.1). Note that monotonicity is not a requirement for this refinement approach.

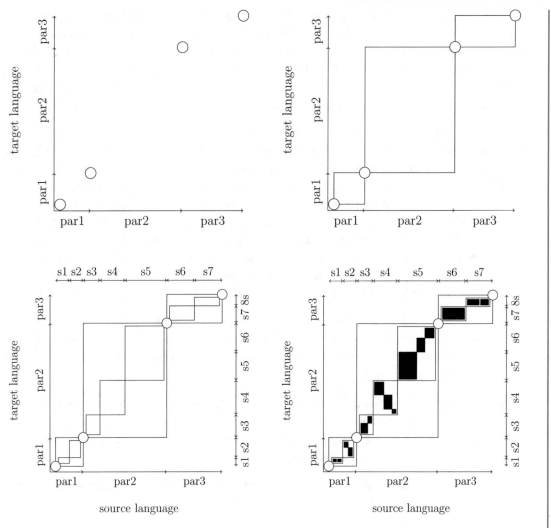

Figure 2.6: Iterative refinement of bitext alignments on various levels of granularity: use paragraph boundaries as anchor points and aligned sentences as word alignment sub-space.

2.4   CORRELATIONS AND CUES

In order to align automatically, it is necessary to discover correlations and cues that explain the correspondence between segments from the bitext. Various types of information can be explored, including pre-defined cues, recurrent patterns, linguistic similarities, and distributional features. Some of them require external resources or training data, and all of them are based on certain conditions and assumptions. In general, alignment cues are easier to discover for coarse-grained segmentations than for more fine-grained ones. Mappings between larger segments such as documents and paragraphs are often rather obvious whereas mappings between words and phrases are much more debatable (and often not possible at all). This is another argument for the hierarchical refinement strategies, as explained in the previous section, as they simplify the complex alignment task on lower levels. The largest difference between alignment approaches can be seen in the correlation features they employ and how they are discovered. Common cues used in various algorithms are, for example:

Lexical cues: Segments that contain pairs of lexical items which are known to be equivalents are more likely to correspond to each other than segments without them. Lexical knowledge can be taken from external resources (for example, bilingual lexicons) or can be discovered using distributional extraction techniques. Especially in the latter case, it is advisable to attach weights to these items according to the strength of their association. A special kind of lexical cue is the so-called *cognate* match. In related languages that share large portions of their alphabets, it is possible to find candidates for lexical matches by measuring string similarities between text elements. This is not only useful to identify candidates of etymologically related words (for example, the German/Swedish "Regierung" – "regering") but also to match named entities ("GNU/Linux" – "GNU-Linux") or numerical values ("20 000,00" – "20,000.00").

Segment length: In many cases there is a strong correlation between the lengths of corresponding segments especially for coarse-grained segmentations such as paragraphs and sentences. Length can be measured in various ways using tokens, characters or bytes or any other type of fine-grained segmentation.

Position: The relative position difference of text elements is often used as a strong cue assuming that most correspondences are to be found close to the diagonal of the bitext space. This is especially true for monotonic alignments but also useful for other types of alignments in which a certain amount of distortion is allowed.

Distributional cues: Corresponding items are assumed to have similar distributions within a bitext. Statistics are often used to measure distributional similarity.

Linguistic features: Alignment cues can be derived from linguistic similarities. For example, morphological features can be used to identify matches between lexical items, or syntactic similarities can be used to map constituents from a pair of analyzed sentences. Syntactic constraints can also be part of a generative alignment model.

Contextual cues: Contextual relations are very important for the identification of correspondence relations. Information from the context on both sides needs to be considered for a proper mapping between individual text elements. Links also strongly depend on each other, and any prediction has to be seen in connection with the entire alignment structure.

Formatting cues: Alignment can also be guided by stylistic information. Many documents include a rich set of markup and layout information that can be used for matching corresponding points. Typical examples are headers, paragraph boundaries, lists, tables and figures. Even information such as font styles and other minor stylistic features can be useful to improve bitext mappings.

Of course, the strength of an algorithm lies in the combination of various cues and the search algorithm that is used to find the optimal segment mapping. Lexical cues, for example, produce a lot of false hits (especially ambiguous and uncertain ones) and need to be combined with other ones such as positional distance and cues from the contextual surroundings. Many cues are language specific even though algorithms that employ those features are often claimed to be language independent. Some of them are more universal (like sentence length correlations) but often depend on the genre and style of the material to be aligned (see for example Figure 2.2). Negative cues are also possible that can help to prevent erroneous links.

Furthermore, alignment algorithms make often use of the interaction between links on higher levels and on lower levels, not only in the manner of a strict hierarchical refinement strategy. For example, document alignment algorithms make heavy use of lexical mappings [Enright and Kondrak, 2007, Patry and Langlais, 2005, Resnik and Smith, 2003]. In Chapter 4.2 we will also see sentence alignment algorithms that apply lexical matching techniques in iterative steps such that alignments on higher and on lower levels influence each other in circles.

2.5   ALIGNMENT MODELS AND SEARCH ALGORITHMS

The dominant approaches to alignment are based on statistical models. They can, in general, be divided into discriminative and generative models. Discriminative models can be seen as *task-oriented* models in which the actual prediction of the target (in this case alignment) is emphasized. In generative settings the general idea is to explain the set of observations (here the bitext) with the help of some underlying generating model. The prediction of targets (here alignments) is more like a bi-product of applying such a model to a specific data set.

DISCRIMINATIVE ALIGNMENT MODELS

Discriminative models try to predict a target y given observable information x. In a stochastic framework, this is done by modeling the conditional probability distribution $P(y|x)$ which is usually learned from labeled training data. For alignment, one can model the target y to be the set of links describing the bitext map, and x is information derived from the bitext. Discriminative models often use a feature-based representation of the observed data. Selecting an appropriate representation of the data is called **feature engineering** and is often the most crucial step that influences prediction performance.

Alignment is a typical structured prediction task. Links often highly depend on each other and interact with contextual features and other link decisions. The capability of dealing with local predictions in their global context is a crucial factor that determines the success of a discriminative aligner. The great advantage of discriminative models is the possibility to employ a rich feature set without making the training procedure intractable. Discriminative models do not need to model the distribution of observable data and can express more complex relationships between target and observations without the need of explaining all dependencies in the data. The disadvantage is that discriminative models usually require labeled training data and that their performance may suffer badly from data sparsity especially due to the structured nature of the prediction tasks.

GENERATIVE ALIGNMENT MODELS

Alignment can be modeled using a *generative story*. In generative models, observable data is generated from an underlying structure. For generative models, a **hidden alignment** between bitext segments is part of that structure. The task is to discover this hidden structure in order to fully explain the generative process. We can distinguish two types of generative alignment models: asymmetric and symmetric models. Asymmetric models try to explain the generation of observable (emitted) data on one side of the bitext from the corresponding parts of the other side of the bitext. Correspondence is captured by the alignment model which is not observable. Symmetric alignment models try to explain the generation of both parts of the bitext from an underlying hidden structure that includes the alignment model for linking bitext segments.

The difference between discriminative and generative frameworks is that the latter fully describe the joint probability distribution including both target and observable data. This complete model is explained by a generative process that can be factorized according to various steps, each of them only depending on the generation history. In this way, the likelihood of observed data can be used as a training criterion which enables unsupervised learning strategies (learning with incomplete data). The disadvantage is, however, that a generative model requires a proper description of all observable variables with all their interdependencies, which are usually very complex in the case of natural languages. Therefore, it is often necessary to make a lot of compromises between reality and model complexity when defining the generative story. Model parameters are then restricted to the ones that fit the underlying generative process and its factorization. This often leads to very strong independence assumptions and limits such models to a few local features.

Conceptually, both types of generative alignment models (symmetric and asymmetric) may be plausible. In translation, one may think of a generative process that produces a translation from a given source language text. This task is usually split into several (but related) subtasks of translating text fragments (for example sentences, phrases, words) which corresponds to an asymmetric alignment model connecting bitext segments. Another possibility is to think of an underlying conceptual layer that generates both versions of the text, the original source text and the translated target language text. This idea is related to the classical interlingual approaches to machine translation that assume the existence of an abstract meaning representation from which any other language can be generated. In such a symmetric model, both texts are generated independently given the common meaning representation. Alignment is then established through the relations of each bitext half to the hidden interlingual structure.

Asymmetric alignment models often do not make much sense, considering the fact that the original translation direction of the bitext is usually ignored when aligning parallel data. In many cases, the source language is unknown or not even included, for example, when aligning two translations of a common source with each other. However, asymmetric alignment models have some interesting properties that makes them very efficient due to the constraints of the generative story as we will see, for example, in the word alignment models discussed in Chapter 5.1. Nevertheless, this leads to some restriction of their expressive power, and we will describe several possibilities to reduce the negative effects of this asymmetry on alignment quality in Chapter 5.2.

OTHER ALIGNMENT MODELS

There are other approaches to alignment that do not rely on explicit statistical alignment models. Some techniques are based on pattern matching, for example, using string difference measures for alignment decisions. Other techniques are based on co-occurrence measures, significance testing and greedy link strategies using score thresholds. The latter are often used for lexical extraction tasks rather than (complete) bitext alignment. Another term for such an extraction is **translation spotting**, coined by Véronis and Langlais [2000]. Approaches to mining parallel sentences from comparable corpora also fall into this category (see Chapter 3.3). In this book, we will focus on statistical alignment models designed for complete bitext alignment. However, most lexicon extraction techniques are immediately useful for statistical word alignment as we will see in the discussion on feature functions for discriminative alignment models in Chapter 5.3. Some other pattern-based approaches are discussed in Chapter 5.4.

SEARCH ALGORITHMS

Essentially, all alignment approaches are implemented as some kind of search algorithms trying to optimize the mapping between segments according to the underlying model and its cost function (or link likelihood model). Independent of the model type (generative or discriminative), the actual alignment algorithm has to consider alternative hypotheses within the alignment space from which it has to select the most promising one. Previously, we have discussed how to define and restrict the hypothesis space and how to define features to guide the alignment program. Now, we also need to say a few words about the actual search algorithm that can be employed. Naturally, the type of search that can be performed highly depends on the underlying model and the size of the hypothesis space. However, some general strategies can be mentioned here.

Dynamic programming: Exhaustive search using dynamic programming can be used if the global decisions can be divided into overlapping reusable subproblems that can be solved locally. This usually implies that strong independence assumptions have to be made and subproblems need to be easily solvable in order to allow efficient computing. Strong alignment space constraints (such as monotonicity and segment length restrictions) are necessary to allow reasonable time complexities. Various well-known instances of dynamic programming exist (for example, the *Viterbi algorithm*) depending on the data structure and the underlying model employed.

Global dynamic programming solutions can often be approximated using more efficient (but suboptimal) beam search strategies.

Greedy best-first: A very efficient heuristic search strategy is greedy optimization. In this strategy, an algorithm selects greedily the best local choice and continues iteratively with the remaining decisions. Together with strong alignment space constraints (for example, the one-to-one mapping constraint), greedy best-first strategies can find a solution in less than quadratic time even with naive implementations. However, greedy search is a heuristic strategy that does not guarantee finding the best global solution. It can still perform quite well especially due to the fact that starting with the most reliable data point provides some security.

Beam search: Another popular search heuristics is based on beam search. In this type of search strategy, a pre-defined number of partial hypotheses is stored in a *beam* and the algorithm expands them iteratively keeping only the best N candidates at each step. Similar to greedy search and dynamic programming we base solutions on incrementally collected local decisions but compared to greedy search we keep a number of alternatives alive to improve the chance of finding the global solution by not committing to just one track.

Backtracking: Search algorithms can also allow backtracking strategies in which incrementally created candidates are abandoned if they cannot possibly solve the given problem or if there is good reason that they will lead to suboptimal solutions. Backtracking is especially useful in constrained optimization problems.

Iterative alignment refinement: Another idea is to divide the alignment process into several steps.[1] The basic principle is to perform an initial alignment of reliable and easy to detect data points based on a simple model and then to adjust the current model iteratively using the knowledge from the previous step. This may be used to reduce the alignment space to make the search more efficient. An example for alignment space reduction is the application of simple greedy search heuristics in which reliable alignments are established first using an initial alignment model and in the following step a new model is computed for the remaining items (assuming that the links from before are fixed and accurate).

Iterative model refinement: Iterative strategies can also be used to move from simple alignment models to more complex ones. In this way, we may find more reliable parameters in complex hypotheses spaces. For example, the IBM models for word alignment (see Chapter 5) follow this strategy starting with simple alignment models first and then moving to more complex ones in order to guide the parameter optimization by previous results.

---

[1] Note that this is not the same as the hierarchical iterative alignment procedure discussed in section 2.2 which refers to alignment steps at different levels of granularity. However, the hierarchical procedure can be seen as a special instance of the general iterative refinement strategy.

2.6   EVALUATION OF BITEXT ALIGNMENT

Quantitative evaluation of alignment is tricky. There are two reasons for this. First of all, alignment concerns an entire structure and it is not always obvious how to divide it into smaller parts that can be evaluated individually. Secondly, alignment in terms of bisegmentation combines two tasks, a proper segmentation into alignable units and the proper mapping of those units to corresponding ones. Additionally, the possibility of empty links, i.e., unaligned elements, complicates quantitative analyses. On the other hand, alignment evaluation is easier than, for example, the evaluation of machine translation. It is in principle possible to define a gold standard for a specific alignment task even though annotator agreements might still be low for fine-grained alignments such as word-level alignments. However, there are several questions that have to be answered:

- What kind of mapping errors are more severe than others?

- Do we require full alignment or high-precision but partial alignment?

- How do we measure mappings which are partially correct/incorrect?

- Does the algorithm have to explicitly mark deletions and insertions, and how do we count elements with no correspondence?

- How do we measure questionable mappings that have been marked as such in the gold standard (for example those marked as *fuzzy links*)

There are no simple answers to any of these questions. In the end, evaluation depends a lot on the applications for which the alignment will be done. The most trusted evaluation is often an extrinsic one, i.e., measuring the performance of an application which is based on the alignment of a bitext (for example, the performance of a statistical machine translation model). This is true because alignment is often just an intermediate step in a larger training procedure. The overall end-to-end performance in that case is more important than the performance of individual sub-tasks.

However, this is not always the case, and alignment quality as such can be interesting because aligned bitexts are often useful for various applications. For intrinsic alignment evaluation, it is now common to concentrate on the evaluation of individual links in a bitext map using measures derived from information retrieval: **precision** and **recall**. Assuming that we have a **gold standard** of links L_{gold}, we can measure precision and recall for a set of proposed links L:

$$Precision = \frac{|L \cap L_{gold}|}{|L|}$$

$$Recall = \frac{|L \cap L_{gold}|}{|L_{gold}|}$$

Both values can be combined with the so-called F-measure (weighted by β or balanced between recall and precision by setting $\beta = 1$) or, alternatively, the alignment error rate (AER):

$$F_\beta = \frac{(1 + \beta^2) * \textit{Precision} * \textit{Recall}}{\beta^2 (\textit{Precision} + \textit{Recall})}$$

$$F_1 = \frac{2 * \textit{Precision} * \textit{Recall}}{\textit{Precision} + \textit{Recall}}$$

$$AER = 1 - \frac{2 * |L \cap L_{gold}|}{|L| + |L_{gold}|}$$

One serious problem is the treatment of many-to-many mappings. Consider the case of mapping the segments "lost your senses" and "tappat förståndet" from Figure 2.1. A token-link-based gold standard would include the following six links to explain this alignment (check this also in the matrix-based illustration of Figure 2.5):

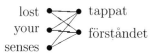

It is not obvious how to evaluate individual token links for such a unit. Assume that our token-based algorithm proposes the following alignment instead of finding all six connections:

lost ●———● tappat
your ●———● förståndet
senses ●

Our alignment algorithm would, therefore, earn only four out of six points for this particular example even though the alignment explains the same bisegment mapping (almost in a more precise way). This seems very harsh, and it also appears that this unit obtains too much weight for the overall measure when averaging over all possible alignment points.

The problem is that there is no straightforward way to specify many-to-many correspondences in the gold standard using individual token links. The only intuitive way to keep the entire unit together in the token-based gold standard is to mark all alignment points even though certain links are quite questionable (for example "your" $\leftrightarrow$ "förståndet" and "your" $\leftrightarrow$ "tappat"). It is therefore common to introduce a new category for *fuzzy links* L_{fuzzy} into the gold standard that is used for all these cases. Regular links are then often called *sure* links L_{sure}. The evaluation measures are then adjusted as follows:

$$L_{possible} = L_{sure} \cup L_{fuzzy}$$

$$Precision = \frac{|L \cap L_{possible}|}{|L|}$$

$$Recall = \frac{|L \cap L_{sure}|}{|L_{sure}|}$$

$$AER = 1 - \frac{|L \cap L_{sure}| + |L \cap L_{possible}|}{|L| + |L_{sure}|}$$

These measures compute precision now in terms of all *possible* links and the recall in terms of solid, generally accepted links. Even though this solution is widely accepted, it still bears a lot of problems related to the same issues of many-to-many alignment evaluations. For example, it has been shown that these measures favor conservative aligners that do not risk adding weak connections as they can quickly cause drops in precision. This tendency is especially apparent if the gold standard contains many more fuzzy links than regular ones. It generally works well if there are mainly one-to-one mappings and no overlapping segments. For more discussions about word alignment quality measures, please look at [Fraser and Marcu, 2007a]

2.7   SUMMARY AND FURTHER READING

Above, several basic concepts related to bitexts and bitext alignment have been introduced. In the literature, a wide variety of notations and descriptions can be found. Some of the terms are used in different ways. We tried to discuss the uses of related terms such as bitext and parallel corpora, alignment, links and bisegmentation. In general, it is important that the concepts of bitext and alignment belong together. Automatic bitext alignment is essentially the task of making the textual correspondences explicit by linking segments that are equivalent according to some pre-defined type of relation. Important is the connection between segmentation and alignment, which can be seen in the two intertwined tasks that we have to deal with: (i) Find segments of appropriate size that can be linked to corresponding segments in the other bitext half. (ii) Find corresponding segment pairs and link them together.

To sum up, here is a list of important concepts and terminology that we have introduced above:

Segmentation: A division of text into meaningful units. Special segmentation types are flat contiguous segmentations and nested segmentations.

Basic text elements: Special type of segment which can be seen as an atomic unit for a certain task. They refer to base units that can be linked together, i.e., they are part of aligned segments (bisegments). They are identified by a segmentation process, and they are part of a global structure (for example a sequence of word tokens in a sentence or a tree of constituents in a syntactic parse).

Bisegments: Aligned segment pairs in a bitext, one from each half of the bitext. Segments are composed of basic text elements that may also individually be linked with each other.

Bitext links: Mappings between text elements from a bitext. Links may express partial relations and uncertainty using attached weights or labels.

Alignment: The entire structure that connects both bitext halves with each other according to some notion of correspondence. Alignments are described by a set of bisegments or a set of links between corresponding elements (bitext map).

Alignment space: The hypothesis space in alignment optimization algorithms containing all possible alignment candidates. The alignment space depends on segmentation and model constraints (*restriction bias*).

Alignment model: Defines the alignment space, the features used for alignment discovery and the interactions between links.

Alignment algorithm: A search procedure that minimizes the alignment costs (or maximizes the alignment likelihood) according to a specific model and a given alignment space. The algorithm can be influenced in various ways (*search bias*) in order to increase alignment quality and efficiency.

Important is the interaction between alignment models and alignment algorithms. The search in a given alignment space can be guided in many ways using constraints and search preferences but it can never find solutions beyond the scope of the space defined by the model. In general, alignment models fall into two main categories: generative models and discriminative models. Most of them use some kind of statistical inference.

- Discriminative models focus on the likelihood of bitext links given the observable data. Interactions between links have to be considered which turns alignment into a structured prediction task.

- Generative models focus on the likelihood of observable data given an alignment between bitext segments. A specific alignment (for example, the one that best explains the emitted data) can be seen as a bi-product of the optimal model applied to the observed data.

- Generative alignment models can be asymmetric or symmetric.

Another overview over fundamental concepts in bitext alignment can be found in Wu [2010]. Introductions to the terminology of bitexts and alignment are also given in Melamed [2001], Merkel

[1999], Véronis [2000]. Cherry and Lin [2006a] discuss alignment spaces in connection with a word alignment task. General introductions of discriminative and generative models can be found in various text books on machine learning and natural language processing.

CHAPTER 3

Building Parallel Corpora

Parallel documents exist since ancient history. The Rosetta stone is probably the most well-known historic parallel text. Translations have been produced for many centuries and many types of documents exist in various languages. Parallel documents have been used for various purposes before, like deciphering ancient texts or education (for example, foreign language learning). In the era of computers and the digital world, electronic documents become more and more available with many parallel versions among them. It is now possible to acquire large numbers of parallel documents from the web in numerous language pairs. Before starting a new collection, one has to consider several questions.

1. What is the purpose of collecting bitexts? What will they be used for?

2. How much data do I need and how clean does it have to be?

3. From which domain should the data come and where can I find appropriate documents?

4. How can I extract the information (text) I need and how do I want to store the data including alignments and annotations?

These questions are, of course, related to each other, and there are certainly more specific issues to consider. However, it is a good start to think about the purpose of any document collection. Dedicated cross-linguistic studies have other requirements than applications that need example data for learning patterns in natural languages. Data for academic research or for testing and developing algorithms can be quite different from data needed for commercial products. Unfortunately, many parallel documents are not freely available. Many valuable collections are closed behind copyrights and private (company) ownerships. Large amounts of public parallel data are only available for a few language pairs and for certain types of domains. Some collections are available (see the appendix for a list of resources). Good sources for translations are international organizations such as the United Nations or the European Union, who produce large amounts of translated material. Other sources can be found among public documentation and translation efforts of software manuals, guidelines, copyright-free books or localization of open-source software. Classic books for which the copyright has been expired are another interesting resource. However, the domains and genres covered are still very limited.

Several strategies can be used to create bitexts. Parallel documents can be downloaded directly from the sources that are known to contain such resources. This makes it possible to control the contents of the extracted material. Another strategy is to use web crawling techniques to fetch parallel websites and other parallel documents automatically from a wide variety of locations. However, this may lead to much nosier data sets which require substantial cleaning efforts.

In any case, it is important to mention that there is a continuum between strictly parallel documents to comparable corpora [Fung and Cheung, 2004a]. Completely parallel documents are actually rather rare and most of the translated material available on-line is only partial. There are also various degrees of faithfulness to the original version, and it is common that translations are out-dated, incomplete or simply wrong. The quality of the document collection is crucial for the success of the alignment approaches that we are going to discuss.

A typical setup for building parallel corpora looks like this:

1. Identify appropriate sources of parallel documents and fetch them (**data collection**).

2. Convert all documents (might even include scanning and OCR) and extract the information we need (usually text) and store it in some unified format (for example, XML-based schemas) (**pre-processing**).

3. Find an appropriate mapping between documents (**document alignment**). This could be harder than it sounds as these mappings are not necessarily obvious especially for diverse material from the web.

4. Align paragraphs and sentences for each parallel document pair (**alignment**).

Further steps for more fine-grained alignments and additional annotation may follow. Especially the complexity of the pre-processing task should not be underestimated. Problems with character encoding, layout detection, and removal of non-textual content can be quite challenging. Furthermore, for subsequent alignment steps, it is necessary to identify appropriate units. The tasks of breaking documents into sentences and breaking sentences into words are not only language dependent but also depend on the text type and the document domain. Another difficult task is the detection of missing parts and other non-parallel sections that need to be filtered out. This is typically done by hand, which is a tedious and time-consuming task.

Finally, it is necessary to decide how to store the alignment information. A flexible way is to use some kind of stand-off annotation to make it possible to adjust alignments and to add several layers of annotation without touching the original data sets. Figure 3.1 shows an example for an XML-based stand-off annotation of sentence alignment.

Keeping separate alignment files has many advantages. For example, it is possible to combine several parallel documents into one bitext as we can see in the example. Furthermore, alternative alignments can be stored simply by creating additional stand-off alignment files. Certain alignment types can easily be filtered out (for example non-one-to-one mappings when processing a bitext). Finally, it is also straightforward to create alignments between multiple documents (for example, translations into various languages) without repeating any document content. Certainly, the storage format depends very much on the application the data is collected for. However, it can be an important

```
<?xml version="1.0" encoding="utf-8"?>
<!DOCTYPE cesAlign PUBLIC "-//CES//DTD XML cesAlign//EN" "">
<cesAlign version="1.0">
  <linkList>
    <linkGrp targType="s"
             fromDoc="Europarl/xml/eng/ep-00-01-17.xml"
               toDoc="Europarl/xml/fre/ep-00-01-17.xml">
      <link xtargets="1;1" />
      <link xtargets="2;2" />
      <link xtargets="3;3 4" />
    ...
      <link xtargets="904;888" />
      <link xtargets="905;889" />
    </linkGrp>
    <linkGrp targType="s"
             fromDoc="Europarl/xml/eng/ep-00-01-18.xml"
               toDoc="Europarl/xml/fre/ep-00-01-18.xml">
      <link xtargets="1;1" />
      <link xtargets="2;2" />
      <link xtargets="3;3" />
```

Figure 3.1: Stand-off annotation of sentence alignments. Parallel documents are specified in the 'linkGrp' tag using 'fromDoc' and 'toDoc' attributes. 'link' tags include the actual links between sentences (that should be marked with 's' tags in the aligned documents). Sentences are identified by their IDs. Linked fromDoc and toDoc sentences are separated by ';' in the 'xtargets' attribute.

advantage to select a format that can easily be transformed into another to make the data collection more versatile.

3.1   DOCUMENT ALIGNMENT

The first alignment task when building parallel corpora is to link corresponding document with each other. In some cases, the mapping between documents is given. However, in many other cases, especially when mining on-line resources, this is not the case, and data collection leaves us with a set of documents in various languages and/or versions. The task of identifying parallel documents among them may be trivial or hard, depending on the source and the meta information available for the data collection. We may not even know the language of each collected document when building a bilingual bitext from web resources. This, however, can be done quite reliably with automatic language identification classifiers (see, for example, van Noord [2006]).

For now, we assume that we have two sets of documents, S and T, that need to be aligned. Typically, we expect one-to-one mappings between documents. However, alternative versions of the same text may exist in the collection, which could lead to multiple mappings, but usually one tries to avoid such settings and opts for removing duplicates and alternative revisions. Document collections are usually not sorted; therefore, we cannot assume any monotonic mapping strategy. Hence, in

00_70221.isv	Swedish (sv)
03_70821.pl	Polish (pl)
03_70221.isf	Swedish and Finish (sf)
03_70421.ien.ny_utg_970627	English (en), new edition ("ny utgåva")
02_60422.idenyutg.960626	German (de), new edition
08_80505.ity	German (ty = tyska)
08_80505.iho	Dutch (ho = holländska)
01_60123.pnl	Dutch (nl)
12B_help_sd_sve.rtf	Swedish (sve=svenska)
12B_help_sp_eng.rtf	English (eng)
om10aen.01	English (en)

Figure 3.2: Inconsistent filenames of parallel documents (originals and translations) from a real-world task of building a parallel corpus.

the general case, we need to select parallel documents from the cartesian product $S \times T$ of both sets according to some similarity measure that reflects the correspondence relation we aim for (for example translational equivalence).

The matching criterion can be based on various features derived from the content of each document and meta-information available for each of them. One obvious feature is the name of a document if available. One typically assumes that corresponding (translated) documents have similar names (filenames, URLs, etc.). In the easiest case, names of corresponding documents are identical except for one well-defined part identifying the language. For example, corresponding documents may be organized in different sub-directories in standard file-system with otherwise identical names and locations. This is, for example, common in localization data and documents from other internationalization efforts. Another common case is that language identifiers are added as suffixes to file names. Unfortunately, name conventions are often not as consistent as one would like them to be. They may vary substantially even in professional workflows and do not necessarily follow standards like the ISO-639 language codes. Figure 3.2 shows some filename examples of documents used to compile the parallel Scania corpus [Sang, 1996]. They exhibit a lot of inconsistencies and do not clearly follow any standard.

Name mapping heuristics become even more important for data mined from the web [Resnik and Smith, 2003]. Adjusting procedures for name-based mappings often becomes much more tedious then anticipated, and this strategy is an underestimated source of errors.

Another possibility for document alignment is the use of content-based similarity measures. Patry and Langlais [2005] compare three metrics with light linguistic features:

Cosine similarity: A standard measure from information retrieval used for comparing documents and queries.

$$\cos(v_1, v_2) = \frac{v_1 \cdot v_2}{\|v_1\| \, \|v_2\|}$$

Patry and Langlais [2005] use vectors v of numbers, punctuations and named entities in order to be able to compare documents in different languages.

Edit distance: The number of insertions, deletions and substitutions necessary to turn one document into another. A document is represented by a sequence of features. Patry and Langlais [2005] apply the same features as the ones used for the cosine measure above (numbers, punctuations and named entities). The final edit distance is normalized by the length of the longer sequence in each particular comparison to make the metric comparable among documents of different lengths.

Alignment score: The ability of automatically aligning sentences in document pair candidates can be used as a quality measure. Patry and Langlais [2005] use ratios of different alignment types as features. See Chapter 4 for more information on sentence alignment algorithms and typical alignment types.

Using these scores, we now need a decision process that can determine, for any given document pair, whether or not they are parallel. A threshold-based approach and a manually tuned combination of scores would be possible. Patry and Langlais [2005] use a classifier instead (actually, a combination of base classifiers) that has been trained on example data using machine learning techniques. The combination of different features and metrics, and the classifier-based decisions, lead to excellent results in the selected tasks presented by Patry and Langlais [2005].

Note that the list of features and metrics can easily be extended using the same classifier-based framework. Document similarity measures may incorporate features based on internal structure, meta-information, stylistic features such as average sentence length, type-token ratios or word variation and may also use other features based on lexical overlaps. Structure-based similarity measures will be discussed in the next section on web mining. Enright and Kondrak [2007] describe a cognate-based approach to parallel document identification. They optimize the process by looking at *hapax legomena* only, i.e., words that appear only once in a document (hapaxes for short). They add a length threshold of four characters for words to be considered and simply count the number of identical hapaxes in each document pair, assuming that those should be cognates. Documents that share most hapaxes are assigned to each other. This simplistic method performed surprisingly well on a parallel test corpus with 11 European languages Enright and Kondrak [2007]. Diacritics were stripped off, and Greek texts were romanized with a simple mapping scheme. A drawback of this method is that there is no clear way to avoid assigning a document to another one that does not have any corresponding document in the entire collection. The algorithm assumes that there is a corresponding document for any selected source.

Another content-based matching approach is presented by Steinberger et al. [2002]. They use the multilingual thesaurus EUROVOC to map similar documents across European languages. The system assigns semantically associated terms to each descriptor in the thesaurus using statistical techniques. Documents are then compared with these vectors of descriptor terms using standard information retrieval metrics. This produces a list of weighted EUROVOC descriptor assignments for each document. The similarity between documents is, finally, calculated by comparing these assignments using a cosine-based measure.

3.2   MINING THE WEB

A natural source for multilingual data is the WorldWideWeb. Collecting data and information from the web is known as **web mining** and several techniques for mining bitexts from the web have been proposed. Collecting documents from the web requires special procedures. The material that can be found online is very diverse with a lot of variation in style, formats and quality. Resnik [1999] describes techniques for automatic identification of parallel web sites. The author develops a web-mining architecture called STRAND (structural translation recognition acquiring natural data) that is based on the observation that translated web sites have a strong tendency to use the same internal structure. The general procedure includes three steps:

1. Locate possibly parallel web sites

2. Generate candidate pairs of parallel web pages

3. Apply structural filters to the candidate set

For the first step, STRAND uses search engines to identify pages that include specific patterns. The system looks for two types of web pages: *parents* and *siblings*. Parent pages include hyperlinks to different language versions of a document. STRAND uses language-specific boolean search queries to find such web sites, for example: (anchor:"english" OR anchor:"anglais") AND (anchor:"french" OR anchor:"francais"). The system applies simple regular expressions to filter candidates pages by looking for web sites with language links close to each other. Sibling documents are web sites that include links to translations of the same page. Again, boolean search queries (anchor:"english" OR anchor:"anglais") can be used to obtain a candidate list of such pages.

Another option for locating sites with translations is to use a web spider and name matching heuristics. A later version of STRAND includes this option. [Resnik and Smith, 2003]. Another system, called BITS (Bilingual Internet Text Search), uses URL matching techniques for this task. [Ma and Liberman, 1999]. They use the Levenshtein distance [Levenshtein, 1966] to compute the difference between URLs, assuming that translated documents will be stored in similar locations and with similar names. Further filtering steps are required to remove noise. Yet another system, called PTMiner [Chen and Nie, 2000], uses a similar technique. In this system, candidate URL pairs are extracted that differ only in a prefix or suffix, which clearly indicates the language version of the document. For this pre-defined prefix, patterns are used such as (.e|.en|_en|...). This strategy is also exploited by the spider version of STRAND [Resnik and Smith, 2003].

The second step of generating candidate pairs of parallel documents usually involves language and character set identification as well. Furthermore, a text length filter can also be useful to filter out unlikely candidates [Chen and Nie, 2000, Resnik and Smith, 2003].

The final step in STRAND is to apply structural filters to all document pairs collected in the previous steps. The assumption here is that translated documents use a very similar structure expressed by their HTML markup. STRAND uses a markup analyzer that produces a linear sequence of tokens representing tags and chunk lengths. The system produces tokens for HTML start-tags ([START:label], representing any <label ...>), tokens for HTML end-tags ([END:label], representing any </label>) and tokens for character data ([Chunk:length], representing any text of length length between HTML tags). These token sequences are then compared for every document pair. First, STRAND aligns them using standard sequence comparison algorithms. Secondly, the system computes four values that characterize the quality of the alignment:

- The percentage of differences between the two sequences

- The number of aligned non-markup chunks of unequal length

- The length correlation of aligned non-markup chunks

- The significance level of that correlation

Thresholds on all values can be used to perform alignment decisions. In this way, precision and recall of the extraction process can be balanced according to one's needs. Resnik and Smith [2003] discuss both manual settings of parameters and machine learning techniques. In the latter, they applied a decision tree for classifying candidate pairs.

An alternative structural matching approach is described by Esplá-Gomis [2009]. This system generates fingerprints of web documents including information about tags and text chunks. Those fingerprints are compared using a process based on the Levenshtein distance.

Many other web-page matching techniques are similar to the general document alignment methods discussed in the previous section. For example, Nie and Cai [2001] apply automatic sentence alignment to filter multilingual text collections. A large proportion of empty alignments indicate an unlikely candidate in their system. Content-based algorithms are used by Ma and Liberman [1999]. They propose the use of lexical matchings to compute the similarity between texts. For this, they apply string similarity measures to identify cognates and suggest the use of bilingual dictionaries to extend the coverage. Resnik and Smith [2003] also explore the use of lexical matchings applying hand-crafted and automatically generated probabilistic translation lexicons. Naturally, content-based and structural matching techniques can also be combined [Resnik and Smith, 2003].

Another interesting approach for parallel document mining is presented by Uszkoreit et al. [2010]. In this approach, the problem is casted as a cross-language near-duplicate detection. The system relies on a baseline machine translation system that can translate parallel documents into one single language that will be used for similarity calculations. For duplicate detection, they use standard techniques derived from research in information retrieval [Henzinger, 2006]. These techniques are based on discriminating words and phrases, which are usually the relatively rare ones. Unfortunately, rare words are typically the ones that machine translation systems have problems with. Uszkoreit et al. [2010], therefore, extract n-grams with relatively low frequency but which are made out of more common in-vocabulary words. Index structures are then applied to make pair-wise scoring efficient. Uszkoreit et al. [2010] use a distributed system to scale the approach to very large data sets.

3.3   EXTRACTING PARALLEL DATA FROM COMPARABLE CORPORA

The techniques discussed in the previous section basically try to extract parallel parts from large multilingual, comparable text collections. However, the focus there is set on detecting entirely parallel documents. Nevertheless, many documents contain translated sentences even though they are not direct translations of another document.

A lot of work has been devoted to the extraction of parallel sentences from comparable corpora. There is no clear-cut definition of comparable corpora, and we have already mentioned that there is a continuum between parallel data and comparable data. Fung and Cheung [2004b] distinguish between parallel, noisy parallel, comparable and quasi-comparable (very-non-parallel) corpora. Noisy parallel corpora refer to mostly parallel, roughly translated documents and are characterized by some insertions and deletions of some paragraphs and sections. Comparable corpora, on the other hand, refer to collections of non-translated but topic-related documents. For example, news articles from two different sources in different languages within the same time frame (publishing dates) constitute a typical comparable corpus. Wikipedia pages in different languages about the same topic are other examples of comparable documents. Finally, quasi-comparable corpora refer to multilingual text collections with overlapping domain coverage but without topic alignment. All these data types can be valuable sources for mining parallel resources but need to be treated in slightly different ways.

Rapp [1995] is probably the first who demonstrates the possibilities of extracting word translations from comparable corpora. Since then, these ideas have attracted a lot of attention [Chiao and Zweigenbaum, 2002, Diab and Finch, 2000, Fung and Yee, 1998, Gaussier et al., 2004, Otero, 2007, Sproat et al., 2006]. Zhao and Vogel [2002] and Munteanu et al. [2004] independently present strategies to mine parallel sentences from comparable news collections. A common strategy for this task is to use bilingual lexical information to measure similarity between textual units. Munteanu et al. [2004] use a three-step procedure:

- First, they select comparable articles by querying an indexed version of the comparable corpus with document-specific terms and their translations. Term translations are taken from a probabilistic translation lexicon that can be generated from a parallel corpus using standard word alignment techniques (see Chapter 5). They refine the selection by adding the constraint that the publication date of the selected news article pairs must not differ by more than five days.

- The second step is the selection of candidate sentence pairs from the selected article pairs. For this, Munteanu et al. [2004] use a simple word-overlap filter in combination with a length ratio filter. The same probabilistic dictionary from step one is used for the word-overlap filter.

- The final step is parallel sentence selection from the previously extracted candidate set. For this, Munteanu et al. [2004] apply a maximum entropy classifier, much in the spirit of the document alignment approach by Patry and Langlais [2005]. This classifier models a binary decision whether or not two given sentences are parallel according to features extracted from the sentence pair sp. The decision is based on a conditional probability distribution $P(c|sp)$, which is parametrized as a log-linear combination of weighted real-valued feature functions $f_i(c, sp)$.

$$P(c|sp) = \frac{1}{Z(sp)} \exp \sum_i \lambda_i f_i(c, sp)$$

$Z(sp)$ is a normalizing factor, and λ_i are the feature weights that need to be optimized in training. The basic decision rule with such a model is $\hat{c} = \underset{c}{\mathrm{argmax}}\, P(c|sp)$ where $c = 1$, in our case, refers to the affirmative decision that the two sentences are parallel and $c = 0$ rejects the sentence selection. Munteanu et al. [2004] exploit the following features to discriminate between parallel and non-parallel sentences: sentence lengths, lengths ratios, percentage of word translations according to the translation lexicon and several word alignment features derived from automatic word alignment.

Fung and Cheung [2004b] extend this idea by turning the procedure into an iterative bootstrapping strategy. In their system, word translation overlap is also the main property for parallel sentence extraction after extracting candidate pairs from similar documents. However, they use a cosine similarity measure for the final extraction of parallel sentences. The main improvement of their approach comes from a bootstrapping loop that they add to the procedure. First of all, translation lexicons are learned from extracted sentence pairs in order to enrich this resource for the next iteration. They also introduce the principle of "find-one-get-more", which refers to the intuition that documents, which contain known parallel sentences, have a good chance to contain more parallel sentences even though they were judged to be dissimilar in previous steps. The system runs in several iterations and stops when the parameters of the translation lexicon do not change anymore and no more parallel sentence pairs are extracted.

The success of these extraction techniques stimulates a lot of current research. Comparable corpora become increasingly important especially due to the limited amount of truly parallel data available. In particular, a lot of effort is spent to support under-resourced languages that require parallel data, for example, for training statistical translation models.

3.4   SUMMARY AND FURTHER READING

In this chapter, we have discussed a number of practical issues to be solved when building parallel corpora. We have seen various techniques for matching documents and extracting parallel texts from different types of sources. Many of these techniques are closely related with each other and exploit similar properties even when applied to very different data collections. A lot of on-going research could be added here and new approaches and ideas for parallel text mining appear constantly. Several workshops dedicated to building and using parallel/comparable corpora have been organized [Fung et al., 2009, Koehn et al., 2005, Kranias et al., 2004, Mihalcea and Pedersen, 2003a, Pinkham et al., 2001, Rapp et al., 2010, Zweigenbaum et al., 2008]. Further techniques for retrieving parallel web documents are described in, for example, Fukushima et al. [2006], Nie et al. [1999], Yang and Li [2004], and Li and Liu [2008]. The system presented by Esplá-Gomis [2009] is freely available and can be used to create translation memories from translated websites. Nadeau and Foster [2004] propose techniques for mining parallel texts from real-time news feeds. Hassel and Dalianis [2009] use document signatures (*fingerprints*) made out of prefix frequencies to compute document similarities between related languages. Utiyama and Isahara [2003] describe techniques based on cross-lingual information retrieval to align news articles. Vu et al. [2009] present another approach to align documents in comparable news corpora.

CHAPTER 4

Sentence Alignment

A sentence is probably the most well-studied linguistic unit in the history of linguistics and natural language processing. A sentence is usually characterized by a meaningful grammatical structure expressing some kind of statement, question, exclamation, request or command. Sentences are especially interesting in computational linguistics because they are, in many respects, self-contained and informative enough to make it possible to perform extensive syntactic and semantic analyses. On the other hand, they are restricted enough to allow efficient processing techniques (still complex enough to leave many open research questions). Therefore, many NLP applications focus on processing sentences (in isolation) instead of larger textual units; machine translation is one of them. Bitexts had been discovered for translation studies and soon thereafter also for data-driven techniques in automatic and semi-automatic translation. This created a lot of attention in the field of computational linguistics and brought a wide range of alignment techniques to appear in the late 1980's and early 1990's. Today, sentence-aligned bitexts are the most important resources for statistical machine translation but also for computer-aided translation (translation memories) and other machine translation approaches.

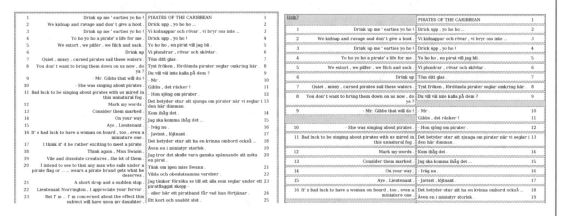

Figure 4.1: A raw bitext with sentence segmentation (to the left) and the monotonic sentence alignment (to the right).

With the term sentence alignment, we usually refer to mappings of adjacent sentences to their corresponding sentences in a bitext. Beside this restriction to a *flat contiguous segmentation*, it is commonly assumed that alignments are *monotonic* (without crossing links). However, many-to-many mappings are usually allowed but often dispreferred. The atomic unit in sentence alignment is, naturally, a sentence but, in a broad sense, including sentence fragments or other textual elements such as headers, lists or table cells.

The input to a sentence alignment algorithm is a bitext, and the output is the mapping between corresponding sentences. Due to the assumption of monotonicity and the strong preference for one-to-one links, it is easy to visualize sentence alignments as parallel segment pairs (see Figure 4.1). Simple cues such as length correlations and incomplete lexical constraints are often sufficient to perform reasonably well. However, in many cases, a previous alignment on a larger textual unit (paragraphs, sections, chapters) is useful to improve alignment quality and speed. The techniques that we will discuss below will also be applicable for those units but often even simpler techniques are sufficient. The accuracy is often very high and, therefore, supports this *hierarchical refinement approach* well.

4.1   LENGTH-BASED APPROACHES

It is generally accepted that sentence alignment can be handled sufficiently by monotonic mappings. It is not common to reorder sentences when translating which would scramble part of the information included in the text. In the rare cases where local reordering occurs, a simple operation of merging sentences to larger units could be performed to find a monotonic mapping for the corresponding parts. Due to the monotonicity constraint, we can rely on very simple cues. Sentence length is one of them which has been explored in a number of alignment approaches. Length-based approaches were introduced in 1991 by two research teams simultaneously [Brown et al., 1991, Gale and Church, 1991b]. Both approaches are based on the correlation between the lengths of parallel sentences. Gale and Church [1991b, 1993] examined bitexts in English and German and found a high correlation between the lengths of corresponding (short "pseudo") paragraphs. A similar correlation can be found between corresponding sentences for various language pairs. Figure 4.2 plots the lengths of translated system messages (in number of characters) from localization data of the KDE platform (`http://kde.org/`) for four different language pairs. In all cases, there is a strong linear correlation above $r = 0.9$. The largest difference can be seen in English and Chinese, which is probably to be expected.

Certainly, this correlation depends not only on the language pair but also very much on the bitext source and the strength of equivalence between both bitext halves. Nevertheless, correlations do not have to be perfect as long as they give enough information for correct alignment decisions. In order to show a different picture, sentence lengths can also be seen as a signal from the underlying text, and the correlation between signals coming from parallel texts becomes apparent when looking at the plots in Figure 4.3.

Using the assumption that the same information is present in both bitext halves (everything is translated), the length signal will be enough, in most cases, to make local decisions about mapping corresponding segments.

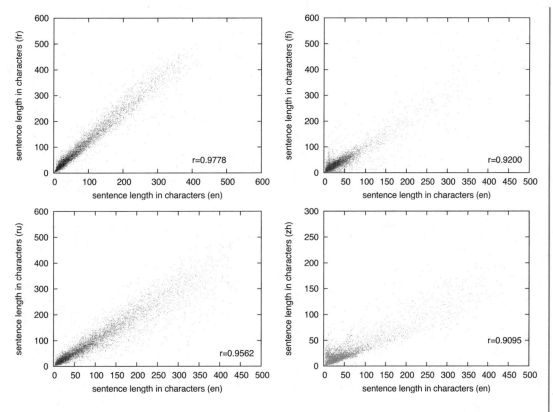

Figure 4.2: Correlation of sentence length differences in 10,000 parallel KDE system messages: English–French (en-fr), English-Finnish (en-fi), English-Russian (en-ru) and English-Chinese (en-zh).

Using these findings Gale and Church [1991b] define a dynamic programming algorithm that finds sentence mappings according to a generative model with sentence lengths as the only observable features. Their model describes the process of generating characters in the target language from characters in the source language. They assume that the number of characters generated follows a pre-defined distribution, independent of type and context. In order to estimate this distribution, they computed the character ratio of a small trilingual corpus (French, English, German) and found a value that was close to one (1.1 for German/English and 1.06 for French/English). They also plotted the frequencies of length differences in their aligned parallel data in order to check the density distribution, which in their case was approximately normal. Assuming that this is true for all parallel data sets, we can now describe the generative model by a normal distribution with the sample mean computed as the length ratio ($c \approx 1$) and the sample variance ($s^2 \approx 6.8$) estimated from the same data. For simplicity, these values are fixed in the general algorithm proposed by Gale and Church [1991b]; therefore, no additional training data is required to optimize those parameters when ap-

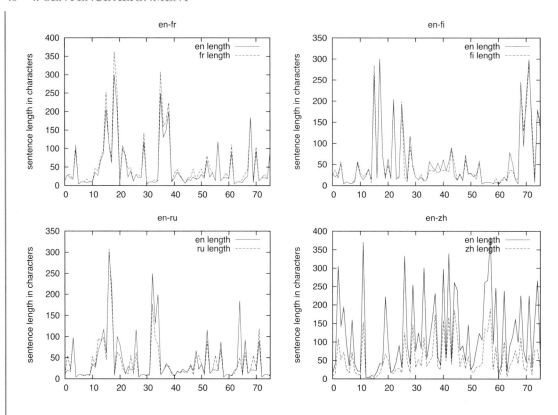

Figure 4.3: Comparison of *sentence length signals* (KDE system messages): English-French (en-fr), English-Finnish (en-fi), English-Russian (en-ru) and English-Chinese (en-zh). (Note: the figures do not illustrate the same set of sentence pairs for each language pair!)

plying the algorithm to new data sets. Putting everything together, we obtain a normalized length difference $\delta(l_i, l_j)$ that can be treated as a random variable X with a normal distribution and zero mean:[1]

$$\delta(l_i, l_j) = \frac{l_j - cl_i}{\sqrt{\frac{1}{2}(l_j + cl_i)s^2}} \approx \frac{l_j - l_i}{\sqrt{3.4(l_i + l_j)}}$$

Here, l_i is the length of segment $\mathbf{p_i}$ in one half of the bitext, and l_j is the length of segment $\mathbf{r_j}$ in the other half, and the variance is proportional to length. The probability for a specific length

---

[1]The formula given below is slightly different from the original paper in which the standard error is estimated as $\sqrt{l_i s^2}$, which can lead to zeros in the denominator of the length difference value. Taking, instead, the average of adjusted segment lengths, $\sqrt{\frac{1}{2}(l_j + cl_i)s^2}$ avoids this problem as we do not allow alignments between two empty strings.

difference for a given pair of segments (which is of alignment type *type*) is then defined according to the probability density function:

$$\hat{P}(\delta(l_i, l_j)|type) \quad = \quad P_N\left(|X| \geq |\delta(l_i, l_j)|\right)$$

$$= \quad 2\left(1 - P_N\left(X < |\delta(l_i, l_j)|\right)\right)$$

In other words, we ask how likely it is to observe a length difference, which is at least as big as our observed δ. The length difference clearly depends on the link type that determines the values for l_i and l_j. We, therefore, add the dependency on *type* in the $\hat{P}(\delta(l_i, l_j)|type)$ notation above. The second line in the equation explains how this probability can be calculated using values that can be obtained from standard tables and software packages, which usually provide the integral of a standard normal distribution as $P_N(X < x) = \frac{1}{\sqrt{2\pi}} \int_{-\infty}^{x} \exp(-\frac{1}{2}x^2)dx$.

To illustrate the algorithm, consider the following tiny bitext, $B = (B_{src}, B_{trg})$, with three sentence fragments in B_{src} and two sentence fragments B_{trg}:

length$_{src}$	B_{src}	B_{trg}	length$_{trg}$
3	**Hej**	**Hi and hello**	12
5	**Hallo**	Goodbye	7
5	Hejdå		0

The segment pair marked in bold face (sentence one and two in B_{src} and sentence one in B_{trg}) has a normalized length difference of $\delta(8, 12) \approx 0.485$, which corresponds to a match probability of $\hat{P}(|X| \geq 0.485) \approx 0.63$. Figure 4.4 shows a graphical illustration of this value within the probability density function of a standard normal distribution.

Another observation that was made by Gale and Church [1991b] is that there is a very skewed distribution of sentence alignment types. In their test corpus, they found a strong preference for one-to-one mappings and only a few other types with much lower frequencies. Table 4.1 lists the approximate values found in their study.

Table 4.1: Sentence alignment types and their relative frequencies found by Gale and Church [1991b].		
Link type	$\hat{P}(type)$	Operation type
1-1	0.89	substitution
1-0 or 0-1	0.0099	insertion or deletion
2-1 or 1-2	0.089	expansion or contraction
2-2	0.011	swap or merge

Note that these alignment types intuitively fit quite well to editing operations as indicated in the last column of the table. Using these results, Gale and Church [1991b] added these estimated

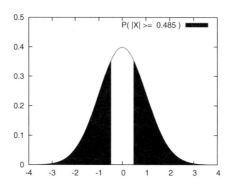

Figure 4.4: The probability density function of a standard normal distribution. The filled area represents the cost of the alignment match in the Gale & Church algorithm according to a normalized length difference of approximately 0.485.

likelihoods of link types as prior knowledge $\hat{P}(type)$ to the system to create the final cost function of the alignment algorithm:

$$Cost(\mathbf{p_i}\|\mathbf{r_j}) = cost(type, l_i, l_j) = -\log \hat{P}(type)\hat{P}(\delta(l_i, l_j)|type)$$

We can now define a recursive algorithm based on dynamic programming in which the overall cost is simply the sum of individual costs.

$$Cost(\mathcal{A}_{(B_{src}, B_{trg})}) = \sum_i Cost(\mathbf{p_i}\|\mathbf{r_i})$$

Note that the segmentation into appropriate $\mathbf{p_i}$ and $\mathbf{r_i}$ is not given. The objective is actually to find the proper segmentation such that the segmented texts are perfectly aligned with each other. Let us denote the lengths of sentences in B_{src} as s_x and the lengths of sentences in B_{trg} as t_y. We can then write the following algorithm to compute the overall alignment cost based on distance scores $D(x, y)$ with $0 \leq x \leq N$ and $0 \leq y \leq M$ with N and M being the number of sentences in B_{src} and B_{trg}, respectively):

1. Initialize:

$$D(0, 0) = 0$$

2. Recursion:

$$D(x, y) = \min \begin{cases} D(x, y-1) & + & cost(0 : 1, 0, t_y) \\ D(x-1, y) & + & cost(1 : 0, s_x, 0) \\ D(x-1, y-1) & + & cost(1 : 1, s_x, t_y) \\ D(x-1, y-2) & + & cost(1 : 2, s_x, t_{y-1} + t_y) \\ D(x-2, y-1) & + & cost(2 : 1, s_{x-1} + s_x, t_y) \\ D(x-2, y-2) & + & cost(2 : 2, s_{x-1} + s_x, t_{y-1} + t_y) \end{cases}$$

After the computation of all distance scores, we can recursively read out the path through the matrix. This requires to store the alignment *type* that minimizes the distance measure in yet another variable for every table cell. The recursive nature of the algorithm is illustrated in Figure 4.5. Here we can see how the distance measures refer back to previous positions in the bitext.

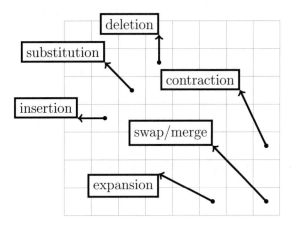

Figure 4.5: An illustration of the search space in the length-based sentence alignment algorithm.

Applying this algorithm to our example bitext from above, we obtain the results shown in Figure 4.6. Note that several slots are empty because they refer to undefined back references.

We can quickly see that the algorithm has a roughly quadratic time complexity as it explores the entire bitext space with its segmentation into sentences. Further improvements can be achieved by restricting the search to reasonable regions avoiding exhaustive explorations of paths that are most likely not leading to optimal solutions. Mainly, this means that we try to stay close to the main diagonal possibly guided by some anchor points as the lowest cumulative cost is to be found along this line (more details about anchor point strategies will be given later).

The algorithm clearly falls into the category of bisegmentation. It explores several possible segmentations (containing sequences of sentences) of the bitext and tries to map them one-to-one (empty segments allowed). Looking at this strategy together with the cumulative cost function, it becomes apparent how important the prior alignment type probabilities are for this algorithm. Simply

		Hej		**Hallo**		**Hejdå**	
	0	$5.67^{1:0}$	–	$11.78^{1:0}$	–	$18.09^{1:0}$	–
		–	–	–	–	–	–
		–	–	–	–	–	–
Hi	– –	$13.10^{1:0}$	–	$7.79^{1:0}$	$\mathbf{2.88^{2:1}}$	$9.19^{1:0}$	$8.19^{2:1}$
and	– –	$1.69^{1:1}$	–	$6.82^{1:1}$	–	$12.71^{1:1}$	–
hello	$7.42^{0:1}$	$13.10^{0:1}$	–	$19.20^{0:1}$	–	$25.51^{0:1}$	–
	– –	$19.60^{1:0}$	–	$11.27^{1:0}$	$9.96^{2:1}$	$8.40^{1:0}$	$4.60^{2:1}$
Goodbye	– –	$8.25^{1:1}$	–	$2.09^{1:1}$	$5.89^{2:2}$	$\mathbf{3.13^{1:1}}$	$11.03^{2:2}$
	$13.93^{0:1}$	$8.19^{0:1}$	$5.16^{1:2}$	$9.39^{0:1}$	$10.20^{1:2}$	$14.69^{0:1}$	$16.04^{1:2}$

Resulting alignment (one 2-to-1 match & one 1-to-1 match):

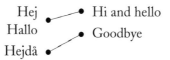

Figure 4.6: The distance matrix according to the Gale & Church algorithm for a small example bitext (with approximate values).

adding the individual match costs ($\hat{P}(\delta(l_i.l_j)|type)$) would always favor two-to-two mappings over one-to-one mappings. However, in the alignment task, we like to focus on the smallest possible unit that can be reliably linked. Therefore, the alignment type probabilities can be seen as a way to introduce **penalties** for odd alignment pairs such as the two-to-two match.

WEAKNESSES AND STRENGTHS OF THE LENGTH-BASED APPROACH

The strongest advantage of the length-based approach is its simplicity. Due to the strong assumptions, it allows efficient search strategies that guarantee to find the global optimum under this model. Furthermore, it is basically language independent as long as characters can be counted. Surprisingly, the length-based approach has proven to be quite robust when tested on various language pairs and textual genres even though most of the assumptions are clearly violated and the fixed parameters from the original study do not fit the new data very well. Look, for example, at the plots in Figure 4.7, which illustrate the distribution of length differences for four language pairs. The shapes differ quite dramatically and, especially for English-Finnish and English-Chinese, they do not look like normal distributions with the typical bell-shape.

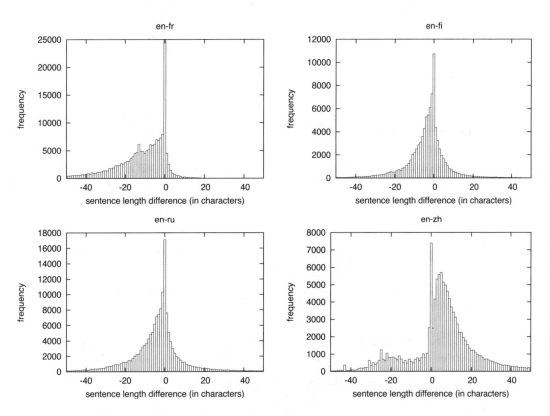

Figure 4.7: Distribution of sentence length differences in parallel KDE system messages: English-French (en-fr), English-Finnish (en-fi), English-Russian (en-ru) and English-Chinese (en-zh).

Furthermore, mean and variance as commonly used in the Gale & Church algorithm do not necessarily meet the reality in all bitexts (see Table 4.2). Nevertheless, sentence length seems to be such a strong signal for well-behaved bitexts that alignment, based on this feature alone, can achieve quite high accuracy. Length difference can be measured in various ways, but the performance is rather stable as long as the measure favors similar lengths. Furthermore, it is possible to measure length in terms of words or bytes instead of characters. However, previous studies have shown that character-based measures are more robust [Gale and Church, 1993], which, however, do not need to be true for all language pairs. Using characters or bytes has the big advantage that it reduces the language dependence as it avoids any decisions on word boundaries and the dependence on specific writing systems.

Table 4.2: Length ratios for different language pairs measured on translated KDE system messages.

source language	target language	length ratio
English	French	0.738
English	Finnish	0.862
English	Russian	0.907
English	Chinese	1.573

The largest weakness of the length-based approach is the risk for error propagation especially in connection with noisy bitexts (for example, with incomplete translations, especially with insertions and deletions in the beginning and at the end). This problem is even increased in cases where neighboring segments have similar lengths such that the length signal is not strong enough anymore to make the correct decisions (remember Figure 4.3). Figure 4.8 shows an example of wrongly aligned movie subtitles due to error propagation from previous alignment decisions.

Help? 1	Drink up me ' earties yo ho !	Sjörövare är jag	1
2	We kidnap and ravage and don' t give a hoot	Vi rövar , vi bränner , vi tar allt guld Drick upp ...	2
3	Drink up me ' earties yo ho !	Tyst , lilla fröken !	3
4	Yo ho yo ho a pirate' s life for me	Det finns sjörövare här .	4
5	We extort , we pilfer , we filch and sack ..	- Du vill väl inte locka hit dem ?	5
6	Drink up	- Mr Gibbs , det räcker .	6
7	Quiet , missy , cursed pirates sail these waters	Hon sjöng om sjörövare .	7
8	You don' t want to bring them down on us now , do ya ?	Att sjunga om sjörövare i denna dimma ger otur , om jag får säga det .	8
9	- Mr. Gibbs that will do !	Nu har ni fått säga det ...	9
10	- She was singing about pirates ..	- Iväg med er .	10
11	Bad luck to be singing about pirates with us mired in this unnatural fog	- Ja , löjtnant .	11
12	Mark my words ..	Att ha kvinnor ombord ger också otur , även om hon är en miniatyr ...	12
13	Consider them marked ..	Att träffa en sjörövare vore spännande .	13
14	On your way .		
15	Aye , Lieutenant .	Tänk efter , miss Swann .	14
16	It' s bad luck to have a woman on board , too , even a miniature one ..	De är avskyvärda och lastbara allihop .	15

Figure 4.8: Error propagation with length-based sentence alignment: Subtitle translations out of sync. The Swedish sentence number 1 should be aligned with the English sentence number 4, and other sentence mappings should be shifted down accordingly.

A typical strategy to prevent such an effect is to guide the alignment by adding synchronization points into the alignment space. One way is to apply hierarchical refinement strategies as mentioned earlier (see Figure 2.6). Aligned paragraph boundaries can be used to constrain the search space and to avoid error propagation beyond these anchor points. However, in many cases, there is no obvious choice for an alignment on a coarser segmentation level. In those cases, lexical cues can be applied to find appropriate pre-segmentations. For language pairs that share alphabetic characters, a so-called **cognate filter** can be quite efficient to perform such a task. A scan through the bitext with a sliding window and pre-defined offset thresholds can be used to identify matching or highly similar pairs of lexical items. In this way, it is possible to identify matching named entities and etymologically related words that can be used to synchronize the alignment algorithm at certain points in the bitext space. (see Figure 4.9 for an illustration).

9	- Mr. Gibbs that will do !	- Mr Gibbs , det räcker .	6
10	- She was singing about pirates .	Hon sjöng om sjörövare .	7
11	Bad luck to be singing about pirates with us mired in this unnatural fog .	Att sjunga om sjörövare i denna dimma ger otur , om jag får säga det .	8
12	Mark my words .	Nu har ni fått säga det ...	9
13	Consider them marked .	- Iväg med er .	10
14	On your way .	- Ja , löjtnant .	11
15	Aye , Lieutenant .	Att ha kvinnor ombord ger också otur , även om hon är en miniatyr ...	12
16	It' s bad luck to have a woman on board , too , even a miniature one .	Att träffa en sjörövare vore spännande .	13
17	I think it' d be rather exciting to meet a pirate .		
18	Think again , Miss Swann .	Tänk efter , miss Swann .	14
19	Vile and dissolute creatures , the lot of them .	De är avskyvärda och lastbara allihop .	15
20	I intend to see to that any man who sails under a pirate flag or ... ... wears a pirate brand gets what he deserves .	Jag ska se till att alla som seglar under sjörövarflagg får vad de förtjänar :	16
21	A short drop and a sudden stop .	Kort fall med snabbt stopp ...	17
22	Lieutenant Norrington , I appreciate your fervor .	Löjtnant Norrington , jag förstår er iver -	18
23	But I' m ... I' m concerned about the effect this subject will have upon my daughter .	- men jag är orolig för hur ämnet påverkar min dotter .	19
24	My apologies , Governor Swann .	Jag ber om ursäkt , guvernör Swann .	20

Figure 4.9: Cognate matches for pre-segmentation. Matching named entities are often good candidates for alignment synchronization.

The risk with such a procedure is naturally the possibility of false friends. It is important to carefully set thresholds and search parameters in order to minimize this risk and maximize precision. Other techniques that combine length features and lexical matches are listed in Chapter 4.4.

Finally, it may also not be sufficient to restrict the search algorithm to the six alignment types presented in Table 4.1. In some cases, other match types may be necessary and also the distribution of alignment types may also be quite different. In a study on movie subtitles (see Figure 4.3), for example we found a large number of non-1-to-1 mappings and a distribution that differed quite a lot from the findings of Gale and Church [1991b].

The standard approach rarely finds deletions and insertions (because of the low prior probabilities); whereas, they occur rather often in this data set. Furthermore, three-to-one mappings are necessary from time to time. However, the increased complexity due to added alignment types may also decrease the performance in terms of accuracy, and purely length-based approaches are not sufficient anymore [Tiedemann, 2007].

Table 4.3: Distribution of sentence alignment types in English, German and Swedish movie subtitles (with relative frequency > 0.001).

alignment type	count	relative frequency
1:1	896	0.6829
2:1	100	0.0762
0:1	91	0.0694
1:0	74	0.0564
1:2	72	0.0549
1:3	24	0.0183
3:1	16	0.0122

4.2   LEXICAL MATCHING APPROACHES

Another idea for sentence alignment is to use lexical cues to guide the alignment along the diagonal of the bitext space. The intuitive assumption is that corresponding sentences contain many lexical translational equivalents, and the monotonicity constraint leads to an alignment in the neighborhood of the bitext diagonal. The bitext is treated as a two-dimensional space with a common origin at the beginning of each bitext half, and the diagonal connects the origin with the terminus, defined by the end of both bitext halves. The neighborhood of the diagonal can be defined in various ways, for example, using a corridor with constant width (see Figure 4.10); however, it is more common to refine this search space dynamically using iterative procedures.

In general, a lexical matching approach has to solve two tasks: i) Translational equivalents (*anchor point candidates*) have to be identified by some robust and efficient algorithm. ii) Alignments between sentences have to be optimized according to the anchor points identified in step i). This procedure naturally allows iterations between both steps. The differences between the various algorithms come down to the following questions:

What is the definition of a lexical item? In order to find lexical matches, we first have to define what a lexical item is. Sentence alignment approaches using lexical cues may apply a variety of linguistic units ranging from surface words [Kay and Röscheisen, 1988, Melamed, 1996a], word stems/substrings [Kay and Röscheisen, 1993, Simard and Plamondon, 1996] to arbitrary character N-grams [Church, 1993].

How do we match lexical items? The task of identifying translational equivalences can be approached in various ways: Bilingual lexicons can be used to identify translation candidates. These lexicons can be derived from external resources or automatically induced from bitexts (even the one to be aligned). They may be stochastic (including translation likelihoods), and they may be dynamic (changing contents within an iterative procedure) or static throughout

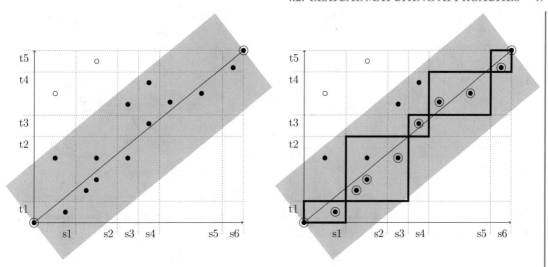

Figure 4.10: Lexical matches in bitext space. Source language sentences are represented along the x-axis and target language sentences along the y-axis. The gray area illustrates a possible search area in the neighborhood of the bitext diagonal. Dots symbolize lexical matches. The right-hand side illustrates a possible sentence alignment (in form of framed boxes) based on the observed lexical matches. Encircled dots refer to anchor points in a smooth monotonic alignment chain.

the alignment process. Another common technique for lexical matching is *cognate filtering* (more details further down).

How do we exploit the alignment space? The bitext space around the diagonal can be searched in various ways. A common strategy is to iteratively refine (reduce) the alignment space by collecting more and more evidence for alignment points. Details will be explained below.

How do we use lexical mappings to create sentence alignments? After lexical matching, the actual alignments have to be established. This can be done in a separate step using, for example, similarity statistics based on lexical matches ([Kay and Röscheisen, 1988]), length-based approaches ([Simard and Plamondon, 1996]) or geometric interpretations of lexical translation chains ([Melamed, 1996a]).

The first algorithm based on lexical matching was presented by [Kay and Röscheisen, 1988] later published in [Kay and Röscheisen, 1993]. The authors propose an iterative refinement algorithm that starts with an initial set of anchor alignments (including only the origin and the terminus of the bitext space if nothing else is given) and then tries to reduce the alignment space around the diagonal between adjacent alignment points by looking for lexical evidence using co-occurrence statistics. The general idea of this process is illustrated in Figure 4.11.

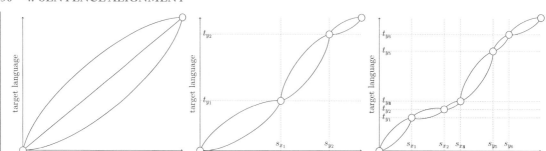

Figure 4.11: An iterative refinement approach to sentence alignment. Dots represent known points of correspondence in the bitext space, and the pillow-shaped area between adjacent dots represents the search space of the alignment algorithm in that region.

The algorithm proposed by Kay and Röscheisen [1993] uses correlation statistics to find lexical matches. They apply the Dice coefficient [Dice, 1945] to measure the degree of correlation between source language word w_s and target language word w_t:

$$Dice(w_s, w_t) = \frac{2N_{AST}(w_s, w_t)}{N_S(w_s) + N_T(w_t)}$$

where $N_{AST}(w_s, w_t)$ is the co-occurrence count of w_s and w_t within the current search space (which they call the *alignable sentence table* AST). $N_S(w_s)$ and $N_T(w_t)$ are the frequency counts of w_s and w_t in the bitext. In fact, this procedure produces a rough stochastic bilingual lexicon that will be used to find alignment points in the next step. Basically, we now look for sentence pairs that can be aligned with some confidence based on the word associations extracted in the previous step. There are many possibilities to use the lexical evidence for inducing alignments. In the original paper, Kay and Röscheisen [1993] focus on sentence pairs that can be mapped based on word associations without any ambiguities, i.e., other possible mappings. They also use simple frequency thresholds to filter out unreliable lexical relations.

Important in the algorithm is the construction of the alignment space that need to be explored. It is constructed from a subset of all sentence pairs using the following restrictions:

- Sentences may not cross any existing alignment point (anchor).

- The position of each sentence in an accepted pair relative to the closest anchor may not differ more than a certain value. This value grows with the relative distance d (in number of sentences) to the anchor which creates the pillow-shaped space depicted in Figure 4.11. Kay and Röscheisen [1993] define the difference to be bound by $\sqrt{d}$.

After each iteration, a new set of aligned sentences is created which is used as the set of anchor points for the next iteration. The procedure is continued until no new alignment points can be identified anymore. Other stopping criteria are also possible. One of the distinctive properties of this iterative approach is that it may stop before all sentences have been aligned. It simply refuses to map sentences for which there is not enough evidence to be collected. This can, indeed, be an advantage and makes the algorithm very robust and less prone to error propagation as we have discussed in the previous section on length-based approaches. The disadvantage is the higher complexity of the algorithm which, in fact, has made this approach less widely used.

The general algorithm can also be adjusted in various ways. For example, lexical association can be measured with several metrics and the significance of lexical cues can be tested statistically. Haruno and Yamazaki [1996] use pointwise mutual information, t-scores and augment lexical matching with information from external dictionaries. Kay and Röscheisen [1993] also propose the use of substrings to improve lexical matching and to avoid data sparseness problems in the statistical association measures.

Another common cue for lexical sentence alignment is based on simple string matching techniques. For pairs of related languages, it has been observed that the amount of cognates in corresponding sentences is significantly higher than for other sentence pairs [Simard and Plamondon, 1996, Simard et al., 1993]. Here again, cognates refer to pairs of highly similar strings which can be found by simple string matching techniques. In other words, we include matching numbers, names and other similar entities besides etymologically related words that happen to be similar in spelling. Matching words, in this respect, can now be used again to guide the sentence alignment procedure. Several heuristics can be applied to improve the discriminative nature of these cues. Simard and Plamondon [1996], for example, use fixed-sized search corridors close to the diagonal between aligned anchor points to find possible cognates. Furthermore, they require that acceptable candidates are *isolated*, i.e., similar words do not appear in the close neighborhood of the given candidate. This reduces ambiguity that may lead to wrong alignment decisions. Another possibility is to use a geometric interpretation that focuses on finding a smooth path through the bitext running through discovered corresponding points [Melamed, 1996a].

Naturally, string matching techniques are only applicable to language pairs that share large parts of their alphabets. It is possible to define mappings between characters from different alphabets but the chance of finding cognates is lower for historically less related languages. However, cognate filters and other lexical cues can easily be combined and may complement each other.

FINAL REMARKS ON LEXICAL MATCHING APPROACHES

The weakest point about iterative lexical matching approaches is the strong assumption about anchor points. Using matches in bitext space as hard constraints is risky and may harm alignment performance more than it improves efficiency. The evaluation of the alignment task in the ARCADE campaign showed how fragile these techniques are when applied to a novel with an abridged translation. It is wise to allow a certain amount of flexibility and to use lexical anchor points as guiding soft constraints instead (see, for example, Langlais [1998]). A nice tool for visually exploring matching points in bitext space is the dot-plot method [Church and Helfman, 1993]. Figure 4.12 shows an example plot for localization data (KDE) in four languages.

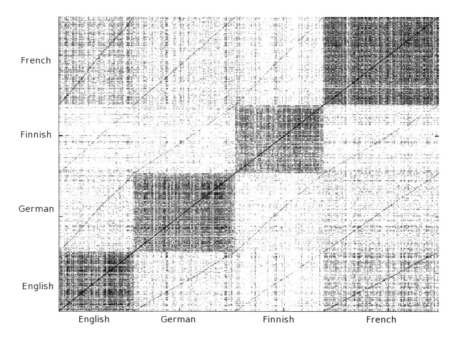

Figure 4.12: A dot plot of matching character 4-grams for 400 lines of KDE system messages in English, German, Finnish and French. The plot includes dots for every matching character 4-gram. Squares indicate string matches for sentences from the same language (high density of unordered matches). Diagonals indicate string matches between different languages (high density of ordered matches).

A dot plot simply shows the similarity of the data with itself. For a parallel corpus, we concatenate all texts to one long string and look for matches of each pair of string positions. A dot plot of parallel data visualizes several interesting properties. Dark squares indicate similarities of strings within one language. In those regions, matches appear everywhere without any particular order and, therefore, create this shape. We can also see that the French and the German texts are longer (in terms of characters) than their English and Finnish counterparts (smaller squares). Furthermore, the similarity between languages is also visible. Some language pairs are more distant than others and resulting squares are lighter. Compare, for example, the region representing English and French with the region representing English and Finnish. Diagonal lines indicate matches in corresponding parts of the bitext. Strongest, of course, is the similarity of corresponding sentences with themselves. However, still quite strong is the match between corresponding sentences across languages (for all language pairs). This pattern can also be seen between more distant language pairs such as English and Finnish due to names, numbers and other named entities.

The dot plot method has several other features that makes this technique interesting, not only for visualization. First of all, it is straightforward to apply this technique with any textual unit and with any similarity measure. In the picture above, we used a sliding window of character N-grams of size four and a simple string matching procedure. We could also use regular words and measure any other type of similarity between them. Secondly, dot plots do not require any text boundaries (like paragraphs, sentences, etc.). The entire corpus is just a long string that is compared with itself. Church [1993] further demonstrates how this technique can also be used for bitext alignment using a program called `char_align`.

4.3   COMBINED AND RESOURCE-SPECIFIC TECHNIQUES

Above we have discussed two of the most common techniques for automatic sentence alignment. Certainly, both ideas can be combined in order to yield higher accuracy. Combinations can be implemented in different ways, either using several types of features in a common search procedure or defining a multi-step approach. For example, Wu [1994] uses a generative model that combines length features with lexical cues. [Simard and Plamondon, 1996] and [Moore, 2002] are examples of multi-step procedures. Evidence from a third language can also be useful [Simard, 1999].

Other types of features, which we have not discussed yet, can also be applied. So far, we always assumed that we have nothing besides the raw text to base our alignment decisions on. In the length-based approach, we already mentioned the use of paragraph alignments as a pre-processing step. Other types of formatting information can be very useful when guiding a sentence alignment program. Many documents come with rich layout information that can be explored to find matching points in the bitext space in the same way lexical cues can be explored. Martínez et al. [1998], for example, propose an alignment algorithm that uses tags from document markup as cognates for matching corresponding segments. The main problem here is that the availability of such information cannot be assumed, and, hence, alignment approaches using these features depend very much on the source and its data formats.

Some source-specific features may also require dedicated alignment algorithms. One example is the alignment of translated movie subtitles. The next sub-section is devoted to this kind of parallel resource in order to include a typical resource-specific approach in our discussions.

SUBTITLE ALIGNMENT

Movie subtitles in various languages are available online in ever growing databases. They can be compiled into diverse collections of parallel corpora useful for many cross-lingual investigations and NLP applications [Armstrong et al., 2006, Lavecchia et al., 2007, Volk and Harder, 2007]. However, translated movie subtitles are very different from other parallel resources and need some special treatment in pre-processing and alignment. Subtitles are not as well-formed as many other textual resources. They contain space-constrained summaries of transcribed dialogues and background information. Translations are often very different from the original manuscript and may vary a lot from language to language as well. They contain a lot of sentence fragments, short expressions of similar length and repeated content. Several studies have shown that traditional alignment techniques do not work very well for these resources [Armstrong et al., 2006, Tiedemann, 2007]. However, subtitles are aligned with the movie and, therefore, should be synchronized with each other. Hence, an obvious idea is to use the time information from subtitle files for the alignment. Tiedemann [2007, 2008] proposes an approach which is entirely based on timing information. The general idea is illustrated in Figure 4.13.

Figure 4.13: Subtitle alignment using time information. Each *subtitle frame* has a start time and an end time. A comparison to neighboring frames can be used to find segment matches with a maximum of time overlap.

The principle of time-overlap alignment is straightforward: segments that are shown at the same time are assumed to be translations of each other. Timing information is, of course, never really identical, and there are some complications when mapping time slots. However, it is easy to see how simple greedy techniques can be used to find segments with the largest overlap among neighboring slots. The alignment approach used in Tiedemann [2007] iteratively extends segments if necessary to find the perfect mapping to the corresponding segments in the other language. Alignments can be found in a linear run through the data. Although this seems very easy, there are several other issues that have to be addressed:

Segmentation: Dividing subtitle frames into suitable segments to be aligned is not as straight-forward as it may seem. One option is to use frames as they are, aligning everything that is marked with a unique time slot. However, in many cases, this does not correspond to a natural sentence segmentation. There are several possibilities:

- Sentences may run over several subtitle frames. This is often marked with special symbols indicating the connection (for example ". . .").

- Sentences may start in the middle of a time slot and run over to the next one.

- One time slot contains several sentences and sentence fragments, which is often the case in fast dialogues.

The layout may be quite different from language to language. Committing to the time slots may make it impossible to link appropriately because text divisions are not compatible. Furthermore, concatenating several sentence fragments into one unit may not be appropriate when, for example, training a translation model on the data.

Synchronization: The synchronization between subtitles may not be as perfect as one would expect. This is especially true for resources that are available online. Small time differences quickly add up and make time-based alignment useless.

To address the first problem, Tiedemann [2007] opted for aligning actual sentences (as opposed to subtitle frame alignment). This means that a sentence may span several time slots or may start or end within a time slot. Therefore, it is necessary to estimate appropriate time information for sentence start and end positions that do not happen to be at time slot boundaries. For this, Tiedemann [2007] proposed the use of a simple linear interpolation between the surrounding time stamps by distributing the length of the time slot evenly over all characters in the slot. This seems to work sufficiently well.

The second problem can be tackled by adjusting time information to fix the synchronization. Time differences are due to two parameters: time offset and speed. Both parameters can be calculated using two fixed anchor points of true correspondence using the formulas given below.

$$time_{ratio} = \frac{(trg_1 - trg_2)}{(src_1 - src_2)}$$

$$time_{offset} = trg_2 - src_2 * time_{ratio}$$

Here, src_1 and src_2 correspond to the time values (in seconds) of the anchor points in the source language and trg_1 and trg_2 to the time values of corresponding points in the target language. Using $time_{ratio}$ and $time_{offset}$, we can now adjust all time values in the source language file before aligning them using the standard time overlap approach. Anchor points can be found in various ways. Tiedemann [2008] proposes the use of lexical matching techniques. Cognate filters and bilingual dictionaries (possibly based on automatic word alignment) can be used to find possible candidates. Tiedemann [2008] uses sliding windows, one from the beginning of the bitext and one from the back, to find anchor points near to the beginning and near to the end. It is also possible to use further heuristics to select among multiple anchor points: Tiedemann [2008] selects the two anchor points that adjust time information in such a way that the time-based alignment algorithm produces the least amount of empty alignments (sentences with no overlap). Fortunately, the linear time-based alignment algorithm is fast enough to allow such a brute-force solution.

An alternative approach is presented in [Itamar and Itai, 2008]. The authors propose to use a combination of string length and time frame length in a standard length-based alignment approach. In this way, the synchronization problems are not an issue. The interpolation between both length parameters needs to be optimized. A problem with this approach appears when one of the subtitles has many omissions. A combination with absolute time information may be a solution for this.

REMARKS ON RESOURCE-SPECIFIC TECHNIQUES

The purpose of this section is to make the reader aware of the necessity of resource specific techniques when creating parallel corpora. Off-the-shelf tools are available for sentence alignment. However, these standard approaches need to be adjusted in many cases. For example, length-based alignment approaches often require hard boundaries to make the alignment approach efficient enough for large-scale text collections and less error-prone on noisy parallel data. However, detecting reliable hard boundaries can be difficult and depends very much on the source. Various types of cues may be used (markup, document structure, lexical anchor points). Furthermore, it is useful to consider other types of information. Some sources come already with some kind of alignment. For example, Bible texts are numbered by verses and chapters that can be mapped across languages [Resnik et al., 1999]. Another example is localization data that is aligned to common identifiers [Tiedemann, 2009a]. Structural information can also be very useful for any alignment procedure but their use depends very much on document formats and available markup. In any case, it is useful to consider the use of markup and meta-data before throwing away all this extra information in the initial conversion process. A final remark is that noisy data collections that include many non-parallel parts always need special treatment before and during alignment. Often some manual work cannot completely be avoided.

4.4   SUMMARY AND FURTHER READING

Sentence alignment attracted a lot of attention in the early developments of data-driven machine translation [Brown et al., 1991, Gale and Church, 1991b, Wu, 1994]. Good results can be achieved with very simple techniques. Sentence alignment is now standard for most parallel corpora, and tools for automatic alignment are widely available. Two main strategies are used: length-based approaches and lexical matching approaches. Both achieve similar alignment quality for clean, completely parallel resources. Some techniques depend on language-pair specific properties, for example, the inclusion of cognates [Simard et al., 1993]. However, most features that are applied are rather language independent or at least flexible enough to make it possible to use similar techniques for a wide range of language families (see, for example, Singh and Husain [2005]). Several authors propose combinations of length-based features and lexical information [Chuang and Chang, 2002, Haruno and Yamazaki, 1996, Ma, 2006, Moore, 2002, Wu, 1994]. The use of string matching techniques has been proposed by Church [1993], Davis et al. [1995], and Melamed [1996a]. Iterative segmentation approaches have been suggested by Xu et al. [2006], and Deng et al. [2006]. A sentence alignment approach that does not assume monotonic mappings is presented by Semmar and Fluhr [2007]. They use a cross-lingual information retrieval approach to find sentence pairs from linguistically analyzed parallel corpora.

The real challenge with sentence alignment comes with noisy parallel corpora. Standard approaches usually fail badly when applied to incomplete parallel resources or collections of mixed quality. Chang and Chen [1997], Fung and McKeown [1994] propose techniques for handling such resources. Much of recent research is devoted to the extraction of parallel parts from comparable corpora (see Chapter 3.3).

CHAPTER 5

Word Alignment

Many applications require alignments on a more fine-grained level. For example, many lexical extraction and statistical machine translation techniques are based on word-level alignments. Word alignment refers to a wide range of techniques for sub-sentential alignment of lexical items. Similar to sentence alignment, we assume a flat segmentation of bitexts into text elements to be aligned. However, such an element now refers to a *word* but in a rather broad sense. Here we try to avoid any further discussion about the term *word* that would lead us to language-specific definitions and complicated linguistic discussions. We will simply require that there is some kind of division of sentences into sequences of smaller meaningful units (**tokens**). These units may refer to punctuations, multi-word units or meaningful character-sequences in the case where clear orthographic word boundaries do not exist.

The largest difference to sentence alignment is that we cannot reasonably assume monotonic mappings anymore, at least not for the majority of language pairs. Furthermore, correspondences are less likely to refer to one-to-one token mappings. Finally, word alignment is not as clear-cut as sentence alignment or other alignments at higher segmentation levels. Alternative mappings may be acceptable, some relations between tokens may be very questionable, and it is often required to leave tokens unaligned because no correspondence can be found. All of these issues but especially the possibility of reordering increases complexity of automatic alignment algorithms at the word level compared to higher-level alignment tasks. One way to reduce the search space is to assume perfect sentence alignment. All approaches that we will discuss consider word alignments within pairs of aligned sentences only.

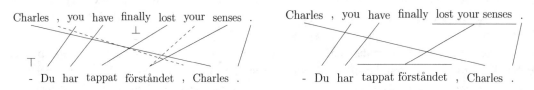

Figure 5.1: Alternative word alignments. A word-to-word linking model on the left and a partial alignment with multi-word units on the right-hand side (sentence pair from *Alice in Wonderland*).

The focus in word alignment is usually set on the smallest alignable units. In other words, we look for the smallest units for which a corresponding unit in the other text can be found. However, it is not always straightforward to identify such units of minimal size as we can see in Figure 5.1. Actually, word alignment depends very much on the application one has in mind. In some cases, it might be necessary to find a complete mapping in terms of token links and some noise is acceptable (high recall) where, in other cases, a partial alignment consisting of accurate bisegments with various sizes is preferred (high precision). Alignment is only a tool for extracting bilingual information for some applications but other applications may use aligned corpora directly, for example, for cross-lingual studies.

Most word alignment algorithms emphasize complete mappings with individual token-to-token links and some special treatment for deletions and insertions. The task of word alignment that focuses on partial but high-precision alignments is also called **translation spotting** [Véronis, 2000], which is often used for the extraction of lexical knowledge.

In the following, we will discuss two common approaches that are used for finding links between individual tokens. The first one is based on a generative word-to-word alignment model and has its origin in the research on statistical machine translation. Thereafter, we will look at discriminative models including a discussion of alignment heuristics and constraints. Finally, we conclude this chapter with a summary and references for further reading.

5.1 GENERATIVE ALIGNMENT MODELS

Generative word alignment models have been developed in the research on statistical machine translation (SMT). In SMT, one tries to build a stochastic model that can be used to translate arbitrary sentences from one language to another. The translation process is modeled as a search problem in which we seek the most likely translation for a given input sentence according to that model. For this, any SMT engine includes a **translation model** which refers to the probabilistic distribution $P(\mathbf{t}|\mathbf{s})$ that assigns a probability to target strings $\mathbf{t}$ given source strings $\mathbf{s}$.[1] Other details of statistical machine translation are not important here as this is not the focus of this book. However, there is a strong connection to bitexts and alignment. SMT is essentially data-driven and the parameters of SMT models are estimated from large amounts of example data. Translation model parameters are usually estimated from collections of translated documents (bitexts). Furthermore, because we focus on the translation of sentences, we require sentence aligned bitexts, and each sentence pair in that corpus is used as an example for training the system. Hence, a sentence aligned bitext becomes the essential training data set for most SMT systems.

One of the crucial questions in SMT is how to create a translation model that assigns proper probabilities to possible translation candidates, given any input sentence. Estimating translation probabilities for complete sentences by looking at their frequencies in a large parallel corpus is not an option as most sentences are unique and proper statistical evidence cannot be found. Therefore, it is necessary to decompose translation models into smaller sub-sentential units (*tokens*) for which appropriate relations can be observed.

The translation between source and target can then be explained on the basis of the relations between these tokens, and the relations can be expressed as the *token alignment* between source and

---

[1]Traditionally, the letters **e** (for English) and **f** (for French or "foreign") are used in the SMT literature. We will stick to **s** (for source) and **t** (for target) to be consistent with other parts of the book.

target sentences. In the framework of SMT, this means that we add another variable $\mathbf{a}$ into the model that represents the alignment between source and target. Together with the target sentence and a given source sentence, this constitutes a stochastic alignment model $P(\mathbf{t}, \mathbf{a}|\mathbf{s})$. Alignments are not given (that is why $\mathbf{a}$ is also referred to as a **hidden variable**); therefore, we need to consider several alternatives and their probabilities. We can infer the translation model that we need for SMT by summing over all possible alignments and their likelihoods according to the alignment model.

$$P(\mathbf{t}|\mathbf{s}) = \sum_{\mathbf{a}} P(\mathbf{t}, \mathbf{a}|\mathbf{s})$$

Similarly, we can also infer the best alignment $\hat{\mathbf{a}}$ according to this model which is called the **Viterbi alignment** between $\mathbf{s}$ and $\mathbf{t}$.

$$\hat{\mathbf{a}} = \operatorname*{argmax}_{\mathbf{a}} P(\mathbf{t}, \mathbf{a}|\mathbf{s})$$

In other words, we can obtain a token-level alignment for any pair of sentences once we have a proper translation model for that language pair. Hence, an alignment can be seen as a by-product of statistical translation modeling.

WORD-BASED ALIGNMENT MODELS

In the discussion above, we avoided the following questions:

1. How do we divide sentences into appropriate units to be aligned?

2. How do we represent the alignment between these units?

3. How do we find appropriate parameters of the stochastic alignment model?

The foundations of statistical machine translation were introduced by [Brown et al., 1988, 1993]. In this work, the authors propose several word-level alignment models for word-based SMT. The segmentation of sentences into words (in the sense of meaningful lexical units which we will call *tokens* from now on) is often a natural way of dividing sentences (also called **tokenization**). With this, we can say that a source sentence $\mathbf{s}$ consists of a sequence of N tokens $(s_1, ..., s_N)$, and a target sentence $\mathbf{t}$ consists of M tokens $(t_1, ..., t_M)$. It is common to abbreviate token sequences by the shorthand $s_a^b = (s_a, ..., s_b)$ with $1 \leq a \leq b \leq N$, which makes it possible to refer to a sentence as s_1^N (and likewise t_1^M for a target sentence). In word-based SMT, this segmentation is fixed, and the alignment models discussed below are all based on such a static segmentation.

The second question is concerned with the representation of alignments between tokens. In general, one could describe a token-level alignment by a set of individual links $\mathcal{L} = \{(n_1, m_1), ..., (n_K, m_K)\}$ as we have discussed before. However, Brown et al. [1993] base their translation models on the generation of words in one language from words in the other. These models, therefore, define an alignment function $a : m \rightarrow n$ to formalize the mapping between source and target tokens. In other words, the function a assigns a unique source token s_n to each target token t_m. This functional constraint (see Chapter 2.3) makes it possible to represent the alignment between two sentences as the vector of source token positions in sentence **s**: $\mathbf{a} = a_1^M = (a_1, ..., a_M)$ where $0 \leq a_m \leq N$ for all $a_m \in \mathbf{a}$. Note that we allow the value of 0 which refers to a non-existing position in sentence **s**. This is a convenient way of allowing unaligned tokens by mapping them to an artificial NULL token at the beginning of the source sentence. Note that placing the NULL token at the beginning of the sentence is not essential and just an arbitrary choice for a position that cannot exist, otherwise. Altogether, this kind of representation has the following properties:

- Each target token can be linked exactly once. Linking to 0 refers to not assigning any source token.

- Each source token can be linked to several target tokens.

- Source tokens do not need to be linked at all.

- Crossing links are allowed without any further restrictions.

In terms of bisegmentations we, therefore, allow many-to-one mappings in one direction but not in the other. Consequently, many-to-many mappings are not possible. To give an example, the left alignment in Figure 5.1 would be represented by the following mapping from English to Swedish (assuming that Swedish is the source sentence **s**).

$$a : \{1 \rightarrow 7, 2 \rightarrow 6, 3 \rightarrow 2, 4 \rightarrow 3, 5 \rightarrow 0, 6 \rightarrow 4, 7 \rightarrow 5, 8 \rightarrow 5, 9 \rightarrow 8\}$$

The same alignment is not possible in the other direction as we can easily see. The two words linked to "förståndet" cannot be represented with the functional representation for a. This shows already the dilemma of this kind of generative approach which necessarily leads to asymmetric alignment models. However, the functional constraint applied here allows efficient training as we will see later and, therefore, outweighs the representational deficiency. There are also ways of combining asymmetric alignments which we will discuss in section 5.2.

The third question is related to the training process in which we need to find appropriate parameters for an alignment model that can be used in statistical machine translation. Alignments consist of individual links between tokens. However, these links depend not only on the tokens they connect but also on the surrounding context and on each other. The entire alignment has to be seen as a complex structure mapping one sentence to another. This structure needs to be decomposed again to allow statistical inference in the training procedure. Without loss of generality, the alignment model can be decomposed as follows using the chain rule for joint probability distributions:

$$P(\mathbf{t}, \mathbf{a}|\mathbf{s}) = P(M|\mathbf{s}) \prod_{m=1}^{M} P(t_m, a_m | t_1^{m-1}, a_1^{m-1}, s_1^N)$$

$$= P(M|\mathbf{s}) \prod_{m=1}^{M} P(a_m | t_1^{m-1}, a_1^{m-1}, s_1^N) P(t_m | t_1^{m-1}, a_1^m, s_1^N)$$

where s_x^y and t_x^y are sequence of source/target language tokens from position x to y and a_u^v is the vector of alignment positions for target tokens u up to v. As the result of this decomposition, we obtain three types of probabilities:

Length probabilities: $P(M|\mathbf{s})$ – the probability of a translation with length M given our source language sentence $\mathbf{s}$

Link probabilities: $P(a_m | t_1^{m-1}, a_1^{m-1}, s_1^N)$ – the probability of an aligned position a_m for target token t_m given all previous target language tokens with their alignments and given the source language sentence $\mathbf{s} = s_1^N$

Lexical probabilities: $P(t_m | t_1^{m-1}, a_1^m, s_1^N)$ – the probability of a target language token t_m given its alignment and all previous target tokens and their alignment and given the source language sentence.

So far, this decomposition did not help us to reduce complexity any further. Individual parameters are still conditioned on the entire context, and all dependencies are part of the model. We will discuss several simplifying assumptions that drastically reduce model complexity which makes it possible to estimate parameters directly from unaligned bitexts. Let us first look at the general principle of training generative alignment models before going into details of specific parametrizations.

PARAMETER ESTIMATION

Statistical modeling involves the task of developing specific models that capture relevant properties for the problem domain. Such a model includes a number of unknown parameters that need to be estimated in some kind of training procedure. In other words, we seek the parameters ϕ of the model $\hat{P}_\phi(\mathbf{t}, \mathbf{a}|\mathbf{s})$ such that

$$\hat{P}_\phi(\mathbf{t}, \mathbf{a}|\mathbf{s}) \approx P(\mathbf{t}, \mathbf{a}|\mathbf{s})$$

The parameters are usually estimated in a training procedure based on statistics from a representative data set of examples, in the case of alignment models, a bitext. Setting parameters to values that explain the training data in the best possible way is called **maximum likelihood estimation** (MLE). In terms of alignment, this would mean that we need to find the parameters $\hat{\phi}$ that maximize the probability of our training set B (our bitext containing K sentence pairs (s_k, t_k)) with respect to the alignment model:

$$\hat{\phi} = \underset{\phi}{\mathrm{argmax}} \prod_{k=1}^{K} P_\phi(\mathbf{t}_k, \mathbf{a}_k | \mathbf{s}_k)$$

This assumes that all sentence pairs are independent and identically distributed training examples that sufficiently represent the entire population of translated sentences. It is often convenient to use the logarithm of this likelihood which produces exactly the same result (because logarithmic functions are monotonic and, therefore, do not change the outcome of the argmax function). In this way, the product of individual likelihood scores can be reduced to a computationally cheaper sum of logarithmic scores:

$$\hat{\phi} = \underset{\phi}{\mathrm{argmax}} \sum_{k=1}^{K} \log P_\phi(\mathbf{t}_k, \mathbf{a}_k | \mathbf{s}_k)$$

In this setup, we assume that our training set is fully specified, which means that all variables can be observed. For our task, this means that the token alignment is given for every sentence pair in the bitext. This is called **supervised learning**, and maximum likelihood estimations are often trivial (simply based on counting observations). The challenging part is now that alignments are not present in the training data. We can say that they are *hidden,* and the training set is incomplete because the alignment variable **a** is not observable (**latent**). For statistical MT, this leads to the dilemma that translation models depend on the alignment between tokens, which we cannot observe. Fortunately, there are techniques that can learn reasonable model parameters even from incomplete data sets, and it is still possible to train a proper translation model $P_\phi(\mathbf{t}|\mathbf{s})$ with an underlying alignment model $P_\phi(\mathbf{t}, \mathbf{a}|\mathbf{s})$. The difference is now that we do not have a fixed and given alignment **a** for each and every sentence pair, but instead we need to consider alternative alignments that might be possible as well. Some of them are more likely than others. Altogether, they describe a probabilistic distribution that we have seen before: $P(\mathbf{t}|\mathbf{s}) = \sum_{\mathbf{a}} P(\mathbf{t}, \mathbf{a}|\mathbf{s})$. Changing our training procedure to an **unsupervised learning** setup where bitexts are given without explicit token alignments, our objective can be formulated as follows:

$$\hat{\phi} = \underset{\phi}{\mathrm{argmax}} \prod_{k=1}^{K} \sum_{\mathbf{a}} P_\phi(\mathbf{t}_k, \mathbf{a}|\mathbf{s}_k) \tag{5.1}$$

$$= \underset{\phi}{\mathrm{argmax}} \sum_{k=1}^{K} \log P_\phi(\mathbf{t}_k, |\mathbf{s}_k) \tag{5.2}$$

One of the techniques (but not the only one) for learning with incomplete data is called EM – the **expectation maximization algorithm** [Dempster et al., 1977]. EM is an iterative re-estimation procedure that tries to adjust model parameters in such a way that the likelihood of observable data improves (the one that we specified in the formula above) in each step. The trick is that we start with an arbitrary initial model and apply it to the training set in order to fill the gaps of the incomplete data with values that would be expected according to the current model. In order to get these *expectations*, it is necessary to compute the posterior probabilities of individual alignments **a**:

$$P_\phi(\mathbf{a}|\mathbf{t}_k, \mathbf{s}_k) = \frac{P_\phi(\mathbf{t}_k, \mathbf{a}|\mathbf{s}_k)}{P_\phi(\mathbf{t}_k|\mathbf{s}_k)} \tag{5.3}$$

These alignment probabilities are used as weights for counting expected observations over all possible alignment for all sentence pairs in the training data. This gives us fractional counts that can be used to estimate new model parameters using standard maximum likelihood estimation in the *maximization* step. The maximization step is essentially the same as in the supervised learning approach with the difference that unsupervised techniques consider all alignments for each sentence pair, while supervised techniques consider only one. Hence, in the supervised setting $P_\phi(\hat{\mathbf{a}}|\mathbf{t}_k, \mathbf{s}_k) = 1$ for the given alignment of $(\mathbf{t}_k, \mathbf{s}_k)$ in bitext B and 0 for all other theoretically possible alignments $\mathbf{a}'$.

With the new model parameters, we can now repeat the entire process. The new model is applied to the bitext and expected values for the missing counts are computed. From this, we can estimate model parameters again and start with the next iteration. A nice property about EM is that there is a theoretical guarantee that the data likelihood is never decreased in any iteration. It will climb the objective function (the data likelihood) until it reaches a stable point from which it cannot be improved anymore (a **local maximum**). We can, therefore, apply this re-estimation process until no (significant) changes of the data likelihood can be observed anymore. However, there is one risk with EM: the local maximum that we find may be sub-optimal and possibly far away from the best setting globally. EM has no possibility to get out of a local maximum; therefore, there is no guarantee to find the **global optimum** even in infinite amounts of time. This is no problem as long as the target function is convex, meaning there is only one local maximum. In that case, we will always find it. However, this is rarely the case. Hence, it is crucial to guide EM in such a way that it is close to the global maximum from the beginning to have a larger chance of finding it. This is one of the reasons why proper initialization is essential for the success of this technique. Note, that there are other methods that allow to jump out of local optima in iterative optimization algorithms, which we will not discuss here.

For statistical MT, we have now a way of finding a translation model from unaligned training data. From an alignment point of view, we can use this method to find token-level alignments for a given sentence-aligned bitext without additional knowledge about the language pair involved (assuming that we know how to tokenize the bitext). However, this is not entirely true because we still need to find a proper parameter set for our alignment model that captures the properties we need for finding the best possible approximation of the true translation process. This is what we will discuss in the following sections.

IBM TRANSLATION MODELS

Brown et al. [1988, 1990, 1993] pioneered the work on statistical machine translation and the alignment models presented there are still used as the main standard in word alignment for training various statistical translation models. The models proposed in Brown et al. [1993] are commonly referred to as the **IBM models 1 - 5** – a series of alignment models with increasing complexity. The starting point is the generative word alignment model and the EM-based training procedure explained above. The five models differ basically in their parametrization which corresponds to certain assumptions about the data and the generative translation process.

IBM model 1   is the simplest model with the strongest independence assumptions between tokens and their alignments. The model is entirely based on lexical translation probabilities $p_t(t|s)$, which are independent of any other information. The *length probability $P_{ibm1}(M|\mathbf{s})$* is assumed to be a small constant ϵ and its value is actually not important for the training procedure (and, hence, does not influence alignment either). *Link probabilities $P(a_m|t_1^{m-1}, a_1^{m-1}, s_1^N)$* are assumed to be independent of individual tokens, their positions and their alignments. We simply assume a uniform distribution over the $N + 1$ possible alignment positions (N source tokens plus the additional NULL token at position 0):

$$P_{ibm1}(a_m|t_1^{m-1}, a_1^{m-1}, s_1^N) = 1/(N + 1)$$

Lexical translation probabilities are assumed to only depend on the aligned token s_{a_m}:[2]

$$P_{ibm1}(t_m|t_1^{m-1}, a_1^m, s_1^N) = p_t(t_m|s_{a_m})$$

Putting this all together gives us the alignment model of IBM 1:

$$P_{ibm1}(\mathbf{t}, \mathbf{a}|\mathbf{s}) = \frac{\epsilon}{(N + 1)^M} \prod_{m=1}^{M} p_t(t_m|s_{a_m}) \tag{5.4}$$

The simplicity of this model makes it possible to compute alignment likelihoods efficiently, which is needed for the EM algorithm outlined in the previous section. We need to sum over all possible alignments to estimate our model parameters (as we know from the equations 5.1 and 5.3). For IBM model 1 and a given sentence pair, this can be simplified in the following way:

---

[2]Note that we use a slightly different notation compared to the descriptions in the background literature. We denote model parameters with the lower-case letter p to mark the probabilistic nature of each parameter, and we use the subscript index to refer to the parameter type, using the same letter as is used in the original literature for that parameter.

$$P_\phi(\mathbf{t}_k|\mathbf{s}_k) \quad = \quad \sum_{\mathbf{a}} P_\phi(\mathbf{t}_k, \mathbf{a}|\mathbf{s}_k)$$

$$= \quad \sum_{a_1=0}^{N} \cdots \sum_{a_m=0}^{N} \frac{\epsilon}{(N+1)^M} \prod_{m=1}^{M} p_t(t_m|s_{a_m})$$

$$= \quad \frac{\epsilon}{(N+1)^M} \prod_{m=1}^{M} \sum_{n=1}^{N} p_t(t_m|s_n) \qquad (5.5)$$

This little trick reduces the computational complexity from $\mathcal{O}(N^M)$ to a roughly quadratic operation ($\mathcal{O}(NM)$) with respect to sentence lengths. Hence, the re-estimation procedure of EM can be performed very efficiently even for large amounts of data. For implementational details, we refer to the presentations in Brown et al. [1993], Knight [1999], and Koehn [2010].

Another nice thing about model 1 is that it describes a convex function [Brown et al., 1993]. As we know from our previous discussions, this gives us the guarantee that we will find the global optimum for our model parameters using EM training. However, model 1 is still not very useful for neither translation modeling nor alignment. The model parameters are too simplistic, and the underlying independence assumptions are too strong to capture important properties of natural languages and translations between them. Figure 5.2 illustrates an example of alternative alignments for a given pair of sentences. Using model 1, all these alignments will obtain the same likelihood, which, of course, is not satisfactory. We need some additional parameters that can capture the differences between these possible solutions.

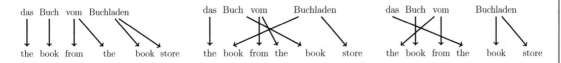

Figure 5.2: Alternative IBM model 1 word alignments that would lead to the same likelihood score due to the position and context independent lexical parameters in the alignment model.

IBM model 2 is a natural extension of the model above by introducing link parameters that are dependent on absolute token positions:

$$P_{ibm2}(a_m|t_1^{m-1}, a_1^{m-1}, s_1^N) = p_a(a_m|m, N, M)$$

The other parameters are the same as in IBM model 1, and the final alignment model is formulated as follows:[3]

$$P_{ibm2}(\mathbf{t}, \mathbf{a}|\mathbf{s}) = \epsilon \prod_{m=1}^{M} p_a(a_m|m, N, M)p_t(t_m|s_{a_m}) \tag{5.6}$$

This model can also be trained efficiently similar to model 1 by replacing the uniform link distribution in equation 5.5 with the newly defined alignment parameters.

$$P_{ibm2}(\mathbf{t}_k|\mathbf{s}_k) = \epsilon \prod_{m=1}^{M} \sum_{n=1}^{N} p_a(a_m|m, N, M)p_t(t_m|s_n)$$

However, this model is not convex anymore; therefore, we are not guaranteed to find the global maximum with EM training. As we have discussed before, proper initialization will be important to increase the chance of finding a maximum close to the global optimum. Fortunately, model 1 can be seen as a special case of model 2; therefore, its parameters are fully compatible. Hence, the optimal parameters found in training model 1 can directly be used as initial parameters for running EM on model 2, assuming that the lexical translation probabilities settled at some reasonable values.

Figure 5.3 illustrates the differences between model 1 and 2. Model 2 can be seen as a two-step procedure with lexical translation as one step and linking (reordering) as the second. There are no dependencies between the parameters as we can see from the graphical representation. The arrows describe the dependences expressed by the individual parameters. Note that the link probabilities predict source positions for each given target token position as defined by the alignment function a and, therefore, point in the opposite direction of the generative process. This will be changed in the following model below.

IBM model 3   adds a new type of parameter $p_n(\phi|s)$ to the alignment model which is called **fertility**. It refers to the number $\phi = 0, 1, 2, ...$ of target tokens that can be generated by a given source token s. With this kind of parameter, it is possible to capture the specific property of some tokens to align to multiple tokens more often than others. It also explicitly models the possibility of dropping tokens ($\phi = 0$). Fertility can be seen as an additional step in the generative procedure which *duplicates* source tokens that will give rise to the target tokens generated on the other side. Figure 5.4 tries to illustrate this process (fertility is the first step on the top).

A special case is the fertility of the artificially inserted token NULL, which refers to the number of insertions that we try to cover. This parameter is modeled separately because the amount of insertions is likely to depend on the sentence length. In particular, instead of adding a fertility parameter for NULL, model 3 includes a special NULL-insertion probability p_1 that is applied together with each generated token. NULL tokens are thus inserted with probability p_1 at all positions. The complementary probability $p_0 = 1 - p_1$ represents the chance of not inserting any NULL token. The NULL insertion step is illustrated as the second step in Figure 5.4.

---

[3]Note that it is common practice to ignore the dependence on M in p_a to reduce the number of parameters.

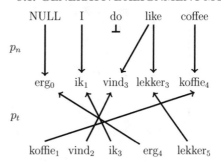

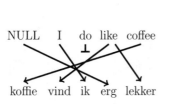

Figure 5.3: A comparison of IBM model 1 (left) and IBM model 2 (right) illustrated for a given English-Dutch sentence pair "I do like coffee" – "koffie vind ik erg lekker". The arrows correspond to model parameters used in these models. The position indexes are indicated for the reordering step in which they become important. As a matter of fact, only the positions are used in that step, and all lexical knowledge is ignored when moving tokens to new places. One can think of just copying generated tokens along the lines.

Lexical translation probabilities p_t are the same as in models 1 and 2. Reordering is also based on absolute positions as in model 2. However, model 3 uses a new class of parameters $p_d(m|n, N, M)$ called **distortion**, which predicts the target position m, given the position n of the source token it is generated from (instead of doing this the other way around in model 2). Distortion fits the generative story that models the movement of tokens to new target positions as we can see in Figure 5.4. Note that we still use the same definition of alignment which is a function that maps a source position to every target position.

As the consequence of this multi-step procedure, there are multiple ways to arrive at the same generated sentence with the same token-level alignment. This is due to the fertility which leads to alternative productions in the translation step. See Figure 5.4 for an example of two alternative translation processes with the same underlying alignment (in terms of our asymmetric alignment function). Therefore, it is necessary to sum over all such possible productions when computing $P_{ibm3}(\mathbf{t}, \mathbf{a}|\mathbf{s})$. Multiple productions occur only for source tokens s_n for which a fertility $\phi_n > 1$ is chosen. The individual productions are the same (see Figure 5.4) and because they are independent of each other, we simply have to consider the $\phi_n!$ permutations of generated target tokens that origin from one specific source token. Putting everything together, we can now formulate the translation model for IBM 3 as follows:

$$P_{ibm3}(\mathbf{t}, \mathbf{a}|\mathbf{s}) = p_n(\phi_0) \prod_{n=1}^{N} \phi_n! \ p_n(\phi_n|s_n) \prod_{m=1}^{M} p_t(t_m|s_{a_m}) p_d(m|a_m, N, M) \qquad (5.7)$$

The first term of this formula refers to the special NULL insertion probability. ϕ_0 refers to the number of insertions that are made (i.e. tokens generated from NULL). Insertion of NULL is allowed at

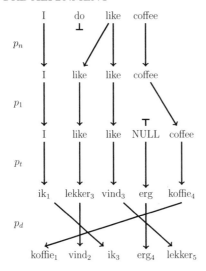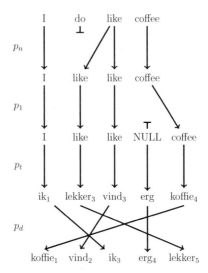

Figure 5.4: An illustration of IBM model 3 including the 4 steps, *fertility* (p_n), *NULL insertion* (p_1), *lexical translation* (p_t) and *distortion* (p_d). The two figures show two alternative productions for the same sentence pair and identical token alignment (look at the position indexes in the last step).

each target token generated from a real source token. Hence, there are $\sum_{n=1}^{N} \phi_n = M - \phi_0$ decisions whether to insert a NULL token or not. Using a binomial distribution, we arrive at the following probability for $p_n(\phi_0)$:

$$p_n(\phi_0) = \binom{M - \phi_0}{\phi_0} p_1^{\phi_0} p_0^{M - 2\phi_0}$$

In IBM model 3, it is, unfortunately, not possible to simplify the marginal probability distribution $P_{ibm3}(\mathbf{t}_k|\mathbf{s}_k)$ in the same way as we did for models 1 and 2. However, enumerating all possible alignments for all sentence pairs is prohibitively expensive. Consequently, exhaustive collections of counts are not possible and complete EM cannot be carried out. A solution is to use approximations by sampling plausible alignments. One technique for finding useful candidates is to use alignments produced by model 2 as a starting point for heuristic hill-climbing techniques. Neighboring alignments in the vicinity of good model 2 alignments can be explored, using swap and move operations. Other techniques are possible as well. More details about transferring model 2 parameters to model 3 and about approximation techniques can be found in various publications and text books [Brown et al., 1993, Koehn, 2010, Och and Ney, 2003].

Although IBM model 3 is already a quite powerful alignment model covering some essential properties of token correspondences, it still makes a lot of assumptions. Its parameters are still independent of surrounding contexts and interactions between alignment decisions are not explicitly considered.

IBM model 4   introduces several extensions to the fertility-based model 3. First of all, it moves from distortion parameters based on absolute positions to a relative distortion model. Absolute positioning does not generalize very well even though these parameters could reasonably be estimated with sufficient statistics. However, there will always be cases for which the counts are too sparse especially for long sentences. It is also not very intuitive to model the placement of target language tokens at absolute positions in a sentence solely depending on the position of the generating source language token (and the sentence length). Model 4, therefore, introduces relative distortions based on the placement of target tokens generated by preceding words. With this, we introduce a **first-order dependence** between links whereas all the previous models ignored any interaction between them. The property that model 4 tries to capture, in this way, is the tendency of chunks to move together. The model therefore defines two types of distortion parameters based on the concept of **cepts**, which refer to chunks τ_n of target tokens generated from non-zero fertility tokens s_n. The position $\pi_{n,1} = m$ of the *head* token $\tau_{n,1}$ (the left-most token) of a cept τ_n is chosen relative to the center c_{n-1} of the previous cept τ_{n-1}, using parameter $p_{d_1}(m - c_{n-1})$. The center of a cept is defined as the ceiling of the average target position of all tokens in that cept. The position $\pi_{n,k+1} = m$ of any other token $\tau_{n,k+1}$ in cept τ_n is chosen relative to the position of the previous token $\tau_{n,k}$ in the same cept with probability $p_{d_{>1}}(m - \pi_{n,k})$. In model 4, we require a left-to-right order of target positions of in-cept tokens (but not necessarily in consecutive order).

Another innovation introduced by model 4 is the dependence on word classes. So far, distortion is independent of any lexical information. This is not satisfactory; therefore, the new model introduces additional lexical dependencies. A straightforward dependency on surface tokens is tempting but statistically prohibitive as we will suffer from sparse counts. Therefore, more general word classes are introduced which can be seen as functions $class_s(s)$ and $class_t(t)$, mapping unique classes to each source and target language token. Usually, one applies a small number of automatically induced classes (using clustering techniques). The final distortion model becomes, then, for initial cept tokens $\tau_{n,1}$

$$p_{d_1}(m - c_{n-1}|class_s(s_{n-1}), class_t(t_m))$$

and for all preceding tokens $\tau_{n,k+1}$ in the same cept

$$p_{d_{>1}}(m - \pi_{n,k}|class_t(t_m))$$

Using such a class-dependent distortion, it is possible to capture consistent structural differences between certain languages. Brown et al. [1993] discuss, for example, the difference of placing adjectives before or after a noun in English and French, respectively. They can observe that the learned distortion parameters, indeed, reflect the intuitive properties for such cases in their experimental setup. The second type of distortion parameters ($p_{d_{>1}}$) models how strongly chunks should stay together when generated from the source. Brown et al. [1993] give the example of the French "ne pas" (generated from the English word "not"), which often occurs with an intervening verb instead of staying next to each other. Again, they can confirm that the model is able to learn this property by putting more weight on larger distortions, for example, $p_{d_{>1}}(2|class_t(pas))$, than for similar distortions of other chunks that tend to stick together.

Once again, training is very expensive and exhaustive count collection is impossible. Hill-climbing techniques, based on model 3 alignments, are used in the same manner as training is performed for model 3, based on model 2 alignments.

In this description we omit a discussion of model 5, which basically models the same properties as model 4. It fixes, however, a problem that arises with the introduction of fertility-based models, which is called **deficiency**. This refers to the problem of impossible outcomes (target token placements that are undefined), which are actually permitted in model 3 and 4. "Wasting" part of the probability distribution for such outcomes may influence training results. Model 5 resolves this problem with the drawback of requiring additional alignment parameters that make training even harder. In terms of alignment performance, model 5 usually does not add significantly to the previous ones; therefore, model 4 is often considered to be the final standard alignment model in statistical machine translation.

To conclude our discussion on the IBM models, we can say that statistical translation models can be used to find asymmetric token alignments for a given sentence-aligned bitext. Complex models using a large number of parameters can be based on simpler models and unsupervised training techniques can be used to fit parameters according to the observed parallel data. There is quite a large body of work on variants, extensions and improvements of these models to overcome some of their shortcomings. Below we will discuss some of them starting with one of the most popular alternatives based on a Hidden Markov Model formulation for alignment.

HIDDEN MARKOV ALIGNMENT MODELS

We have discussed earlier that an alignment refers to the entire structure of mapping one half of a bitext to the other one. IBM models 1 to 3, however, do not take care of interactions between individual links. Model 4 introduces first-order dependencies and adds lexical information into the distortion model. Both extensions lead to a substantial boost in alignment quality. Vogel et al. [1996] propose an alternative alignment model based on a Hidden Markov Model (HMM) formulation which includes first-order dependencies between adjacent links. It otherwise uses the same parameter types as IBM model 2 but replaces the reordering model with the following link parameter p_a:

$$P_{hmm}(a_m|t_1^{m-1}, a_1^{m-1}, s_1^N) = p_a(a_m|a_{m-1}, N)$$

The alignment position a_m of the target token t_m in the source language now depends on the alignment position a_{m-1} of the preceding target token instead of depending on the position m of the current token in the target language sentence (model 2). The idea here is similar to the one discussed in model 4: tokens tend to move in chunks and the dependence on previous alignment positions may capture this. Using a simple length model $P_\phi(M|s) = p_l(M|N)$, we can now write the formulation of the new alignment model as follows:

$$P_{hmm}(\mathbf{t}, \mathbf{a}|\mathbf{s}) = p_l(M|N) \prod_{m=1}^{M} p_a(a_m|a_{m-1}, N) p_t(t_m|s_{a_m}) \qquad (5.8)$$

In the HMM, we further assume that the link probabilities $p_a(n|n', N)$ only depend on the *jump width* $(n - n')$ between the two alignment positions. The link probabilities are, therefore, computed using relative jump width counts:

$$p_a(n|n', N) \approx p_d(n - n') = \frac{c(n - n')}{\sum_{n''}^{N} c(n'' - n')}$$

This formulation makes the reordering parameter independent of absolute positions and ensures the normalization constraints of a homogeneous Hidden Markov Model [Vogel et al., 1996]. HMMs have the nice property that they can be trained efficiently with the Baum-Welch algorithm [Baum et al., 1970], a particular case of the EM algorithm. Similarly, the best alignment can be found using the well-known Viterbi algorithm [Forney Jr., 1973, Viterbi, 1967]. One problem is related to the representation of NULL alignments. Och and Ney [2003] propose to double the state space of the HMM in order to support empty words. Each additional *empty-word-state* has an incoming connection from exactly one of the original N states in the HMM with a fixed transition cost p_0. This value has to be optimized in a separate step on some held-out data. Och and Ney [2003] simply set this additional parameter to an arbitrary value (0.2). An alternative is to make p_0 dependent on the input sentence length $p_0 = 1/(N + 1)$ [Liang et al., 2006]. Outgoing transitions from the empty-word states are forced to have identical costs as the transition to the same target state without the intermediate jump to the empty-word state [Och and Ney, 2003].

The HMM alignment model has proven to be very effective. It is, therefore, common to include HMM training in the alignment pipeline, placing HMMs between IBM model 2 and IBM model 3. Furthermore, it is also possible to augment HMMs with additional information. Toutanova et al. [2002] experiments with various extensions, among others, the addition of part-of-speech information as additional linguistic constraint for word alignment. It is also possible to add dependencies on automatically induced word classes similar to the ones used in IBM model 4 [Och and Ney, 2003].

OTHER EXTENSIONS & IMPROVEMENTS

The alignment models presented above can be further improved in various ways. For example, a common variant of IBM model 2 defines link probabilities based on the relative distance to the diagonal instead of absolute alignment positions [Vogel et al., 1996]:[4]

---

[4]$\lfloor x \rfloor$ is the largest integer y with $y \leq \lfloor x \rfloor$ (*floor*).

$$p_a(n|m, N) \approx p_d \left(n - \left\lfloor \frac{mN}{M} \right\rfloor \right) = \frac{c(n - \lfloor \frac{mN}{M} \rfloor)}{\sum_{n'}^{N} c(n' - \lfloor \frac{mN}{M} \rfloor)}$$

Furthermore, we can also group out-of-range values together to reduce the number of link parameters to a fixed number of distortion parameters, assuming that the majority of links will be close to the diagonal. This modified model is also called the *diagonal-oriented* model 2 [Och and Ney, 2000]. Additionally, these adjusted model 2 link parameters can be conditioned on source and target word classes in the same way it is done for model 4 and the HMM.

Och and Ney [2003] propose several other extensions which have positive effects on alignment quality. They introduce smoothing techniques to avoid overfitting of the distortion and fertility probabilities. Distortion in their approach is modified using a linear interpolation with a uniform distribution $p(n|m, N) = 1/N$. Fertility parameters are smoothed using a new fertility distribution $p_n(\phi|g(s))$ that depends on the length $g(s)$ of the input token s assuming that longer words are more likely to have larger fertilities. This distribution is then again combined with standard fertility parameters using linear interpolation. Interpolation weights are determined on held-out data.

Another extension is the use of external bilingual dictionaries to improve alignment quality. Och and Ney [2003] propose to add dictionary entries with a high count to the training corpus if they actually co-occur at least ones in the regular training corpus. A low count or zero should be used for other dictionary entries to avoid a negative impact of out-of-domain words.

Finally, Och and Ney [2003] also propose a model 6 which combines the HMM and IBM model 4. The motivation here is to use complimentary knowledge of these two models especially due to the fact that the HMM includes first-order dependencies along the source language side whereas IBM model 4 adds distortion dependencies on the target side. Och and Ney [2003], therefore, suggest a log-linear combination of these two models with a weight parameter α that has been optimized on held-out data:

$$P_{model6} = \frac{P_{ibm4}(\mathbf{t}, \mathbf{a}|\mathbf{s})^{\alpha} P_{hmm}(\mathbf{t}, \mathbf{a}|\mathbf{s})}{\sum_{\mathbf{a}',\mathbf{t}'} P_{ibm4}(\mathbf{t}', \mathbf{a}'|\mathbf{s})^{\alpha} P_{hmm}(\mathbf{t}', \mathbf{a}'|\mathbf{s})} \tag{5.9}$$

FINAL REMARKS ON GENERATIVE ALIGNMENT MODELS

The generative alignment models have their origin in the *noisy-channel* formulation of word-based statistical machine translation. Today, they are widely used beyond the scope of this particular application. Alignment model parameters are usually not used anymore for direct incorporation in statistical machine translation but merely for creating word-aligned training data for other purposes (like, for example, training phrase-based SMT [Koehn et al., 2003]). For this, the Viterbi alignment of the final model in the training pipeline is commonly used. The popularity of generative approaches is based on the possibility to run unsupervised training procedures as described above. However, there are a number of drawbacks that have to be pointed out:

- The alignment is asymmetric and results depend very much on the alignment direction. We will discuss some techniques to overcome this problem in the next section.

- Parameter estimation is expensive especially for the fertility-based models. Approximate search is required to find model parameters.

- Initialization is important to avoid local maxima. The training scheme has a large impact on the final performance.

- Large amounts of sentence-aligned parallel data are required to obtain reasonable results. Morphologically rich languages suffer easily from data sparseness.

- Distortion is a major reason for misalignment. "Well-behaved" languages that mainly align along the bitext diagonal are preferred.

- It is difficult to integrate additional contextual information and linguistic knowledge into generative models.

- Optimizing the likelihood of observable data does not necessarily lead to a good estimation of the hidden link structure we are seeking in automatic alignment.

5.2   CONSTRAINTS AND HEURISTICS

Generative word alignment models are not satisfactory mainly because of their asymmetric nature. The correspondence relation between words and multi-word units should be seen as a symmetric relation as any other type of alignment. During EM training, rare source words can also become so-called garbage collectors [Moore, 2004] which obtain links to target words that cannot reliably be linked, otherwise. This effect is due to the fact that rare words often have a lot of spare mass in their conditional distribution that can be spend for generating random words. Obviously, the same words cannot act as garbage collectors in the reverse alignment direction due to the definition of the alignment function and the generative model. Hence, symmetric models do not suffer from this problem. Certainly, generative alignment models can be run in both directions. One obvious idea for improvement is to use knowledge from both alignment directions.

SYMMETRIZATION

In general, we like to consider alignments that consist of sets of individual links $l_k = (n, m)$ between tokens s_n and t_m. Viterbi alignments using the asymmetric models introduced above can be used to produce subsets of possible links constrained by the functional definition of the alignment function a. Training alignment models in both directions allows us to obtain two such link sets, $\mathcal{L}_{s \to t}$ and $\mathcal{L}_{t \to s}$. The trick of symmetrization is to merge these two sets in a clever way in order to produce a better symmetric alignment between tokens from the given sentence pair.

One obvious choice is to produce the **intersection** $\mathcal{L}_{s \to t} \cap \mathcal{L}_{t \to s}$ of both sets. The intuition behind this way of combining alignments is to focus on links for which both alignment models agree on. We expect the precision of links to increase in this way. However, we can also expect a drop in recall as we certainly remove possibly valuable links especially in cases of very different Viterbi alignments. The set of aligned segments will also be restricted to one-to-one token mappings, which may even hurt precision when measured in terms of bisegment correspondences.

Another possibility is to create the **union** $\mathcal{L}_{s \to t} \cup \mathcal{L}_{t \to s}$ of both sets. Here we assume that all links are valuable and both alignment directions include complementary information. However, automatic word alignment is not perfect, and the risk of merging all links together is to increase the garbage in the final alignment. Hence, in terms of precision, we expect a drop whereas recall should go up.

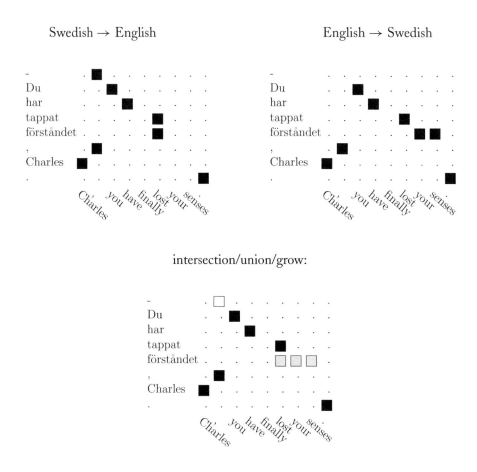

Figure 5.5: Combination heuristics for asymmetric (not necessarily correct) word alignments. In the combined matrix, all boxes are part of the union of links, filled black boxes refer to the intersection, gray boxes refer to links added during the grow symmetrization heuristics.

Figure 5.5 illustrates these two possibilities of combining asymmetric word alignments. There are a number of symmetrization heuristics that try to balance precision and recall by creating sets in between the strict intersection and the general union of token links. An observation that has been made is that good links are often next to other already accepted links. This leads to various heuristics using **link neighbors** from the union set to extend the intersection of links, which is assumed to be most reliable. Such *growing heuristics* have initially been proposed by Och et al. [1999] in connection with the alignment template approach for statistical machine translation. These techniques have been developed further and have shown to be of great value for phrase-based SMT approaches [Ayan and Dorr, 2006a, Koehn et al., 2003].

The difference between the various grow heuristics is mainly the definition of *neighbor* (whether they allow diagonal neighbors or not) and how they treat remaining unaligned tokens. Typical strategies start by iteratively adding neighboring links (horizontal, vertical, possibly diagonal) to existing links and, finally, adding links between source and target tokens which have otherwise not been linked yet. For simplicity, this is run in a left-to-right manner without considering any further measures of confidence. Alternatively, one can also train classifiers for combining various word alignments [Ayan and Dorr, 2006b]. The main drawback of symmetrization techniques is, however, that we base our decisions on independently trained asymmetric models. Heuristic symmetrization as a one-time post-processing step is, therefore, not really satisfactory.

AGREEMENT CONSTRAINTS

Liang et al. [2006] propose a method for incorporating agreement constraints in HMM-based alignment training. The approach is motivated by the observation that intersections of asymmetric word alignments outperform individual alignments in particular in terms of precision. An intersection can be seen as the set of links on which two models agree upon. Therefore, it makes intuitively sense to encourage agreement when jointly training asymmetric alignment models. Let us define binary indicator variables a_{nm} that refer to the link between s_n and t_m, which is set to 1 if the link $l_k = (n, m)$ is established.[5] The task is now to find the distribution over $P(\mathbf{a}|\mathbf{s}, \mathbf{t})$ that corresponds to the data and its alignment structure. The alignments created by the generative alignment models can be seen as special cases in which $P(\mathbf{a}|\mathbf{s}, \mathbf{t}) = 0$ for all instances of $\mathbf{a}$ that do not fulfill the functional constraint of a.

Liang et al. [2006] quantify the agreement between two alignment models $P_{\phi_1}(\mathbf{a}|\mathbf{s}, \mathbf{t})$ and $P_{\phi_2}(\mathbf{a}|\mathbf{s}, \mathbf{t})$ by summing over all alignment probabilities on which both models agree:

$$\sum_{\mathbf{a}} P_{\phi_1}(\mathbf{a}|\mathbf{s}, \mathbf{t}) P_{\phi_2}(\mathbf{a}|\mathbf{s}, \mathbf{t})$$

---

[5]We abuse notation here to refer to those binary variables with the same letter a as we have previously used for specifying the word alignment function in IBM models. Essentially, alignments are still represented by these indicator variables and should not cause too much confusion.

Adding this agreement measure to the individual log-likelihood estimations of each alignment model we arrive at the following objective:

$$\max_{\phi_1,\phi_2} \sum_{k=1}^{K} \left[\log P_{\phi_1}(\mathbf{t}_k, |\mathbf{s}_k) + \log P_{\phi_2}(\mathbf{t}_k, |\mathbf{s}_k) + \log \sum_{\mathbf{a}} P_{\phi_1}(\mathbf{a}|\mathbf{s}_k, \mathbf{t}_k) P_{\phi_2}(\mathbf{a}|\mathbf{s}_k, \mathbf{t}_k) \right]$$

In order to run the EM algorithm with this augmented objective function, we need to sum over the set of alignments with exclusively one-to-one mappings (corresponding to possible intersections) in order to obtain accurate counts in the expectation step. This is, however, intractable and Liang et al. [2006] propose to use a simple approximation using individual link probabilities:

$$P_{\phi}(\mathbf{a}|\mathbf{s}, \mathbf{t}) \approx \prod_{n,m} P_{\phi_1}(a_{nm}|\mathbf{s}, \mathbf{t}) P_{\phi_2}(a_{nm}|\mathbf{s}, \mathbf{t})$$

In Hidden Markov Models, these posterior link probabilities correspond to the *state occupation probabilities* [Matusov et al., 2004] which can be computed efficiently using the Baum-Welch algorithm. The marginal probability of source token s_n being connected to the target token t_m is estimated using the following sum:

$$p_m(n, \mathbf{t}|\mathbf{s}) = \sum_{\mathbf{a}:a_m=1} P_{hmm}(\mathbf{t}, \mathbf{a}|\mathbf{s})$$

The state occupation probability then becomes

$$P_{\phi_1}(a_{nm}|\mathbf{s}, \mathbf{t}) = p_m(n|\mathbf{t}, \mathbf{s}) = \frac{p_m(n, \mathbf{t}|\mathbf{s})}{\sum_{n'=1}^{N} p_m(n', \mathbf{t}|\mathbf{s})}$$

Using a similar computation for the HMM in the other alignment direction, we can compute $P_{\phi}(\mathbf{a}|\mathbf{s}, \mathbf{t})$ using the link posteriors as described above. Due to the approximation, this procedure is not guaranteed to increase the joint objective in each training step. However, Liang et al. [2006] show experimentally that this technique indeed improves alignment quality.

The final issue that has to be addressed now is the actual prediction of links using the jointly trained model. Finding the Viterbi alignment of the combined HMM $\text{argmax}_{\mathbf{a}} = P_{\phi_1}(\mathbf{a}|\mathbf{s}, \mathbf{t}) P_{\phi_2}(\mathbf{a}|\mathbf{s}, \mathbf{t})$ is intractable [Liang et al., 2006]. One possibility would be to use a hard intersection between individual alignment predictions, but this would hurt recall as discussed above in the standard symmetrization heuristics. Liang et al. [2006], therefore, propose to apply **posterior decoding** instead, using a simple threshold δ for selecting links:

$$\mathbf{a} = \left\{ a_{nm} = 1 : P_{\phi_1}(a_{nm}|\mathbf{s}, \mathbf{t}) P_{\phi_2}(a_{nm}|\mathbf{s}, \mathbf{t}) \geq \delta \right\}$$

This is similar to the approximation used for count collection in the joint training procedure. Individual links are still influenced by the entire alignment distribution and δ can be adjusted to balance the trade-off between precision and recall. Liang et al. [2006] show that there is large range of settings where posterior decoding outperforms Viterbi decoding.

ALIGNMENT SEARCH CONSTRAINTS

So far, we have focused on statistical techniques for unsupervised training of generative alignment models. These models are described by a set of parameters, and the actual alignment has to be inferred using some decoding techniques such as Viterbi decoding or posterior decoding as presented in the previous section. This *alignment inference procedure* can actually be constrained in various ways. For simplicity, let us consider the case where individual links can be evaluated independently. Posterior decoding as presented in the previous section has shown that such an approach can be quite successful. Let us assume that there is a way to produce scores c_{nm} for each individual alignment position for a given sentence pair.[6] These scores could be, for example, posterior link probabilities $P_\phi(a_{nm} = 1|\mathbf{s}, \mathbf{t})$ from the previous section. Hence, various kinds of source, target and alignment dependencies may contribute to this score. The task of the inference procedure is now to use the evidence collected in the link matrix

$$C = \begin{bmatrix} c_{11} & c_{21} & \cdots & c_{n1} \\ c_{12} & c_{22} & \cdots & c_{n2} \\ \vdots & \vdots & \ddots & \\ c_{1m} & c_{2m} & & c_{nm} \end{bmatrix}$$

to extract the overall best alignment for the given sentence pair. Simple thresholding as used in the previous section is one way to perform this task.

With the generative sequence models, the Viterbi algorithm can be used to fully exploit the alignment space. However, it can also be useful to constrain the inference procedure in order to guide the algorithm to make even better decisions. Search constraints can be seen as additional prior knowledge which are built into the alignment procedure. The same constraints do not necessarily have to be part of the training procedure as they often lead to increased complexities and inefficient training algorithms. For example, interactions between variables in the output space (links in our case) can be modeled without explicitly including the same dependencies in training.

Constraints can be either hard constraints (conditions that cannot be violated) or soft constraints that can be used to act as a preference mechanism. This can be seen as adding *restriction bias* and *search bias* to the final inference step. Ignoring the procedures of obtaining scores or costs for individual links, we can now explore several algorithms with various types of constraints and restrictions. Cherry and Lin [2006a] discuss some possibilities to restrict the alignment space in a word alignment task (see also the discussion on alignment spaces in Chapter 2.3). One observation that has been made is that simple thresholding can lead to wrong alignments because of spurious relations discovered by the training procedure. This is similar to the effect of garbage collectors in generative alignment models [Moore, 2004] which we have discussed already. It can, therefore, be

---

[6]We omit the dependence on the current sentence pair to simplify notation.

beneficial to restrict alignments to one-to-one token mappings. A search which is constrained in this way can be implemented in various ways. One way is to treat the alignment problem as a weighted bipartite matching problem (more details will be discussed in section 5.3). Another alternative is to use a simple greedy algorithm which is known as competitive linking Melamed [2000]. The procedure is very simple, and it can easily be combined with other constraints like score thresholds δ or structural constraints. Using our matrix C as a set of indexed link scores $\{c_{nm}\}$, we can run competitive linking as described in Figure 5.6. The algorithm simply looks for the highest score in turn, links corresponding items with each other, and removes them from the search space for the next iteration. Additional constraints can be added to avoid links that do not satisfy certain conditions.

$sorted \leftarrow$ reverse_sort_index_pairs_by_value(C)
$links = \{\}$
$linkedSrc = \{\}$
$linkedTrg = \{\}$
while $(n, m) \leftarrow$ pop $sorted$ **do**
   if $c_{nm} < \delta$ **then**
      return $links$
   end if
   if not $(n \in linkedSrc$ **or** $m \in linkedTrg)$ **then**
      if meets_other_constraints$((n, m), links)$ **then**
         $links \cup \{(n, m)\}$
         $linkedSrc \cup \{n\}$
         $linkedTrg \cup \{m\}$
      end if
   end if
end while
return $links$

Figure 5.6: Competitive linking with additional constraints. The algorithm starts with a list of link candidates (n, m) sorted by their association scores c_{nm} and pops iteratively candidates from that list. Linked items are removed from the search space to avoid multiply linked elements. This is done until a certain threshold δ is reached. Further alignment constraints can be checked in the *meets_other_constraints* function.

Matusov et al. [2004] define another inference procedure based on alignment costs. Local alignment costs are defined as weighted sums of various link cost functions $c_{nm} = \sum_m \lambda_m h_m(n, m)$, which is similar to the *clue alignment algorithm* presented in Tiedemann [2003a]. For their experiments, Matusov et al. [2004] use the negative logarithm of posterior link probabilities from HMM alignment models as follows:

$$c_{nm} = \alpha(-\log p_m(n|\mathbf{s}, \mathbf{t}; \phi_{hmm1})) + (1 - \alpha)(-\log p_n(m|\mathbf{s}, \mathbf{t}; \phi_{hmm2}))$$

The interpolation weight α is estimated on some held-out data and reflects how well one alignment direction can capture the true alignment compared to the other alignment direction.[7] Tiedemann [2003a] shows further how arbitrary real-valued features of possibly overlapping pairs of multi-word units can be combined to create the individual alignment costs. Using such a cost matrix, Matusov et al. [2004] present edge cover algorithms which are essentially identical to the greedy algorithms presented in Tiedemann [2004]. They also present a minimum-cost edge cover algorithm which is based on maximum-weight bipartite matching which we will discuss in section 5.3. Edge-cover algorithms can produce many-to-one or one-to-many alignments whereas the bipartite matching approach is restricted to one-to-one mappings.

Another type of constraint that can be integrated in alignment inference is based on syntactic restrictions. Cherry and Lin [2006a] define, for example, dependency constraints based on parsed sentences on one side of the bitext. They force phrases in the dependency tree to move together when being aligned to the other language based on findings about *phrasal cohesion* [Fox, 2002]. The size of the restricted search space depends very much on the provided tree structure but is usually much smaller than the unrestricted alignment space. The additional constraints seem to have a positive effect on alignment accuracy. Another possibility is to use restrictions based on grammar formalisms used for synchronous parsing. Inversion transduction grammars (ITGs) Wu [1997] are widely used for this purpose (see Chapter 6.2 for more details). The shared tree structures of synchronous ITG parses also implies a word alignment which restricts the alignment space according to the capacity of the grammar formalism. Wu [1997] includes a detailed discussion about permutations and the restrictions implied by the ITG formalism. Cherry and Lin [2006a] show how dependency constraints and ITG constraints can be combined to improve alignment search accuracy.

5.3   DISCRIMINATIVE ALIGNMENT MODELS

The discussions on alignment constraints and link costs from above naturally leads to discriminative word alignment models. Word alignment can be seen as a general **structured prediction problem** in which we like to use a target function f that maps instances of input objects coming from a space $\mathcal{X}$ to target values y coming from the output space $\mathcal{Y}$. In alignment, $\mathcal{X}$ contains pairs of sentences $(\mathbf{s}, \mathbf{t})$, and target values y are alignments $\mathbf{a}$ for given sentence pairs.

$$f : (\mathbf{s}, \mathbf{t}) \rightarrow \mathbf{a}$$

The task of learning refers to finding an approximation $\hat{f}$ of this unknown target function (also called **discriminant function**) that minimizes the expected error when applied to arbitrary data instances from $\mathcal{X}$. In **supervised machine learning**, we try to find such a target function by optimizing parameters of a chosen class of functions such that the prediction error on a given training set $\{(\mathbf{s}_1, \mathbf{t}_1, \mathbf{a}_1), ..., (\mathbf{s}_K, \mathbf{t}_K, \mathbf{a}_K)\} \subseteq \mathcal{X} \times \mathcal{Y}$ is minimized. Training data is usually a limited (hopefully representative sample) of the entire population of data instances. In machine learning, it is therefore

---

[7]Note that costs can also come from only one alignment model or more than two models.

important to use models and to apply learning algorithms that generalize well in order to minimize the **expected loss** of the final target function $\hat{f}$.

Target functions can be defined in various ways leading to decisions that can be made about given input objects. In a statistical framework, we can use probabilistic density functions. In the generative models discussed earlier, we have seen already that target predictions can be based on the following search procedure over the joint probability distribution of **t** and **a** given **s**:

$$\hat{\mathbf{a}} = f_{gen}(\mathbf{s}, \mathbf{t}) = \underset{\mathbf{a}}{\operatorname{argmax}} P_{\phi_1}(\mathbf{t}, \mathbf{a}|\mathbf{s}) \qquad (5.10)$$

Discriminative models define the function instead as the maximization over posterior target probabilities:

$$\hat{\mathbf{a}} = f_{discr}(\mathbf{s}, \mathbf{t}) = \underset{\mathbf{a}}{\operatorname{argmax}} P_{\phi_2}(\mathbf{a}|\mathbf{s}, \mathbf{t}) \qquad (5.11)$$

The crucial difference here is that this model does not need to fully explain the observable data anymore with all its complexities and internal dependencies. Discriminative models have instead the freedom to chose whatever information and evidence there is (usually in form of a feature-based representation) to improve the prediction performance without the need to worry about proper input data modeling. A lot of the structure in complex data sets may not be important for the prediction task; therefore, it is unnecessary to make the effort to cover it all. Furthermore, it is usually necessary to have large amounts of data to compute sufficient statistics for reasonable parameter estimates of complex data structures. We have already seen in our discussion about the IBM models how even simple parameters with strong assumptions can lead to complicated models and difficult parameter estimation strategies. On the other hand, generative models have a natural way to estimate marginal probabilities $P_{\phi_1}(\mathbf{t}|\mathbf{s})$ that allow unsupervised learning strategies by maximizing the data likelihood (using EM, for example). Discriminative models usually require labeled training data, which is one of their major drawbacks. Nevertheless, their performance is often superior, due to the rich information that can be incorporated and their target oriented definition. This makes it often worthwhile to spend the effort of manually creating sufficient amounts of fully specified training examples. The success of supervised learning and discriminative models has been shown in various sub-fields of natural language processing such as tagging, named entity recognition and statistical parsing, to name a few examples.

STRUCTURED PREDICTION

In contrast to standard classification tasks, we are now concerned with an instance of a **structured prediction** problem. The task is not to predict isolated links of independent data objects but to predict the entire structure **a** of an alignment between sentences **s** and **t**. The alignment can still be represented as a set $\{l_1, ..., l_i\}$ of individual links $l_i = (n, m)$ between tokens, and we assume that all input objects $(\mathbf{s}, \mathbf{t})$ are independent of each other. However, the links aligning them form a rather complex structure with many dependencies among them. We will use the same notation again and refer to alignments as the set of binary indicator variables $\{a_{11}, ..., a_{nm}\}$ for which $a_{nm} = 1$ if and only if $l = (n, m) \in \mathcal{L}$. The alignment structure is too complex to be predicted as one unit, and its prediction needs to be broken down into smaller sub-problems. However, we still need to respect the global structure with its internal dependencies, and this is the general challenge of structured prediction problems.

Finding the global solution is the task of the search procedure (inference) in our target function which plays a crucial role in structured prediction models. This search needs to be optimized because of rich target structures that lead to very large output spaces. Efficient search is especially important because it is usually part of the training procedure. In training, one tries to adjust parameters to minimize **prediction loss** measured on labeled example data. This is generally been done with numerical techniques using iterative methods or search heuristics as it is often not possible to solve the given optimization problem analytically. One can also use **maximum-likelihood training** in which the likelihood of the fully-observable (labeled) training data is maximized. In either case, we need efficient search algorithms to find appropriate model parameters.

One way to improve efficiency is to apply output space restrictions, for example, based on the Markov assumption (restricting structural dependencies to local context). This enables efficient dynamic programming algorithms for an optimal search under the given assumptions. Another possibility is to rely on approximate search methods and heuristics to explore an unrestricted output space. For example, it is possible to apply incremental beam search strategies to find a subset of possible output targets that can be evaluated. Another strategy is to apply greedy sequential search based on local decisions, constraints and additional **history features**. The latter are taken from previous predictions and may influence further decisions made by the local prediction models. Such an approach is also referred to as a **recurrent sliding window** strategy [Dietterich, 2002].

Naturally, the complexity of global search influences the efficiency of training. It is possible to ignore the inference step in training and to train structured prediction models locally. Punyakanok and Roth [2005] study the influence of inference on prediction performance. The conclusion is that global inference in training can be skipped if local models are sufficiently accurate and the output space dependencies do not add a lot of predictive power to the model. This statement may not be very surprising but re-assuring about the capacity of local prediction models. In any case, local models can still cover some output dependencies using history features as mentioned above. These dependencies can directly be learned from the annotated training data even without global inference. However, this may lead to a problem called **label bias** [Bottou, 1991], a kind of error propagation that is due to incorrect predictions that enter the pipeline in terms of history features. A local classifier trained on entirely correct labels may overestimate the value of these history-based features. A solution for the label-bias problem is to apply adaptive learning strategies [Daumé III, 2006, van den Bosch, 1997] in which parameters are adjusted iteratively to reflect the history during *prediction* rather than taking history labels from the gold standard. Some learning frameworks, for example conditional random fields [Lafferty et al., 2001], allow full global inference in training to avoid the label bias problem from the start at the cost of output space restrictions.

Let us now first have a look at typical features that can be explored for predicting word alignments before looking at some specific discriminative frameworks that have been proposed in the literature.

FEATURE FUNCTIONS

Very important for the success of discriminative models is the design of appropriate features that capture discriminating properties (with relation to the problem definition) of given data sets. Weighting these features according to their importance for the target prediction is the task of the learning procedure, which we will consider later. Features can directly be taken from the data. For example, we could use the actual tokens from all sentence pairs and couple them together to create binary features. This would not only lead to an explosion of features (and appropriate weights are difficult to learn especially from limited amounts of training data) but also mean that these features are very specific and not very helpful in many cases. Hence, we need to be careful to define features that generalize well for the given task in such a way that small amounts of labeled training data are sufficient to find relations between input space and output space even for unseen data instances. In sentence alignment, we have seen already how effective a simple feature such as sentence length can be for predicting links. Similarly, token length could be a useful feature for discriminative word alignment models. Many other features are possible. The utility of each of them is not necessarily important as long as the training procedure can figure out how much weight it should give to every feature when predicting alignments. This is the beauty of discriminative models. The danger, however, is to introduce features that mislead the training procedure due to spurious relations that they may capture.

In most discriminative frameworks, features are used in terms of binary or real-valued feature functions over the input data. In structured prediction, we also need to add a dependency on the output variables in order to take care of structural dependencies. Furthermore, we may add additional variables and information from external sources, which we will call $\mathbf{v}$ in our description:

$$h(\mathbf{a}, \mathbf{s}, \mathbf{t}, \mathbf{v})$$

Many models assume a simple linear combination of weighted features (λ_l being appropriate weights for the current task and feature set):

$$P_\Lambda(\mathbf{a}|\mathbf{s}, \mathbf{t}) \propto \sum_l \lambda_l h_l(\mathbf{a}, \mathbf{s}, \mathbf{t}, \mathbf{v})$$

Non-linear relations between certain properties can be captured by creating complex features. Using this model, we can formulate the decision function from equation 5.11 as the following search procedure:

$$\hat{\mathbf{a}} = \underset{\mathbf{a}}{\operatorname{argmax}} \sum_l \lambda_l h_l(\mathbf{a}, \mathbf{s}, \mathbf{t}, \mathbf{v})$$

Note that feature functions do not necessarily need to depend on all variables, and they may not be attached to the entire structure. For example, many useful features can be extracted for particular token pairs without considering context or relations to the rest of the alignment structure. Symbolic features can easily be converted into binary feature functions, indicating whether a specific symbol occurs or not. Some feature functions may require some computation; others do not. External resources such as taggers, parsers, and dictionaries may be used to create additional information that can directly be incorporated in feature functions. In general, we can distinguish between **local features**, **history-based features**, and **global features**. Below we give some examples.

Local Alignment Features

Local features should capture some properties of token pairs (s_n, t_m) in their context that help to decide whether these tokens should be linked or not. We now consider features that are independent of the overall link structure but may depend on surrounding context in the input space (source or target language). We can write such features as

$$h(a_{nm}, n, m, \mathbf{s}, \mathbf{t})$$

with n and m specifying the token positions within the sentences $\mathbf{s}$ and $\mathbf{t}$, respectively. These features should generalize well as we have discussed above but still need to be specific enough to capture discriminating properties. To add pairs of surface strings is usually not very useful, but features derived from each token could easily be created in various ways. For example, we could use suffix pairs taken from aligned tokens to capture derivational similarities. For example, we might find a feature useful for matching German and English nouns using the following binary function:

$$h_{\text{suffix}}(a_{nm}, n, m, \mathbf{s}, \mathbf{t}) = \begin{cases} 1 & \text{if suffix}(s_n) = \text{-ismus} \wedge \text{suffix}(t_m) = \text{-ism} \\ 0 & \text{otherwise} \end{cases}$$

Another possibility is to use external resources and tools to create features like, for example, parts-of-speech correspondence:

$$h_{\text{pos}}(a_{nm}, n, m, \mathbf{s}, \mathbf{t}) = \begin{cases} 1 & \text{if pos}(s_n) = \text{NOM} \wedge \text{pos}(t_m) = \text{NN} \\ 0 & \text{otherwise} \end{cases}$$

Note that we can easily incorporate contextual information to extend the knowledge about individual token pairs:

$$h(a_{nm}, n, m, \mathbf{s}, \mathbf{t}) = \begin{cases} 1 & \text{if pos}(s_{n-1}) = \text{ART} \wedge \text{pos}(s_n) = \text{NOM} \wedge \text{suffix}(t_m) = \text{-ism} \\ 0 & \text{otherwise} \end{cases}$$

These simple examples already show the flexibility of discriminative models and the necessity of proper **feature engineering** to balance complexity and generality for the support of the prediction model.

Many useful alignment features can actually be derived from findings in previous work on the extraction of bilingual lexical information from parallel corpora. A wide variety of **association measures** between words (and phrases) has been proposed. They can be used for word alignment on their own, which is sometimes called the *heuristic* alignment approach (even though association measures are often based on statistics as well). See, for example, Véronis [2000] for a discussion of various techniques and applications.

One important property of corresponding tokens is **co-occurrence**. We can measure co-occurrence using statistics over sentence pairs as we assume to have already sentence-aligned bitexts. Hence, we can "train" co-occurrence features over large amounts of bitexts and do not need to restrict ourselves to small amounts of word-aligned training data. It is possible to compute a wide variety of frequency-based association measures, assuming that corresponding tokens co-occur in aligned sentences more often than it would be expected by chance. Popular metrics are the Dice coefficient [Ker and Chang, 1997, Smadja et al., 1996], pointwise mutual information [Church and Hanks, 1990, Melamed, 2001], t-scores [Ahrenberg et al., 1998] and log-likelihood ratios [Melamed, 2000]. This list could easily be extended (and many more references to background literature could be given). Let us assume that tokens are independent events and that their occurrence probability in a bitext can be estimated from relative frequencies. Co-occurrence of tokens s_n and t_m can then be measured as

$$p(s_n, t_m) \approx \frac{C_B(s_n, t_m)}{|B|}$$

where $C_B(s_n, t_m)$ is the number of aligned sentence pairs in which both tokens appear (in the source or the target sentence, respectively) and $|B|$ is the size of bitext B in terms of sentence pairs. Similarly, we can define occurrence probabilities for the individual tokens

$$p(s_n) = \sum_{t'} p(s_n, t') \approx \frac{C_B(s_n, \bullet)}{|B|}$$

and likewise for $p(t_n)$. $C_B(s_n, \bullet)$ is the number of source sentences that contain s_n. Furthermore, conditional probabilities can be computed in the standard way:

$$p(t_m | s_n) = \frac{p(s_n, t_m)}{p(s_n)} \approx \frac{C_B(s_n, t_m)}{C_B(s_n, \bullet)}$$

The difference between the various co-occurrence-based association measures is how these probabilities are combined based on information-theoretic or distributionally motivated findings. One intuition is to compare the measured co-occurrence probability $p(s_n, t_m)$ with the likelihood of co-occurrence by chance $p(s_n)p(t_m)$. If these two values are identical or similar within a certain range, one can assume that there is no strong relation between the two items. Ahrenberg et al. [1998] measure the significance of this difference using t-scores:

$$t \approx \frac{p(s_n, t_m) - p(s_n)p(t_m)}{\sqrt{\frac{1}{|B|}p(s_n, t_m)}}$$

Pointwise mutual information (PMI) is another measure that can be used to exploit this difference:

$$PMI(s_n, t_m) = \log \frac{p(s_n, t_m)}{p(s_n)p(t_m)}$$

The Dice coefficient is a set-theoretic measure which can also be used for cross-lingual association:

$$Dice = \frac{2|B_{s_n} \cap B_{t_m}|}{|B_{s_n}| + |B_{t_m}|}$$

where B_{s_n} and B_{t_m} are the sets of bitext segments in which s_n and t_m appear, respectively. This can be re-written using our definitions of occurrence probabilities

$$Dice = \frac{2p(s_n, t_m)}{p(s_n) + p(t_m)} = 2\left(\frac{1}{p(s_n|t_m)} + \frac{1}{p(t_m|s_n)}\right)^{-1}$$

which shows that the Dice coefficient is, in fact, the harmonic mean of the two conditional probabilities $p(s_n|t_m)$ and $p(t_m|s_n)$. In practice, it is common to use simple token frequency counts to estimate $p(s_n) \approx freq(s_n)/|B|$, $p(t_m) \approx freq(s_n)/|B|$ and $p(s_n, t_m) \approx freq(s_n, t_m)/|B|$, which can lead to *Dice* scores above 1 because s_n and t_m may occur multiple times in a given sentence pair, but this is usually not a problematic issue. It can actually be an advantage to use the information about multiple occurrences instead of counting sentence pairs.

We should also stress that association measures can be computed over elements other than tokens. We could, for example, explore relations between more general units such as substrings, part-of-speech tags or any other type of information connected with the bitext [Tiedemann, 2005]. Furthermore, it is possible to compute associations between contextual information, for example, previous and next words [Taskar et al., 2005] or other features like parts-of-speech connected to contextual items [Tiedemann, 2009b]. Looking at contextual features makes it possible to implicitly encode first-order dependencies in the way that features that often mark strong relations (positive or negative) between contextual tokens may influence link decisions over other token pairs.

Association measures as the ones above have similar effects as the lexical translation probabilities in IBM model 1. Additionally, similar to other generative alignment models, we would also like to integrate position and reordering properties into the discriminative setting. In spirit of the diagonal-oriented IBM model 2, we can use proximity features such as the absolute difference in relative positions [Taskar et al., 2005]:

$$distance(s_n, t_m) = \left\lfloor \frac{n}{N} - \frac{m}{M} \right\rfloor$$

The flexibility of discriminative models allows to easily include various variants of proximity measures using non-linear combinations of relative positions, absolute position differences, etc.

Other feature types that are not available to generative alignment models can also be integrated without any problems. For example, arbitrary **orthographic features** might be helpful for discrimination between alternative link predictions. For related languages with shared or overlapping alphabets, we can, for example, define cognate features similar to the ones used in lexical sentence alignment (see Chapter 4.2). String similarity measures have been used in lexicon extraction approaches [Melamed, 1995] and can be useful as a word alignment feature here again. The longest common subsequence ratio (LCSR) is one of the popular measures based on edit distance. An LCSR filter computes the longest, not necessarily contiguous, subsequence of matching characters for two given strings and normalizes the lengths of this subsequence by the lengths of the longer string. Figure 5.7 shows an example.

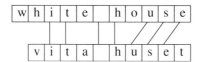

$$LCSR(\text{'white house'}, \text{'vita huset'}) = \frac{|\text{it huse}|}{\max(|\text{white house}|, |\text{vita huset}|)} = \frac{7}{11} \approx 0.64$$

Figure 5.7: The longest common subsequence ratio (LCSR) for the two strings "white house" and "vita huset".

Alternatively, one can use the Dice coefficient again to compare sets of character N-grams.

$$Dice = \frac{2 * |Ngrams(s_n) \cap Ngrams(t_m)|}{|Ngrams(s_n)| + |Ngrams(t_m)|}$$

To give an example, we can compute the similarity between "white house" and "vita huset", based in bigram matches as follows:

$$Dice(\text{'white house'}, \text{'vita huset'}) = 2* \mid \{\text{'it'}, \text{'h'}, \text{'us'}, \text{'se'}\} \mid /10 + 9 = 8/19 \approx 0.42 \ .$$

String similarity matching can be varied in many ways. It can be useful to match only substrings or to change the normalization of LCSR scores. It is possible to ignore certain character classes (for example vowels) or to normalize strings in some way before matching (for example, replacing diacritics with related ASCII characters). It makes also sense to add length thresholds to avoid spurious relations of very short tokens. Furthermore, specific character-matching functions can be introduced to match not only identical characters but to provide a matching cost for any character pair. With this, we can strengthen certain matches (for example between identical non-alphabetic characters), and we can even handle language pairs with disjoint alphabets. Matching regularities can also be learned automatically [Mackay and Kondrak, 2005, Nabende et al., 2010, Tiedemann, 1999a]. Other orthographic features may simply flag whether two strings both start with a capital letter or not, whether there are hyphens or digits included, etc.

All the features mentioned above can describe contextual information as well, and they can also be combined in various ways to explicitly capture interactions between the properties they represent. Some learning strategies may support certain feature relations implicitly. However, many popular models support simple linear combinations of features only.

Generative Alignment Features

Features can be derived from generative word alignment models. For example, it is easy to incorporate predictions from IBM alignment models as additional features in discriminative frameworks. Taskar et al. [2005] introduce several such features in their alignment model using the predictions of both asymmetric alignments of IBM model 4 and the predictions from the intersection heuristics. Each of them acts as a simple binary functions being set to one if the link is included in the generative Viterbi alignments (or their intersection). Another way of incorporating knowledge from generative alignment models is to use link posterior probabilities as explained in Chapter 5.2. Lacoste-Julien et al. [2006] use posterior features from their generative agreement aligner in this way. Yet another possibility is to use individual parameters of generative alignment models to create local alignment features. Tiedemann [2009b], for example, uses lexical translation probabilities from IBM models as one of the discriminating features.

History Features

Depending on the inference strategy, we may also want to add feature functions that store previous alignment decisions. For example, using a sliding window approach, we may use the alignment position of previous tokens. Ittycheriah and Roukos [2005] use what they call *dynamic features* that fire if preceding words have been linked already and integrate those in an incremental beam search algorithm. History features can have a limited horizon and may include additional information about the context of previous prediction states. The difference to global features is that they are solely based on previous steps in incremental search algorithms whereas global features are concerned with the entire alignment structure.

Global Alignment Features

Besides features for specific token-link candidates, we can also introduce global alignment features that may help the overall alignment prediction. Moore [2005], Moore et al. [2006] discuss several features that are concerned with the global alignment structure. For example, they define *monotonicity features* that measure the proportion of links that violate monotonicity in the proposed mapping of words. Furthermore, they introduce a feature that counts the number of unaligned words. They also use a *one-to-many feature* which is related to the ideas of fertility in generative alignment models. Finally, they propose conditional link probabilities that relate the co-occurrence frequencies of token pairs to the actual number of times these tokens have been linked together in the training data. Another possibility is to use generative alignment models as additional global feature function [Liu et al.,

2005]. We have seen this idea already in the proposal of model 6 in Chapter 5.1. Liu et al. [2005] also propose to use the output of a HMM-based part-of-speech tagger to improve their word aligner.

Global features like this require some special attention in the alignment inference step. They introduce dependencies between individual predictions by dynamically changing feature values. Alignment inference can often be solved only by approximate search heuristics. For example, it is common to apply some kind of iterative beam search algorithm for this purpose.

With this, we conclude our general discussion about alignment features. Let us now have a look at some specific discriminative frameworks that have been proposed for word alignment.

ALIGNMENT MODELS

Several discriminative word alignment models have been proposed based on linear combinations of feature functions. Model 6 introduced by Och and Ney [2003] can be seen as the first approach in which IBM model alignments have been combined in a log-linear way. Liu et al. [2005] extend this idea by incorporating various global features derived from other sources. A general conditional log-linear model based on the well-founded maximum entropy framework can be specified as follows:

$$P_\Lambda(\mathbf{a}|\mathbf{s}, \mathbf{t}) = \frac{1}{Z_\Lambda(\mathbf{s}, \mathbf{t}, \mathbf{v})} \exp \sum_l \lambda_l h_l(\mathbf{a}, \mathbf{s}, \mathbf{t}, \mathbf{v})$$

where $\Lambda = \{\lambda_1, .., \lambda_L\}$ is a set of weights that correspond to the L feature functions $h_l(...)$. $\mathbf{v}$ refers again to external resources. $Z_\Lambda(\mathbf{s}, \mathbf{t}, \mathbf{v})$ is the normalization that turns the function above into a proper probabilistic distribution. It is defined as the sum over all possible alignments $\mathbf{a}'$:

$$Z_\Lambda(\mathbf{s}, \mathbf{t}, \mathbf{v}) = \sum_{\mathbf{a}'} \exp \sum_l \lambda_l h_l(\mathbf{a}', \mathbf{s}, \mathbf{t}, \mathbf{v})$$

Using log-linear models for alignment prediction turns out to be based on a simple linear decision function over weighted features:

$$
\begin{aligned}
\hat{\mathbf{a}} &= \underset{\mathbf{a}}{\mathrm{argmax}}\ P_\Lambda(\mathbf{a}|\mathbf{s}, \mathbf{t}) \\
&= \underset{\mathbf{a}}{\mathrm{argmax}}\ \log P_\Lambda(\mathbf{a}|\mathbf{s}, \mathbf{t}) \\
&= \underset{\mathbf{a}}{\mathrm{argmax}} \sum_l \lambda_l h_l(\mathbf{a}', \mathbf{s}, \mathbf{t}, \mathbf{v})
\end{aligned}
$$

This is because $Z_\Lambda(\mathbf{s}, \mathbf{t}, \mathbf{v})$ is constant for any $\mathbf{a}$ given a specific sentence pair $(\mathbf{s}, \mathbf{t})$ ($\mathbf{v}$ is also assumed to be static and independent of specific alignment predictions $\mathbf{a}$).

Liu et al. [2005] use IBM translation models as basic feature functions but add additional features over part-of-speech pairs and information derived from bilingual dictionaries. Ayan and Dorr [2006b] use a similar setup for combining several word aligners. They extract more fine-grained features describing individual links in their context. Besides the individual link decisions, they also use part-of-speech tags (even from surrounding context), neighboring links, fertility features and monotonicity features.

Another related approach based on log-linear models is presented by Ittycheriah and Roukos [2005]. Here the authors divide the global alignment prediction model into a weighted combination of a transition model $P_t(a_m|a_{m-1})$ (a first-order dependency model for adjacent links expressed in the functional format of a) and an observation model $P_o(a_m|\mathbf{s}, \mathbf{t}, a_1^{m-1})$ of individual links given source and target sentences and the link history. The observation model is then defined as a log-linear combination of weighted feature functions over the input space and the link history. They apply various local features such as lexical features over individual token pairs, segmentation features (specific for Arabic in their example), orthographic features and semantic features derived from WordNet. They also use some history-based features that add dependencies on previous decisions.

Finally, there is the discriminative framework proposed by Moore [2005] and Moore et al. [2006]. In this work, the authors propose another model that is based on a linear combination of alignment features. The decision function is exactly the same as above with a weighted linear combination of arbitrary features over input and output space. Moore [2005] applies a mixture of local features and global features. The author uses log-likelihood ratios to incorporate frequency-based word association and introduces monotonicity features and fertility (one-to-many and many-to-many alignment features) inspired by the IBM models. A special feature for counting unlinked tokens is also introduced to control the amount of links that should be established. Furthermore, Moore [2005] introduces features that measures the (inverse) ratio between the co-occurrence frequency (*cooc*) of a given token pair and the number of links that have been established between that specific token pair (*links*).[8]

$$lp(s, t) = \frac{\text{links}_{stage1}(s, t) - d}{\text{cooc}(s, t)}$$

These features can be bootstrapped from some initial alignments that have been created by a simple model, for example, the alignment result without that feature. This creates a two-stage procedure which is further developed in Moore et al. [2006]. In that paper, the authors replace the simple ratio from above with a more complex *link odds* measure over a cluster of words. The idea is essentially the same. They also add a number of additional local features in stage one of the alignment model. They introduce association rank features, jump distance features (distortion), lexicalized features and string matching features. In order to guide the alignment search procedure, they finally add two hard constraints: i) Only 5 alignment patterns are allowed (1-1, 1-2, 1-3, 2-1 and 3-1). Without this restriction, the model would prefer multiple links because of the simple sum over weighted features. More links would inevitable lead to higher overall scores. ii) Links need to include the strongest individual association for at least one token pair. This corresponds to a greedy selection with respect to association scores.

---

[8]A small discounting constant d is used to make the feature work better.

All models listed above have one thing in common: they need to make compromises when training their parameters because of the global features involved. Despite the chosen training paradigm one needs to enumerate all possible alignments in order to make the necessary parameter updates when optimizing the model on a given training set. An exception is Ayan and Dorr [2006b] where they use a strictly local model and ignore global constraints. Otherwise, there are no efficient inference algorithms for global optimization with models that include arbitrary global features. Therefore, one needs to rely on approximate techniques. Liu et al. [2005] use an iterative scaling algorithm for learning feature weights based on an n-best list of highly probable alignments. To obtain those, they use a greedy search algorithm based on a heuristic *gain* function that can be computed incrementally. Moore et al. [2006] use averaged perceptron training [Collins, 2002] which is based on incremental updates based on the difference between proposed ($\mathbf{a}_{hypo}$) and reference alignments ($\mathbf{a}_{ref}$). η is the training rate.

$$\lambda_l' \leftarrow \lambda_l + \eta \left[h_l(\mathbf{a}_{ref}, \mathbf{s}, \mathbf{t}) - h_l(\mathbf{a}_{hypo}, \mathbf{s}, \mathbf{t}) \right]$$

Moore et al. [2006] apply, then, a beam search algorithm with various heuristics to find the best alignment hypothesis according to the current model. Note that perceptron training is a so-called *on-line* strategy that looks at training instances one-by-one to make the necessary adjustments. The result is, therefore, sensible to the order of data instances presented to the learner and may be unstable. Averaging the parameters over all update steps addresses this problem to some degree.

Let us now move from models that require approximate search strategies to decriminative models that allow globally optimal inference. First, we will have a look at a graph-theoretic alignment approach before discussing discriminative sequence models.

WORD ALIGNMENT AS ASSIGNMENT PROBLEM

Word alignment can be modeled as an **assignment problem** [Taskar et al., 2005]. The general task for a linear assignment problem is to distribute N tasks to N agents such that every agent performs exactly one task. Each agent-task assignment has a specific cost, and we seek the distribution of tasks that minimizes the overall cost. This combinatorial optimization problem is the same as the maximum weighted matching problem for bipartite graphs. A **bipartite graph** is a graph that can be divided into two disjoint sets S and T of nodes such that every edge in the graph connects a node in S with a node in T. Matching is the task of finding a set of edges without common nodes (this set is also called a *matching*). See Figure 5.8 for an illustration.

A weighted graph is a graph where each edge has a numeric weight attached to it. A **maximum weighted bipartite matching** is defined as a *perfect matching* where the sum of the edge weights is the maximally possible value. A perfect matching is defined as a matching where all nodes in the graph are covered. We can easily see that this is restricted to bipartite graphs where both subsets S and T have the same cardinality (which is not the case in Figure 5.8). However, it is easy to adjust the setup to cover cases of unequal sets by adding artificial nodes and simply adding zero weights (or maximal costs) to edges connecting those nodes.

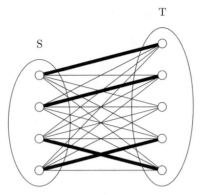

Figure 5.8: Bipartite graphs and the matching problem. Thick lines refer to a *matching* between S and T.

With this setup, it is straightforward to cast word alignment as an instance of the matching problem introduced above. Elements in S and T refer to tokens in source, and target and edge weights refer to individual link scores c_{nm} as we have discussed in section 5.2. The score for an alignment is then defined as the sum over edge scores from the maximum weighted matching in the bipartite graph. Finding this matching is a well-known problem, and efficient combinatorial algorithms exist. The Hungarian method [Kuhn, 1955] is one of them solving this task in polynomial time [Munkres, 1957].

Using binary indicator variables a_{nm}, again to indicate assignments from s_n to t_m, the task is now to find an assignment that maximizes

$$\hat{\mathbf{a}} = \underset{\mathbf{a}}{\operatorname{argmax}} \sum_{nm} c_{nm} a_{nm} \tag{5.12}$$

subject to the constraint that $\sum_n a_{nm} \leq 1$ and $\sum_m a_{nm} \leq 1$ (at most one assignment per token). The score c_{nm} can be modeled as a weighted feature vector using an arbitrary number of real-valued or binary feature functions $h_l(n, m, \mathbf{s}, \mathbf{t})$ over position pairs in a given sentence pair

$$c_{nm} = \sum_{l=1}^{L} \lambda_l h_l(n, m, \mathbf{s}, \mathbf{t})$$

Any of the local alignment features discussed earlier can be used here.

In **training**, one needs to find appropriate weights λ_l to minimize the prediction error on the training data. Taskar et al. [2005] use a weighted Hamming distance to measure the loss between predicted alignments $\bar{\mathbf{a}} = \{\bar{a}_{nm}\}$ and correct alignments $\mathbf{a} = \{a_{nm}\}$:

$$\ell(a, \bar{a}) = \sum_{nm} \left[c^+ (1 - a_{nm}) \bar{a}_{nm} + c^- (1 - \bar{a}_{nm}) a_{nm} \right]$$

where c^+ is the cost for false positives and c^- is the cost for false negatives. In their experiments, Taskar et al. [2005] use a penalty for false negatives which is three times higher than for false positives. Later, when presenting some extensions to the assignment model, Lacoste-Julien et al. [2006] adjust the parameters to a value ten times higher for false negatives than for false positives. These values need to be determined on some independent validation data. Using this loss function, they formulate a **large-margin strategy** to learn appropriate weights λ_l. The upper bound of the loss is given by

$$\hat{\ell}(\mathbf{s}, \mathbf{t}, \mathbf{a}) = \max_{\bar{a}} \left[\sum_{nm} \bar{a}_{nm} c_{nm} + \ell(a, \bar{a}) \right] - \sum_{nm} a_{nm} c_{nm} \tag{5.13}$$

The objective in learning is to minimize this upper bound with respect to the parameters $\Lambda = \{\lambda_1, ..., \lambda_L\}$ (remember that $c_{nm} = \sum_l \lambda_l h_l(...)$) when summing over our training corpus:

$$\min_{\Lambda} \sum_k \hat{\ell}(\mathbf{s}_k, \mathbf{t}_k, \mathbf{a}_k)$$

Taskar et al. [2005] turn the original assignment problem into a linear program in order to find an efficient way to handle the optimization problem. This is possible by relaxing the binary constraints on a_{nm} in equation 5.12 to equivalent constraints on corresponding continues variables z_{nm}.

$$\begin{aligned} \max_{\mathbf{z}} \quad & \sum_{nm} c_{nm} z_{nm} \\ \text{subject to} \quad & \sum_n z_{nm} \leq 1, \ \sum_m z_{nm} \leq 1, \ 0 \leq z_{nm} \leq 1 \end{aligned} \tag{5.14}$$

This problem is guaranteed to have an integral solution for any function c_{nm} [Schrijver, 2003] and, hence, fulfills the requirement of the original binary constraints with $\hat{a}_{nm} = \hat{z}_{nm}$.

Taskar et al. [2005] further show that the loss function based on Hamming distance decomposes over the proposed links in $\bar{\mathbf{a}}$:

$$\begin{aligned} \ell(a, \bar{a}) &= \sum_{nm} \left[c^+ (1 - a_{nm}) \bar{a}_{nm} + c^- (1 - \bar{a}_{nm}) a_{nm} \right] \\ &= \sum_{nm} \left[c^+ \bar{a}_{nm} - c^+ a_{nm} \bar{a}_{nm} + c^- a_{nm} - c^- a_{nm} \bar{a}_{nm} \right] \\ &= \sum_{nm} c^- a_{nm} + \sum_{nm} \left[c^+ - c^+ a_{nm} - c^- a_{nm} \right] \bar{a}_{nm} \end{aligned}$$

Using this derivation, we can now re-write the loss-augmented optimization problem in equation 5.13 (leaving out the constant part $\sum_{nm} a_{nm} c_{nm}$ and the constant $\sum_{nm} c^- a_{nm}$ from the loss function)

$$\max_{\bar{a}} \left[\sum_{nm} \bar{a}_{nm} c_{nm} + \sum_{nm} \left(c^+ - c^+ a_{nm} - c^- a_{nm} \right) \bar{a}_{nm} \right]$$

$$= \max_{\bar{a}} \sum_{nm} \left[c_{nm} + c^+ - c^+ a_{nm} - c^- a_{nm} \right] \bar{a}_{nm}$$

where $\left[c_{nm} + c^+ - c^+ a_{nm} - c^- a_{nm} \right]$ can be seen as a function c' over $\mathbf{a}$. Hence, we can re-write the optimization problem into a linear program in the same way as we did for equation 5.12 (turning it into 5.14) by relaxing binary variables $\bar{a}_{nm}$ to corresponding continuous variables z_{nm}. In this way, we can convert the original combinatorial optimization problem into a standard optimization problem over continuous variables z_{nm} that can be solved using standard algorithms [Taskar et al., 2005].

Even though the linear assignment model defines an effective and computationally tractable approach it has two critical limitations:

- It cannot handle **structural relations** between individual link decisions. The model is essentially a *zero order* model similar to IBM models 1, 2, and 3. Link dependencies can only be included indirectly via contextual features.

- Linear assignment allows only **one-to-one mappings** between tokens. Even though this is often the most common type even in word alignment, it is still a strong limitation.

Lacoste-Julien et al. [2006], therefore, introduce several extensions to the model above by turning the problem into a **quadratic assignment problem**. Scores for *pairs of edges* are included in the new model that connect consecutive tokens in an alignment between $\mathbf{s}$ and $\mathbf{t}$. First of all, we need to fix the **fertility** problem. Unfortunately, simply changing the constraints from $\sum_n z_{nm} \leq 1$ to $\sum_n z_{nm} \leq D$ (where D is the maximum fertility allowed) does not work. Any maximization algorithm would then always select as many links as possible for every token due to the simple sum over individual edges in the objective function $\max_{\mathbf{z}} \sum_{nm} c_{nm} z_{nm}$. Lacoste-Julien et al. [2006], therefore, introduce **fertility penalties** for each source and target language node that have increasing costs for increasing fertilities. Using binary variables, $z_{dn\bullet}$ and $z_{d\bullet m}$, indicating that source node n and target node m have at least fertility d, we can formulate incremental penalties as follows:

$$fp_s = \sum_{n, 2 \leq d \leq D} s_{dn\bullet} z_{dn\bullet}$$

$$fp_t = \sum_{m, 2 \leq d \leq D} s_{d\bullet m} z_{d\bullet m}$$

where $s_{dn\bullet} \geq 0$ and $s_{d\bullet m} \geq 0$ are increasing penalty increments for moving from fertility $d - 1$ to fertility d. These extra costs fp_s and fp_t are then subtracted from the sum of edge scores to adjust the overall score.

$$\max_{\mathbf{z}} \sum_{nm} c_{nm} z_{nm} - f p_s - f p_t$$

The constraints are changed to add the maximum fertility for each node for which the corresponding cost has been subtracted:

$$\sum_{n} z_{nm} \leq 1 + \sum_{2 \leq d \leq D} s_{d \bullet m} z_{dn \bullet}$$
$$\sum_{m} z_{nm} \leq 1 + \sum_{2 \leq d \leq D} s_{d \bullet m} z_{d \bullet m}$$

The difference between this model and the linear assignment model from before is illustrated in Figure 5.9. Maximum weight bipartite matching problems can be reduced to the well-known min-cost max-flow problem in single-source and single-sink flow networks. Figure 5.9 (a) shows the original model with edges leaving the source node and edges going to the sink node that have capacity 1 and cost 0. In Figure 5.9 (b), we have the augmented network with multiple edges connecting source and sink with other nodes. These edges represent the different levels of fertility, and their costs correspond to the fertility penalty introduced above.

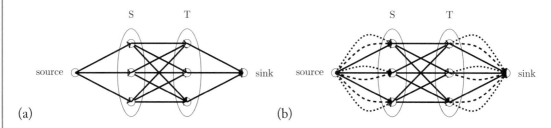

(a)   (b)

Figure 5.9: Bipartite graph matching as flow networks. Figure (a) corresponds to a basic maximum weighted matching problem whereas figure (b)hillustrates the network augmented with fertility edges.

Secondly, [Lacoste-Julien et al., 2006] introduce parameters for **first-order interactions** between links. They add variables z_{nmop} that indicate whether both edges from s_n to t_m and from s_o to t_p are linked or not. Each of them has a corresponding score $s_{nmop} \geq 0$ that can be used to boost certain link pairs. Obviously, setting z_{nmop} makes only sense when z_{nm} and z_{op} are also set. Therefore, we add the constraints $z_{nmop} \leq z_{nm}$ and $z_{nmop} \leq z_{op}$ to the linear program that needs to be solved. We will obtain the desired result $z_{nmop} = z_{nm} z_{op}$ when solving the final problem formulation as an **integer linear program**. The final model including fertility costs can now be formulated as follows:

$$\max_{\mathbf{z}} \quad \sum_{nm} c_{nm} a_{nm} - f p_s - f p_t + \sum_{nmop} s_{nmop} z_{nmop}$$

$$\text{subject to} \quad \sum_{n} z_{nm} \leq 1 + \sum_{2 \leq d \leq D} s_{d \bullet m} z_{dn \bullet}$$

$$\sum_{m} z_{nm} \leq 1 + \sum_{2 \leq d \leq D} s_{d \bullet m} z_{d \bullet m}$$

$$z_{nmop} \leq z_{nm}$$

$$z_{nmop} \leq z_{op}$$

For parameter estimation, we can use the same large-margin formulation as previously for the linear assignment approach. Standard solvers for the resulting quadratic program can be used to estimate appropriate parameters [Lacoste-Julien et al., 2006], and the actual alignments can be created using standard algorithms to solve min-cost max-flow problems. New in this augmented model are the additional scoring functions for fertility and quadratic assignments. Similar to the scores between individual tokens, these values can be parametrized using a feature-based representation. Lacoste-Julien et al. [2006] use a weighted linear combination and introduce various feature functions based on training data. One problem is that fertility highly depends on lexical information. Learning appropriate feature functions requires substantially more labeled training data than the local link features used otherwise. Lacoste-Julien et al. [2006], therefore, propose to use automatically word aligned training data in addition to the correctly labeled training data from which they estimate their scoring functions. For this, they apply the "cheap" alignments created by the generative alignment model of IBM 2. Similarly, they train feature function parameters on the same word-aligned bitext for the quadratic assignment scores. In their approach, they identify features for specific patterns of connected links. They focus on link pairs that connect consecutive words either monotonically, inverted or overlapping in either source or target language. For this, they use both asymmetric IBM 2 Viterbi alignments and their intersection. Finally, they show that adding the more expensive IBM model 4 predictions gives another boost in alignment performance.

DISCRIMINATIVE SEQUENCE MODELS

Another possibility is to model word alignment in a similar way as the generative sequence models do, but in a discriminative way. Conditional random fields (CRF) [Lafferty et al., 2001] provide a discriminative framework for structured prediction with local output space dependencies. CRFs provide efficient inference algorithms which makes global optimization in training tractable. Blunsom and Cohn [2006] present an alignment model based on a CRF that resembles the graphical structure of the generative HMM presented earlier. Their model is based on a log-linear combination of feature functions with a first-order dependency on link assignments:[9]

---

[9]Note that we use a, now again, as a function assigning aligned source positions to each target token position.

$$P_\Lambda(\mathbf{a}|\mathbf{s}, \mathbf{t}) = \frac{1}{Z_\Lambda(\mathbf{s}, \mathbf{t})} \exp \sum_m \sum_l \lambda_l h_l(m, a_{m-1}a_m, \mathbf{s}, \mathbf{t})$$

Feature functions $h_l(\ldots)$ refer again to arbitrary real-valued functions over source and target sentences coupled with adjacent alignments at a specific target position. $Z_\Lambda(\mathbf{s}, \mathbf{t})$ is the normalization which refers to the sum over all possible alignments as before:

$$Z_\Lambda(\mathbf{s}, \mathbf{t}) = \sum_\mathbf{a} \exp \sum_m \sum_l \lambda_l h_l(m, a_{m-1}a_m, \mathbf{s}, \mathbf{t})$$

Conditional random fields are usually trained using maximum likelihood training over labeled training data. Blunsom and Cohn [2006] add a Gaussian prior $P_0(\lambda_l)$ over feature weights for smoothing the likelihood in order to avoid overfitting. This leads to the maximum a posteriori estimation of parameters, which can be expressed as the maximization of the following log-likelihood function

$$\hat{\Lambda} = \underset{\Lambda}{\operatorname{argmax}} \sum_k \log P_\Lambda(\mathbf{a}_k|\mathbf{s}_k, \mathbf{t}_k) + \sum_l \log P_0(\lambda_l)$$

$$= \sum_k \left[\sum_m \sum_l \lambda_l h_l(m, a_{m-1}a_m, \mathbf{s}_k, \mathbf{t}_k) - \log Z_\Lambda(\mathbf{s}_k, \mathbf{t}_k) + \sum_l \log P_0(\lambda_l) \right]$$

Similar to standard log-linear models, this objective function is convex, and the maximization can be solved using iterative methods finding the globally optimal parameter settings in this case. Important here is that the linear chain CRF allows efficient inference procedures based on the well-known Baum-Welch algorithm [Baum et al., 1970] (see our discussion about the generative HMM). Using this inference algorithm, we can compute the marginals necessary in the iterative training procedures without relying on approximate search heuristics.

Finally, after training, we can also use the Viterbi algorithm to obtain the best alignment according to our final model and its parameters.

$$\hat{\mathbf{a}} = \underset{\mathbf{a}}{\operatorname{argmax}} P_\Lambda(\mathbf{a}|\mathbf{s}, \mathbf{t})$$

Altogether, CRFs constitute an efficient framework for training and alignment inference. In contrast to its generative counterpart, it allows the integration of unrestricted features over the input space in connection with local output space dependencies. Blunsom and Cohn [2006] define a set of features which are similar to the ones we have discussed earlier. They use word association features based on Dice scores, orthographic features based on string matching, suffix and prefix features, and length and length difference features. They also employ part-of-speech tags, information from bilingual dictionaries and features derived from IBM model 1 (lexical translation probabilities). They also use fully lexicalized features as indicator variables for every possible token pair, which can be useful for very common words:

$$h(m, a_{m-1}, a_m, \mathbf{s}, \mathbf{t}) = \begin{cases} 1 & \text{if } s_{a_m} = \text{and} \wedge t_m = \text{und} \\ 0 & \text{otherwise} \end{cases}$$

For the output space dependencies, they define a jump-width feature in the spirit of HMM alignments but use it as a real-valued feature instead of defining separate parameters for each jump width. In this way, they do not have to limit the distance measure to a fixed set of values and do not need to bucket together distances beyond certain limits. Furthermore, they also use a feature for the relative difference in sentence positions similar to the diagonal-oriented alignment models. Finally, some special features for treating NULL alignments are introduced as well.

One drawback of the model above is its asymmetry. Blunsom and Cohn [2006] refer to standard heuristics to combine asymmetric alignments in the same way as the output of generative alignments are processed.

FINAL REMARKS ON DISCRIMINATIVE ALIGNMENT MODELS

Finally, we need to add some comments about training data required for discriminative alignment models. All models described above need annotated data sets for optimizing model parameters, which means, in our case, perfectly word-aligned sentence pairs. However, annotation is expensive, and already aligned data is not available in large amounts. Fortunately, all reported studies agree in one point: Appropriate parameters can be found on very limited training sets. In most cases, only a few hundred aligned sentence pairs are sufficient to find reasonable weights to obtain comparable and often superior results compared to the generative alignment models. The reason for this success is that many features are very general and include knowledge from cheap external resources. For example, frequency-based association scores can be computed from large amounts of parallel data. Fertility parameters can be bootstrapped from automatically aligned bitexts. However, discriminative alignment models usually learn quite a lot of language specific and also text-specific knowledge which is difficult to transfer to other domains. In order to make discriminative alignment competitive with unsupervised generative approaches, one needs to show that language-independent features can be used with high confidence on various domains. Such a systematic study has not been presented yet and generative models are still by far the most dominant approach to automatic word alignment.

5.4   TRANSLATION SPOTTING AND BILINGUAL LEXICON INDUCTION

There is a strong relation between approaches to the extraction of bilingual lexical knowledge and word alignment. In fact, automatic word alignment as described above is usually just a first step for the extraction of translation equivalents, probabilistic word/phrase translation tables or other parameters for data-driven machine translation models. Automatic word alignment is almost never used to create fine-grained aligned parallel corpora as a resource of their own. In most cases, the alignment is just too noisy to be useful for qualitative investigations and word alignment results are often stored temporally only until necessary parameters are extracted.

The extraction of bilingual lexical information from bitexts has a long tradition. Many techniques we have discussed already have been applied for this purpose. Different to the general word alignment models introduced above, lexicon extraction techniques do not aim at complete word alignments but rather focus on the extraction of reliable translation equivalents. With this objective, it is possible to leave out questionable cases and to emphasize high precision links between words and multi-word units. Another term for this task is **translation spotting** [Véronis and Langlais, 2000].

Many of the proposed approaches to the extraction of translation equivalents use co-occurrence statistics and statistical significance tests that we have discussed already in connection with features for discriminative alignment models. We will not repeat the description of these measures here and just refer to relevant parts of Chapter 5.3. Extraction is then done by simple greedy search algorithms and score thresholds as we have discussed already earlier as well. Special for lexicon extraction techniques is that they often focus on certain linguistic constructions and phenomena depending on the purpose of the extraction. Hence, they naturally include multi-word units when linking translation units and do not need to consider single words only as it is often the case in statistical alignment models. For example, it is common to extract terminology from domain-specific bitexts by focusing on noun phrases and other language-specific patterns (see for example [Dagan and Church, 1994]).

Furthermore, various simple, non-statistical techniques can be applied for lexicon extraction and translation spotting. For example, many sentence-aligned bitexts include very short sentence fragments, and their alignments can often be used immediately as lexical translation equivalent. These initial entries can then be used to mark other occurrences of known equivalence pairs in the bitext. With the assumption that remaining parts still correspond to each other, we can apply these extraction techniques recursively. Consider the following example of aligned sentences from the Swedish-English subtitles of *Alice in Wonderland*:

> This is *impossible* .
> - Det här är *omöjligt* .
>
> *Impossible* !
> *Omöjligt* !
>
> **Wait** !
> **Vänta** !
>
> **Wait** , this is my dream .
> **Vänta** ... Det här är min dröm .

Ignoring punctuations and casing, we can extract one-to-one word equivalences of "impossible – omöjligt" and "wait – vänta". In the second step, this would give us mappings between "this is" and "det här är" which, finally, leads to the correspondence between "my dream" and "min dröm". This principle of *iterative size reduction* has been introduced by Tiedemann [1999b] and can be combined with other techniques for the recognition of translation equivalents [Tiedemann, 2003b]. Lardilleux and Lepage [2008b] develop this idea further by defining an alignment method purely based on monolingual string differences. Its iterative principle is similar in spirit to the idea presented above but introduces the possibility of comparing arbitrary sentence pairs and their translations to find common substrings. The idea is to find the longest common substring (**LCSubstr**) for all relevant sentence pairs in parallel with the same operation on the translations of these sentences. Consider the following simple example:

> Wait , this is my <u>dream</u> .
> Vänta ... Det här är min <u>dröm</u> .
>
> It' s only a <u>dream</u> , Alice .
> Det är bara en <u>dröm</u> , Alice .

The longest common substring for the two English sentences is "dream". Similarly, the LCSubstr for the corresponding Swedish sentences is "dröm". The method now assumes that LCSubstr in source and target are translations of each other ("dream" and "dröm" in our case) as well as the remaining parts in each aligned sentence pair (for example "It's only a , Alice ." and "Det är bara en , Alice" in the second pair). This assumption is quite strong and often not true. However, a general observation is that longer LCSubstr are quite reliable. Lardilleux and Lepage [2008b], therefore, sort sentence pairs to be considered by the length of their LCSubstr. They use only a pre-defined number of sentences to be examined for a specific alignment candidate, which also reduces the complexity of the algorithm. Certainly, in many cases, the LCSubstr is more than a single lexical unit, but the method can be applied iteratively to further reduce the strings created.

Applying this method to the entire bitext creates alternative results for most lexical units. Lardilleux and Lepage [2008b] use extraction frequencies to select reliable translation candidates. They further normalize this value by the number of sentences required to obtain each candidate as this leads to more reliable LCSubstr's in practice [Lardilleux and Lepage, 2008b].

There are several advantages of this method compared to statistical alignment models. First of all, it is straightforward to align as many languages as available in parallel. The entire process is not restricted to bilingual settings. Secondly, the matching approach can be applied to any character sequence and does not require any tokenization. This advantage is especially relevant for languages that do not have clear word boundaries. It also naturally includes multi-word units on both sides of possible alignments. Finally, this non-statistical method does not require the critical amount of data to obtain reliable statistical parameter estimations. It still requires sufficient repetitions to find common patterns, but it can basically be applied to any size of data collection. Certainly, this technique has also its shortcomings especially due to the strong correspondence assumptions after each string reduction step. This can lead to many ill-formed strings especially in noisy and less literally translated bitexts.

Another observation is that corresponding low frequency words can be extracted with high confidence. Tiedemann [1999b] uses words below a certain frequency threshold in corresponding sentence pairs as possible link candidates. Lardilleux and Lepage [2007] investigate the use of so-called **hapax legomena** (words that appear only once in a corpus) for word alignment and conclude that they can safely be aligned in most cases. This is an important observation as low frequency words constitute a large part of any language (according to Zipf's law) and hapax legomena typically represent around or above 50% of the vocabulary present in a corpus. Statistical methods have problems treating low frequency events and, therefore, may miss or misinterpret a large portion of the language's vocabulary.

Lardilleux and Lepage [2009] use these findings and develop an alignment algorithm that *down-samples* parallel corpora to find what they call *perfect alignments*. These perfect alignments are words that appear exactly in the same aligned sentences (and nowhere else). This is naturally true for hapax legomena that appear in corresponding sentences. For most other words, perfect alignments cannot be found. However, the corpus can be *reduced* in size such that perfect alignments can be found even for high frequency words. Lardilleux and Lepage [2008a] give the following explanatory example (see Figure 5.10).

Figure 5.10: Bitext sampling for word alignment.

In this toy example, *a* and *A* appear only on lines one and four and can therefore be safely aligned. Furthermore, using iterative reduction techniques, we can also conclude that *d* most likely corresponds to *D* and *c* corresponds to *D D* (context alignment). *b* is ambiguous in the global bitext. However, dividing the bitext into two sub-bitexts allows to "perfectly" align *b* to *B* in sample 1 and *b* to *C* in sample 2. This shows that words can be disambiguated by finding appropriate subsets of the parallel data. Note that this procedure is not restricted to language pairs. Any number of parallel languages can be used in the same way. The procedure simply looks for words appearing on the same *line*, which can be composed of any number of aligned sentences (even one language only which would lead to the extraction of monolingual discontiguous collocations).

Lardilleux and Lepage [2009] describe how this conceptually simple method can be applied to real-world data in a truly multilingual setting. They present ways of biasing the sampling techniques for optimal data selection and how to extract translation equivalents efficiently. They also show how to compute weights for extracted translation units in order to create probabilistic phrase translation tables that can directly be used in statistical machine translation. More detailed analyses of extraction results are presented in Lardilleux et al. [2009].

5.5   SUMMARY AND FURTHER READING

The work on word alignment was pushed by two main application areas: the research on statistical machine translation and the research on automatic extraction of multilingual lexical knowledge. Both of them are, of course, related with each other and the techniques proposed for either purpose exploit similar properties and features. Various techniques for the extraction of bilingual lexicons from parallel corpora have been proposed in the literature. Many of them use co-occurrence statistics as their main feature [Ahrenberg et al., 1998, Gale and Church, 1991a, Hiemstra, 1998, Kaji and Aizono, 1996, Kumano and Hirakawa, 1994, Melamed, 1995, 1996b, 1997, Smadja et al., 1996]. Some extraction techniques are focused on specific terminology [Dagan and Church, 1994, Macken et al., 2008, van der Eijk, 1993]. Linguistically motivated features can be integrated together with constrained search algorithms to improve extraction performance [Simard and Langlais, 2003, Tiedemann, 2003a, Tufiş, 2002]. Feature combinations can be optimized using machine learning techniques [Tiedemann, 2005, 2009b], which is similar to the ideas of discriminative word alignment.

Word alignment for statistical machine translation has been presented in numerous publications. A comprehensive overview over the standard models is included in [Koehn, 2010]. Brown et al. [1993] describe the mathematical details of the classical IBM alignment models. A gentle introduction to the concepts of statistical machine translation and statistical alignment models can be found in Knight [1997, 1999]. Several authors propose extensions of the standard models. For example, Pianta and Bentivogli [2004], Popovic and Ney [2004], Toutanova et al. [2002], and Crego and Habash [2008] suggest techniques for integrating linguistic features into the statistical alignment models. Prior knowledge can be integrated in a constrained search strategy [Cherry and Lin, 2006b, Deng and Gao, 2007]. Alignment models can also be extended to cover phrases [Deng and Byrne, 2005] instead of single words.

Further discussions about discriminative linear models for word alignment can be found in [Liu et al., 2010]. The authors propose a minimum-error-rate training procedure with a rich feature set. DeNero and Klein [2010] present discriminative models that extract multi-word correspondences from bitexts. Their model allows the alignment of overlapping bitext segments and is trained using the margin-infused relaxed algorithm (MIRA) to be directly optimized for the anticipated end task. They can show that their model improves the state-of-the-art in unsupervised and supervised word alignment and also leads to higher machine translation performance in a selected task. Recently, Dyer et al. [2011] present an approach to move to unsupervised discriminative techniques with arbitrary features which removes the dependence on available word-aligned training data for optimizing model parameters.

Statistical alignment techniques have been applied to a variety of applications. For example, Dejean et al. [2003], Wu and Xia [1994] use them for the extraction of bilingual lexical knowledge, Bannard and Callison-Burch [2005] apply translation models for the identification of paraphrases, van der Plas and Tiedemann [2010] use automatic word alignment for the identification of term variations. Foster et al. [2003], Oard and Och [2003] investigate the use of SMT technology for language pairs with limited resources.

Alternative statistical alignment models have been proposed by Cherry and Lin [2003], Dagan et al. [1993], Marcu and Wong [2002] and Birch et al. [2006]. Another generative alignment model that is capable of aligning multi-word units has been introduced by Fraser and Marcu [2007b]. Goutte et al. [2004] discuss symmetric word alignment techniques using matrix factorization. Vogel [2005] present phrase alignment techniques as a sentence splitting process. Transduction grammars (which we will discuss in the next Chapter 6.2) can also be used to induce symmetric word alignments [Saers and Wu, 2009, Saers et al., 2010, Wu, 1995, Zhao and Vogel, 2003]. The use of flow networks for word alignment have been proposed already by Gaussier [1998]. The author describes an iterative algorithm to estimate network parameters that can be used for alignment and terminology extraction. Combinations of various techniques are also possible [Ayan et al., 2004, 2005, Liu et al., 2005, Tufiş et al., 2006].

In the descriptions above, we avoided a discussion on performance. Instead, we focused on the introduction of the techniques proposed in the literature. Evaluation of word alignment is tricky and depends very much on training data, language pair and evaluation measures. Various metrics and annotation standards have been proposed [Ahrenberg et al., 2000, Carl and Fissaha, 2003, Lambert et al., 2005, Langlais et al., 1998, Martin et al., 2005, Melamed, 1998, Mihalcea and Pedersen, 2003b,c, Véronis and Langlais, 2000]. Word alignment evaluation depends to a large degree on the particular application for which the alignment has been performed. In statistical machine translation, it is common to apply the standard measures of precision and recall as presented in Chapter 2.6. However, these measures have their shortcomings as we have discussed earlier in that chapter. Word alignment techniques as presented above emphasize the identification of individual links between tokens and usually do not concern the correct establishment of bisegments. It is, therefore, natural that evaluation metrics focus on individual links, but in this way, they do not really capture the overall alignment quality. Several studies have shown that improved alignment error rates do not necessarily lead to improved translation quality [Fraser and Marcu, 2007a, Vilar et al., 2006]. The link between alignment quality and translation performance has been studied intensively in recent years [Ayan and Dorr, 2006a, Ganchev et al., 2008, Lopez and Resnik, 2006]. In most applications (not only machine translation), it is necessary to identify complete translational correspondences which, in the case of sub-sentential alignments, involves phrasal units that cannot be split into smaller alignable segments. Phrase/multi-word correspondences are required for phrase-based statistical machine translation, lexicon extraction and terminology extraction. Approaches that focus on phrases in terms of hierarchical alignment will be addressed in the next chapter.

CHAPTER 6

Phrase and Tree Alignment

So far, we have only considered flat segmentation schemes in the alignment algorithms discussed in the previous chapters. Furthermore, we focused on token-linking approaches in the chapter on word alignment, above. However, especially in word alignment, it is very common that simple one-to-one mapping between tokens are not sufficient. Treating the alignment problem as a simple token-to-token mapping is, therefore, not always very satisfactory. In general, we like to obtain symmetric correspondences in terms of bisegments. Word alignment should therefore include explicit many-to-many mappings where necessary. Hence, we would like to include links between units that span more than just one word on each side.

Additionally, we might be interested in more than just flat alignment structures with disjoint bisegments. For example, in phrase-based machine translation, one tries to extract multi-word correspondences up to a specific size limit. The strength of this approach lies in the fact that it considers overlapping units and builds a large database of translation fragments that can be considered when building translation hypotheses. Additionally, structure-based statistical translation models become increasingly popular because of their strengths to capture syntactic dependencies beyond local context.

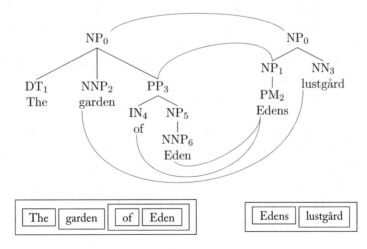

Figure 6.1: The alignment of a tree and the corresponding nested segmentation.

Hierarchical token alignment addresses the task of mapping compositional units of arbitrary size within the sentence limits. The relation between hierarchical structures and compositional segments (the **surface structure**) can be seen in Figure 6.1. In the case illustrated here, the hierarchical structure refers to a projective tree (without crossing edges) which can be represented as a set of nested segments. Without labels, this is also called **bracketing** as we can put brackets around each segment to indicate the hierarchical structure. This is not possible for segmentations with discontinuous segments which correspond to unlabeled non-projective tree structures.

In this chapter, we like to discuss two tasks: we will consider the case of **tree alignment** in which existing hierarchical structures are available on both sides of the bitext that need to be aligned with each other. The general motivation here is to find mappings between linguistically motivated analyses across languages for the purpose of building **parallel treebanks**. These can be useful for cross-linguistic research, translation studies, translator's support or machine translation. Secondly, we also look at inductive hierarchical alignment techniques that do not (necessarily) require additional annotation but instead build a common structure for sentence pairs from a bitext from scratch. In both cases, we assume already sentence aligned bitexts and focus on the alignment of individual sentence pairs.

6.1 PARALLEL TREEBANKS AND TREE ALIGNMENT

Treebanks are corpora with syntactically analyzed sentences. They have raised a lot of interest in the field of computational linguistics especially in connection with the work on statistical parsing. A wide variety of possible annotation formats exist that very much depend on the linguistic theory and grammar formalism used. Common to all of them is that the annotation describes a structure over sentences that can be decomposed into smaller units with relations between them. Discussing different traditions, formalisms and terminologies is beyond the scope of this book. We simply assume that there are substructures, which we call **constituents**, that are related with each other in some way. Constituents refer to either single tokens or several tokens from a sentence. Hence, they impose a segmentation of a sentence into possibly overlapping units. Constituents naturally form a tree if this segmentation is strictly compositional, i.e., each segment s is contained in another one, and there is a (root) segment that spans the entire sentence. Constituents within a tree are called **nodes** with one special node at the root of the tree. Nodes can be labeled (as well as **edges** connecting nodes). Labeled constituents are also called **non-terminals** and single tokens are referred to as **terminal nodes** (as they are usually attached as *leaf nodes* at the end of every branch of the tree). The task of **tree alignment** is now to link constituents (or tree nodes) from one source sentence to corresponding units in the target sentence. For now, we assume that there is a similar structure in the target language, and we aim at finding corresponding constituents among them.

TREE-TO-TREE ALIGNMENT

The idea of coupling constituents in syntactically analyzed sentence pairs dates back to the early developments of example-based machine translation [Nagao, 1984]. Pairs of subtrees can be used as fragmental translation examples with syntactic structure that can be combined with others to translate sentences from one language to another. They can also be used to learn syntactic transfer patterns for classical rule-based machine translation systems. For this, we do not need to care much about the global tree structure as we are mainly interested in extracting as many subtree/constituent pairs as possible to fill our database. Kaji et al. [1992] presents a simple greedy algorithm to perform this kind of extraction.

Recently, the progress in tree-based statistical machine translation pushed a lot of interest in the direction of hierarchical alignment approaches. As a side-effect, any tree alignment approach is also a natural way of producing phrase correspondences which are directly useful for non-structural approaches to machine translation.

For a tree-to-tree alignment strategy, it is required that both sides of the bitext are analyzed syntactically. This is usually done independently using some underlying grammar formalism. However, parallel corpora with syntactic annotation do not exist in large amounts. There are some initiatives for creating such resources [Ahrenberg, 2007, Gonzales et al., 2009, Gustafson-Čapková et al., 2007, Megyesi et al., 2008], but their size is usually very limited. It is, therefore, common to rely on entirely automatic annotation using monolingual hand-crafted or statistical parsers. Usually, one retains only the best tree the parser can find to go ahead with the tree alignment task. Alternatively, one may use an N-best list or a compact representation of parse alternatives (a *parse forest*) to make alignment decisions more flexible. In the description below, we assume that we only have one tree per language and per sentence available.

Tree-to-tree alignment approaches have to tackle the difficult problem of harmonizing independent syntactic analyses to find a common structure. Due to the usually substantial differences in monolingual analyses, it is often impossible to find such a common representation describing a complete mapping from one tree to another. Generative tree-to-tree alignment models are, therefore, not very successful because of the strong constraints given by the monolingual parses. As a consequence, most approaches apply heuristic or discriminative models for constituent mappings aiming at partial alignments of given tree structures.

A common approach is to start with lexical mappings to perform a constrained cost-minimization approach. One important constraint in tree alignment is the **crossing constraint** [Wu, 1997] (which is also sometimes called the *wellformedness constraint* [Lavie et al., 2008, Tinsley et al., 2007]):

> *Descendants/ancestors of a linked non-terminal node in the source tree may only be linked to descendants/ancestors of its linked counterpart in the target tree.*

This ensures that links between constituents may not cross each other in the tree structure. The crossing constraint is quite intuitive and reduces the search space substantially, which makes it possible to run simple greedy alignment strategies. It also implies that every node in a tree may obtain at most one link, which is another important property for efficient alignment strategies. However, it may sometimes be useful to relax this constraint to allow multiple mappings especially in cases of unary productions. For example, consider the edge from NP_1 to PM_2 in the Swedish tree in Figure 6.1. It could be argued that the non-terminal node PM_2 should also be aligned to the English counterpart PP_3 in the same way as NP_1 is aligned to this node. Another way to handle such situations is to collapse unary productions to form one "super-node" [Zhechev and Way, 2008]. Note that we excluded the alignment of terminal nodes in this discussion. However, they can be a natural part of a tree alignment algorithm and, hence, word alignment can be integrated in the alignment procedure. Nevertheless, it is useful to add some additional constraints in that case:

- Non-terminal nodes may only be linked to non-terminal nodes.

- Terminal nodes may only be linked to terminal nodes.

- Terminal nodes may be aligned to multiple nodes as long as they obey the crossing constraints.

The general objective for tree-to-tree alignment is to find the mapping $\mathbf{a}$ that minimizes a dedicated cost function

$$\hat{\mathbf{a}} = \underset{\mathbf{a}}{\operatorname{argmax}} \ cost(\mathbf{a}|\mathbf{s}, \mathbf{t})$$

for a given source tree $\mathbf{s}$ and a target tree $\mathbf{t}$. We simply represent trees as sets of constituents $\mathbf{s} = \{\mathbf{p}_1, ..., \mathbf{p}_K\}$ and $\mathbf{t} = \{\mathbf{r}_1, ..., \mathbf{r}_L\}$ where each constituent refers to a node in the tree. We further represent each constituent by the surface tokens it combines: $\mathbf{p}_k = \{s_{k_1}, ..., s_{k_n}\}$ and $\mathbf{r}_l = \{t_{l_1}, ..., t_{l_m}\}$. For both sentences, there should be a dedicated constituent that spans over all tokens in the sentence ($\mathbf{p}_{root} = \{s_1, ..., s_N\}$ and $\mathbf{r}_{root} = \{t_1, ..., t_M\}$). For sets of non-identical (compositional) constituents, this would be sufficient to reconstruct a tree structure. Otherwise, one could define a function *parent* over constituents, to map each node to its parent node.

Similar to other alignment approaches, the optimization objective above can be seen as a structured prediction task in which we try to find the best alignment structure given some input variables. As usual, it is necessary to decompose the problem into smaller sub-problems to make prediction tractable. A common strategy is to apply greedy alignment search based on local link costs. For this, we assume that the overall cost can be computed out of individual link costs:

$$cost(\mathbf{a}|\mathbf{s}, \mathbf{t}) = \sum_{kl} cost(a_{kl}|\mathbf{s}, \mathbf{t}, \mathbf{h})$$

where $\mathbf{h}$ is the history of the previous link decisions. In many cases, any dependency on prediction history is dropped, and alignment search is guided by the crossing constraints, presented above. Matsumoto et al. [1993] present a greedy top-down search algorithm (starting at the root) in which expected costs are calculated to incrementally expand the currently best alignment hypotheses. Grishman [1994] uses a beam search in a bottom-up approach (starting at the leaf nodes). Groves et al. [2004], Menezes and Richardson [2001] use greedy best-first alignment strategies starting with evidence collected for leaf nodes. Tinsley et al. [2007], Zhechev and Way [2008] experiment with various search heuristics that allow minor corrections in case of blocking links. Yet another approach is presented by Lavie et al. [2008] in which alignment decisions are greedily propagated from leaf nodes to the root.

Ignoring the crossing constraints, it is straightforward to model tree alignment as another instance of an assignment problem [Tiedemann, 2010]. In a sense, this is similar to the local constituent coupling approach by [Kaji et al., 1992] but adding a one-to-one alignment restriction. Using standard maximum weighted bipartite matching algorithms, we obtain the optimal alignment according to the local link costs. Nodes that violate the crossing constraint can be removed in a final post-processing step. Thereafter, additional links can be added using greedy strategies again.

The search strategies above are not very different from constrained search heuristics that we have discussed for word alignment. Interesting for tree-to-tree alignment is the estimation of appropriate link costs (or similarity measure) that we need to base our local decisions on. Basically, all approaches mentioned above rely on association features. Let us have a closer look at some of these features proposed in the literature.

All algorithms mentioned, so far, use lexical matching to compute some kind of alignment cost. Constituents which share a lot of lexical mappings are more likely to correspond to each other than other constituent pairs. The simplest possibility for lexical matching is to use external resources such as bilingual lexicons ($\mathcal{D}$) and monolingual thesauri together with some pre-defined thresholds and constraints. Matsumoto et al. [1993], for example, define a lexical match heuristics with a fixed score and extend matching by looking up words in a monolingual thesaurus ($\mathcal{T}$).

$$sim(s_n, t_m) = \begin{cases} 6 & \text{if } (s_n, t_m) \in \mathcal{D} \\ -\min_{t':(s_n,t')\in\mathcal{D}} dist(t_m, t'|\mathcal{T}) & \text{if } \min_{t'} dist(t_m, t'|\mathcal{T}) \geq d \\ 0 & \text{otherwise} \end{cases}$$

The distance $dist(t, t'|\mathcal{T})$ is measured as the number of steps that have to be made to get from t to t' in the thesaurus $\mathcal{T}$. d is a constant threshold for the permitted distance in $\mathcal{T}$. For non-terminal nodes, one can measure the amount of lexical mappings between all tokens dominated by those nodes. It can be useful to filter tokens, for example, to consider only content words [Kaji et al., 1992].

This approach can easily be extended to use probabilistic lexicons. Zhechev and Way [2008], for example, apply the lexical translation probabilities created by automatic word alignment to compute a score for constituent matching. They combine information about token pairs *inside* the current subtree pair and token pairs *outside*. Let us define $\overline{p_k} = \{s_x : s_x \in \mathbf{s} \wedge s_x \notin \mathbf{p}_k\}$ to be the complementary bag of tokens of $\mathbf{p}_k$ (and likewise for $\overline{\mathbf{r}_l}$). Using this, Zhechev and Way [2008] define a similarity score $sim(\mathbf{p_k}, \mathbf{r_l})$ for arbitrary constituent pairs:

$$sim(\mathbf{p_k}, \mathbf{r_l}) = \alpha(\mathbf{p_k}|\mathbf{r_l})\alpha(\mathbf{r_l}|\mathbf{p_k})\alpha(\overline{\mathbf{p_k}}|\overline{\mathbf{r_l}})\alpha(\overline{\mathbf{r_l}}|\overline{\mathbf{p_k}})$$

$$\alpha(\mathbf{x}|\mathbf{y}) = \prod_{x_i \in x} \frac{1}{J} \sum_{j=1}^{J} p_t(x_i|y_j)$$

where $p_t(x_i|y_j)$ are the lexical translation probabilities of any IBM alignment model. The intuition for using outside scores as well is that strong associations between tokens *outside* the current constituent (subtree) pair also provide valuable evidence for the relation between the constituents under consideration. The score above combines evidence from both asymmetric translation models in a simple uniform way. The score is independent of any context and can easily be computed for all node pairs. Zhechev and Way [2008] apply greedy search strategies with crossing constraints to align trees according to these individual link scores.

Other possible association features that can be included in a greedy alignment algorithm may include matches between constituent labels and substructures. Various manually defined linking rules are explored in Groves et al. [2004], Menezes and Richardson [2001]. The disadvantage here is the dependence on language-specific annotation and the necessity of manual rule writing. Another heuristic search strategy is to use existing word alignments as constraints in a bottom-up alignment algorithm [Lavie et al., 2008].

A natural way to extend these heuristic alignment strategies is to use a discriminative framework in a similar way as we have seen in word alignment. Several features have been discussed above already, and it is desirable to combine them in a unified model in which their contribution to alignment decisions is optimized. Tiedemann and Kotzé [2009a] present a simple model based on a local classifier that can be used to predict constituent mappings. They apply a log-linear model for predicting the link likelihood of individual node pairs (p_k, r_l) based on a linear combination of weighted feature functions.

$$P_\Lambda(a_{kl}|k, l, \mathbf{s}, \mathbf{t}) = \frac{1}{Z_\Lambda(k, l, \mathbf{s}, \mathbf{t})} \exp \sum_l \lambda_l h_l(a_{kl}, k, l, \mathbf{s}, \mathbf{t})$$

Various local feature functions can be applied that make use of association measures, constituent labels, tree position information (vertical and horizontal), consistency with word alignment, constituent labels and so forth. For example, using such a model, it is straightforward to use inside $\alpha(\mathbf{x}|\mathbf{y})$ and outside $\alpha(\bar{\mathbf{x}}|\bar{\mathbf{y}})$ scores defined by Zhechev and Way [2008] as individual feature functions. Using an existing word alignment $\mathcal{L} = \{(n_1, m_1), ..., (n_k, m_k)\}$, we can also define the following alignment consistency feature:

$$align(\mathbf{p}, \mathbf{r}) = \frac{\sum_{(n,m)\in\mathcal{L}} consistent(\mathcal{L}, \mathbf{p}, \mathbf{r}, n, m)}{\sum_{(n,m)\in\mathcal{L}} relevant(\mathcal{L}, \mathbf{p}, \mathbf{r}, n, m)}$$

$$consistent(\mathcal{L}, \mathbf{p}, \mathbf{r}, n, m) = \begin{cases} 1 & \text{if } s_n \in \mathbf{p} \wedge t_m \in \mathbf{r} \\ 0 & \text{otherwise} \end{cases}$$

$$relevant(\mathcal{L}, \mathbf{p}, \mathbf{r}, n, m) = \begin{cases} 1 & \text{if } s_n \in \mathbf{p} \vee t_m \in \mathbf{r} \\ 0 & \text{otherwise} \end{cases}$$

Relative position differences in the tree can also be defined as additional features. Tiedemann and Kotzé [2009b] define a vertical tree-level similarity score (*tls*) and a horizontal tree-span similarity score (*tss*).

$$tls(\mathbf{p}, \mathbf{r}) = 1 - abs\left(\frac{distance(\mathbf{p}, \mathbf{p}_{root})}{\max_{\mathbf{p}'} distance(\mathbf{p}', \mathbf{p}_{root})} - \frac{distance(\mathbf{r}, \mathbf{r}_{root})}{\max_{\mathbf{r}'} distance(\mathbf{r}', \mathbf{r}_{root})}\right)$$

$$tss(\mathbf{p}, \mathbf{r}) = 1 - abs\left(\frac{start(\mathbf{p}) + end(\mathbf{p})}{2 * |\mathbf{p}_{root}|} - \frac{start(\mathbf{r}) + end(\mathbf{r})}{2 * |\mathbf{r}_{root}|}\right)$$

where $distance(\mathbf{p}, \mathbf{p}_{root})$ is the length of the path from constituent $\mathbf{p}$ to the root of the tree. The functions $start(\mathbf{p})$ and $end(\mathbf{p})$ refer to token positions in the respective sentence: $start(\mathbf{p}) = \min_x x : s_x \in \mathbf{p}$ and $end(\mathbf{p}) = \max_x x : s_x \in \mathbf{p}$. Another useful feature is the ratio of segment sizes:

$$leafratio(\mathbf{p}, \mathbf{r}) = \frac{\min(|\mathbf{p}|, |\mathbf{r}|)}{\max(|\mathbf{p}|, |\mathbf{r}|)}$$

Finally, very important information can be coded into binary label pair features which refer to the category labels stored at each non-terminal node and part-of-speech labels at each pre-terminal node.

All these features can be extracted for each constituent pair but also from the surrounding context. Features can also be combined in various ways to create complex feature functions with information about context on both sides. Having this rich set of features, it is now important to find appropriate weights for the classification model. This is done with standard iterative techniques for maximum likelihood learning of log-linear models. Tiedemann and Kotzé [2009a] show that a small data set of a couple of hundred hand-aligned pairs of trees is sufficient for training reasonable model parameters. In the simplest setup, their approach entirely relies on a local classifier trained without consideration of link dependencies. They also introduce a recurrent bottom-up classification strategy that allows the integration of link history features. However, rich contextual features seem to capture much of the structural information needed. The local classifier, together with a greedy search strategy and crossing constraints, performs quite well even without history features involved. A comparison of search strategies is presented in Tiedemann [2010]. Furthermore, these models seem to be quite robust even across domains. Tiedemann and Kotzé [2009b] demonstrate how this discriminative tree alignment approach can be applied to build large (automatically) aligned parallel treebanks.

6.2   HIERARCHICAL ALIGNMENT AND TRANSDUCTION GRAMMARS

Tree-to-tree alignment has its use especially for cross-linguistic research over specific phenomena. The alignment makes it possible to study syntactic divergences and supports quantitative cross-lingual studies. The use for data-driven machine translation, however, is limited. Aligning fixed trees has several disadvantages as pointed out by Wu [2010]:

- Monolingual parsing is not robust enough or not developed at all. For many languages, there are no appropriate grammars and tools for parsing nor large enough treebanks to train stochastic parsers. Even if a parser exists, it must be able to handle even noisy and unexpected input and must produce reasonable results which are worthwhile to process further.

- Grammars do not match very well across languages. Monolingual grammars are usually designed independently following different traditions, formalisms and linguistic theories. Certain grammatical decisions about syntactic categories and constructions may make it impossible to find matching correspondences among the units annotated in two different languages.

- Single-best parse trees may not always be the best choice to find a common structure across languages. Hard decisions about certain ambiguous structures may block possible alignments. Furthermore, heuristic search strategies as the ones presented above may select the wrong mappings, and link errors may propagate to other couplings.

The most severe problem is probably the mismatch of independently designed grammars across languages. Fixed tree structures can be seen as hard constraints that restrict the search space for a hierarchical alignment algorithm. To avoid these blocking mismatches, let us now assume that there is a common structure between source and target sentence, but it is not given. The task of the hierarchical alignment algorithm is now to uncover this hidden structure. Instead of searching for mappings between given structures in a discriminative way, we now search for the common structure that has generated both strings simultaneously. Hence, we are looking at **symmetric generative models** that explain the generation of pairs of strings which are mutual translations of each other. Grammars in terms of declarative rewrite rule sets that generate pairs of strings are called **transduction grammars**. The equivalent procedural automaton is called a **transducer**. They can be used in three modes:

Generation: Rewrite rules are applied starting with a specific start symbol, to generate pairs of strings (also called bistrings). The set of string pairs that can be generated by a specific transducer is called a **transduction**.

Recognition/Parsing: A pair of strings is parsed by a transduction grammar (or transducer). This is also called **biparsing**. Recognition produces a simple binary answer whether or not the pair of string is part of the transduction defined by the grammar. Parsing refers to the task of finding actual structures that can generate the string pair (if there are any).

Transduction: A transducer translates a string into its equivalent string according to the transduction grammar. This is also called **transducing** a string.

As we can see from the descriptions above, transduction grammars can be considered as a principle model for translation. In terms of alignment, the parsing mode is the most interesting one. The common structure produced as a bi-product of biparsing includes the hierarchical alignment structure we are looking for.

SYNTAX-DIRECTED TRANSDUCTION GRAMMARS

Syntax-directed transduction grammars (SDTG) are well-known formalisms from classic compiler theory [Aho and Ullman, 1969, Lewis and Stearns, 1968]. In the machine translation community, they are also known as **synchronous context-free grammars**. Formally, a transduction grammar is defined as the tuple $\mathcal{G} = (\mathcal{N}, \mathcal{W}_s, \mathcal{W}_t, S, \mathcal{R})$ where $\mathcal{N}$ is a finite set of non-terminal symbols, $\mathcal{W}_s$ is a finite set of terminal symbols (words) in the source language, $\mathcal{W}_t$ is a finite set of target language terminal symbols,[1] $S \in \mathcal{N}$ is a designated start symbol and $\mathcal{R}$ is a set of transduction rules of the form:

$$A \rightarrow \alpha, \beta$$

where $A \in \mathcal{N}, \alpha \in (\mathcal{N} \cup \mathcal{W}_s)^*$ (a string of zero or more non-terminal symbols and/or source language terminals) and $\beta \in (\mathcal{N} \cup \mathcal{W}_t)^*$. It is important that non-terminal symbols in α and β are connected with each other, using a one-to-one correspondence relation (or bijection). This is usually marked by using identical symbols for linked non-terminals or indexed non-terminals in cases of name collisions. In generation mode, rewrite rules need to be applied until all non-terminal symbols are consumed (starting with the start symbol S). The non-terminal symbols on the left-hand side replace corresponding (linked) non-terminals on the right-hand side. The final result of a derivation is a bistring, and the set of all bistrings that can be generated in this way is the transduction defined by the grammar.

SDTGs can be divided into classes of different ranks using a normal form for rules permitted in the grammar. The rules of an SDTG of rank k are restricted to

$$A \rightarrow B^1 B^2 ... B^k, C^1 C^2 ... C^k$$
$$A \rightarrow \mathbf{s}, \mathbf{t}$$

where $A, B^i, C^i \in \mathcal{N}, \mathbf{s} \in \mathcal{W}_s^*$ (a sequence of source language tokens), and $\mathbf{t} \in \mathcal{W}_t^*$ (a sequence of target language tokens). The notation above makes it difficult to see the alignment between the k non-terminals. An alternative way of presenting rules is to specify the permutation of non-terminals on the target side when compared to the order on the source side. For example, a rule $A \rightarrow B_1 B_2 B_3, B_2 B_3 B_1$ has the permutation [2 3 1]. We can therefore specify SDTG rules in the following general way to make the non-terminal relations explicit:

$$A \rightarrow B_1 B_2 ... B_k [\pi_1 \pi_2 ... \pi_k]$$
$$A \rightarrow \mathbf{s}, \mathbf{t}$$

where $1 \leq \pi_x \leq k$.

---

[1]The use of "source" and "target" is chosen for explanatory reasons. The grammar is symmetric and does not depend on any direction in generation.

The rank k (maximum number of non-terminal pairs on the right-hand side) determines the expressivity of the transduction grammar.[2] Aho and Ullman [1972] define the hierarchy of SDTGs of various ranks. Basically, SDTGs build an infinite hierarchy of increasing capacity for all ranks $k > 3$. It turns out that the ranks $k = 2$ and $k = 3$ form the same class which is equivalent to the formalism of inversion transduction grammars discussed below. But let us first finish the discussion of general SDTGs. Syntax-directed transduction grammars describe a flexible generative model for translation, and the biparsing mode can be seen as an attractive way of producing aligned hierarchical structures of corresponding strings (sentences). The model still needs some preference mechanism to guide the search through ambiguities and to rank alternative solutions. A natural way of doing this is to add probabilities to each production (rule) defined by the grammar to turn it into a stochastic grammar.

The question is how much flexibility one should allow to make it possible to

- efficiently biparse a given pair of sentences

- induce a grammar from data that we can use for biparsing

- efficiently train parameters of a stochastic grammar

The computational complexity of general SDTGs is very high and search approximations are necessary. A restriction to rank-2 SDTGs (or inversion transduction grammars) seems to be a good compromise between expressive power and computational complexity, which we will discuss further in the next section.

INVERSION TRANSDUCTION GRAMMARS

Inversion transduction grammars (ITGs) have been introduced by Wu [1995, 1997] as a computationally tractable formalism for bilingual transduction. They represent a restriction of SDTGs by limiting rules to one of the following forms:

- At most two non-terminals (rank $k = 2$)

- At most three non-terminals (rank $k = 3$)

- Non-terminals are either ordered in the same way or in inverse order.

The third type leads to the name of inversion transduction grammars. Interestingly enough, it can be shown that either condition produces the same class of grammars [Wu, 1997]. ITGs (using the third rule restriction type) permit arbitrary rule lengths as long as the permutations are monotonic (straight or inverse order). Due to this property, they can be reduced to a rank-2 normal form (which leads to efficient parsing algorithms as we will see later on).

---

[2]The rank does not restrict the number of non-terminals in $\mathcal{N}$.

$$A \rightarrow BC \; [\; 1 \; 2 \;]$$
$$A \rightarrow BC \; [\; 2 \; 1 \;]$$
$$A \rightarrow \mathbf{s}, \mathbf{t}$$

It is common to use yet another alternative notation to compress descriptions of ITGs: straight rules $A \rightarrow BC \; [\; 1 \; 2 \;]$ are written with square brackets as $A \rightarrow [\; BC \;]$ and inverse rules $A \rightarrow BC \; [\; 2 \; 1 \;]$ are written with angle brackets as $A \rightarrow \langle \; BC \; \rangle$. String pairs $\mathbf{s}, \mathbf{t}$ in the third rule type are often specified as $\mathbf{s}/\mathbf{t}$. Note that for rank-2 SDTGs all possible permutations are included (and, therefore, a restriction to rank 2 (=binary) rules is sufficient to specify the class of ITGs). SDTGs (or synchronous grammars), which became very popular in statistical machine translation, are often restricted to binary productions and, therefore, are instances of ITGs. This is, for example, true for models based on hierarchical phrase-based translation proposed by Chiang [2005]. Other models that apply rule binarization are discussed in Zhang et al. [2006].

So much for the formal descriptions of ITGs. The big question is whether the formalism is flexible enough to describe natural language translations or if its restrictions are too strong. Wu [1997] discusses in detail how most phenomena observed in parallel data can be captured by ITGs. For an alignment task this means that we should be able to find appropriate hierarchical mappings between sentences using ITGs as a generative model. Figure 6.2 illustrates a selection of mappings between four adjacent elements that can be produced by ITG parses. Inverted rules are indicated by horizontal bars in the corresponding subtree. Note that there are alternative ways of arriving at the same permutation, depending on the derivations in the tree. For example, the last example could be obtained with a left-branching tree as well.

Figure 6.2: Six of the 22 permutations possible for ITG parses (leaving out all labels) for four elements. Horizontal bars indicate inversion.

Wu [1997] shows how 22 of the $4! = 24$ possible permutations of four elements can be represented by ITG parses and argues further that these constructions cover well common natural language phenomena. We leave it as an exercise to discover the other permutations and their corresponding ITG representation for the example with four elements.

The most important point is that the ITG restriction reduces computational complexity significantly from exponential biparsing complexity for general SDTGs to a (still high but tractable) polynomial complexity for ITGs. This complexity reduction can be seen by the growth of legal ITG

Table 6.1: The number of mappings that can be represented by ITG for n tokens compared to all possible permutations (as allowed in SDTGs/SCFGs) [Wu, 1997].

n	ITG	$n!$	ratio
1	1	1	1.000
2	2	2	1.000
3	6	6	1.000
4	22	24	0.917
5	90	120	0.750
6	394	720	0.547
7	1,806	5,040	0.358
8	8,558	40,320	0.212
9	41,586	362,880	0.115
10	206,098	3,628,800	0.057
11	1,037,718	39,916,800	0.026
12	5,293,446	479,001,600	0.011
13	27,297,738	6,227,020,800	0.004
14	142,078,746	87,178,291,200	0.002
15	745,387,038	1,307,674,368,000	0.001

mappings as shown in Figure 6.1, which is much less dramatic than the one for unrestricted SDTGs. More detailed analyses can be found in [Saers and Wu, 2009, Wu, 1997].

ALIGNMENT THROUGH BIPARSING

Having a stochastic inversion transduction grammar, we can find a shared structure for source sentence **s** and target sentence **t** and thus a hierarchical alignment by **biparsing** the two given sentences and extracting the most likely parse tree according to the grammar. Similar to stochastic context-free grammars (or probabilistic context-free grammars, PCFGs, to avoid the confusion with *synchronous* context-free grammars), the probability of a biparse tree is the product of rule probabilities $P(A \rightarrow \phi)$ applied to generate the tree.

In ITG trees, each node (non-terminal or terminal) corresponds to a unique pair of consecutive token sequences. A node can therefore be represented by the source and target language span it covers. Let us say that a non-terminal $A_{x..y}^{a..b}$ covers (and eventually generates) source tokens $(s_{a+1}, s_{a+2}.., s_b)$ and target tokens $(t_{x+1}, t_{x+2}..., t_y)$.[3] Similarly, terminal $s_{a..b}/t_{x..y}$ spans the same pair of token

---

[3]Spans can be empty in case $a = b$ or $x = y$. Note that ITGs in normal form are not allowed to generate the empty bistring (empty strings on both sides). This additional constraint ensures recursive parsing algorithms to terminate.

sequences. A biparse naturally forms a set of aligned hierarchical bitext segments. Corresponding phrases can easily be extracted from such a structure as depicted in Figure 6.3.

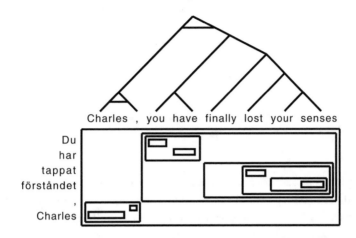

Figure 6.3: A possible ITG parse tree with corresponding word and phrase alignments.

Another way to look at the best parse (and therewith the best alignment) is to define the alignment cost of coupling constituents (sequences of tokens) as the negative log probability of the rule corresponding to that constituent pair. The best alignment (and therewith the best parse) is then the sum of costs for all constituent couplings in the tree. In this way, our objective is not much different from the tree-to-tree alignment approaches discussed earlier except that we do not restrict the search to a fixed set of constituents but instead allow all bisegmentations possible within the grammar.

It is natural to see that the biparsing approach has a larger chance to find a common structure than tree-to-tree alignment approaches with hard constraints on both sides. The problem is, however, to select the most plausible one from the waste amount of possible analyses. The parsing algorithm itself resembles the CKY algorithm [Cocke and Schwartz, 1970, Kasami, 1965, Younger, 1967]. It considers all possible constituents. Conceptually, one can think of dividing string pairs **s**/**t** at arbitrary points to see whether that string pair has been generated by combining the resulting two substrings on each side. In ITGs, there are two ways of combining them, either in the same order on both sides (straight rules) or swapped on one side (inverted rules). Recursively, we now have to explain these new substrings as well with the same procedure until a final terminal production rule is found. The possible inversion at each step allows complex word and phrase order differences which is the power of ITGs. Figure 6.4 illustrates the general procedure in terms of a deductive system in which conclusions can be deduced from evaluating the premises above in each of the three inference rules.

Using this biparsing approach, segmentation is naturally integrated in the alignment procedure (*translation-driven segmentation*). Guided by the costs (probabilities) of grammar rules the parsing algorithm optimizes mapping and segmentation at the same time. [Wu, 1996, 1997] presents a

$$A \rightarrow s_{a..b}/t_{x..y}$$
$$\overline{A_{x..y}^{a..b}}$$

$$\frac{A \rightarrow [\ BC\ ], \ B_{x..j}^{a..i}, \ C_{j..y}^{i..b}}{A_{x..y}^{a..b}}$$

$$\frac{A \rightarrow \langle\ BC\ \rangle, \ B_{j..y}^{a..i}, \ C_{x..j}^{i..b}}{A_{x..y}^{a..b}}$$

Figure 6.4: ITG parsing as deductive system adapted from the presentation in Saers [2011]. The goal item is the start symbol spanning over the entire source and target sentence $S_{0..M}^{0..N}$. The second and the third inference rule illustrate how string pairs can be divided at arbitrary points i, j into two parts that can be either inverted (rule three) or straight (rule two).

bottom-up parsing algorithm that generalizes the monolingual CKY algorithm to the bilingual case of ITGs. In the next section, we will have a closer look at the computation of inside-outside probabilities that enable such dynamic programming solutions of the parsing problem. They are also essential for the induction of transduction grammars from raw data, which will be the focus of the next section. Further details about parsing algorithms and their implementation are given in [Saers, 2011, Saers and Wu, 2009, Wu, 1997].

INDUCING TRANSDUCTION GRAMMARS

In the previous section, we have discussed how inversion transduction grammars can be used for hierarchical alignment via parsing in bitext space. We now address the question of how to obtain such a grammar. Transduction grammars are generative models that try to explain how pairs of strings have been created. Stochastic transduction grammars make it possible to compute the probability of a given string pair (by summing over all possible derivations). Hence, they can be seen as bilingual language models that can be trained on a representative sample of bilingual data. The expectation maximization (EM) algorithm can be used again to estimate grammar parameters by iteratively adjusting rule probabilities. Similar to stochastic context-free grammars, we can use a variant of the **inside-outside algorithm** to compute the necessary variables for efficient computation of rule expectations. **Inside probabilities** are computed as follows:

1. Initialization:

$$\beta(A_{j..j}^{i..i}) = 0 \text{ for all } A \in \mathcal{N}, 0 \leq i \leq N, 0 \leq j \leq M$$

2. Recursions:

$$\beta(A_{x..y}^{a..b}) = p(A \rightarrow s_{a..b}/t_{x..y}) +$$
$$\sum_{B,C \in \mathcal{N}\ a \leq i \leq b, x \leq j \leq y} p(A \rightarrow [\ B\ C\ ])\ \beta(B_{x..j}^{a..i})\ \beta(B_{j..y}^{i..b}) +$$
$$\sum_{B,C \in \mathcal{N}\ a \leq i \leq b, x \leq j \leq y} p(A \rightarrow \langle\ B\ C\ \rangle)\ \beta(B_{j..y}^{a..i})\beta(B_{x..j}^{i..b}) +$$

Outside probabilities are computed with the following recursive definition:

1. Initialization:

$$\alpha(A_{0..M}^{0..N}) = \begin{cases} 1 & \text{if } A = S \\ 0 & \text{otherwise} \end{cases}$$

2. Recursions:

$$\alpha(A_{x..y}^{a..b}) = \sum_{B,C \in \mathcal{N}\ 0 \leq i \leq a, 0 \leq j \leq x} p(B \rightarrow [\ C\ A\ ])\ \alpha(B_{j..y}^{i..b})\ \beta(C_{j..y}^{i..b}) +$$
$$\sum_{B,C \in \mathcal{N}\ b \leq i \leq N, y \leq j \leq M} p(B \rightarrow [\ A\ C\ ])\ \alpha(B_{x..j}^{a..i})\ \beta(C_{y..j}^{b..i}) +$$
$$\sum_{B,C \in \mathcal{N}\ 0 \leq i \leq a, y \leq j \leq M} p(B \rightarrow \langle\ C\ A\ \rangle)\ \alpha(B_{x..j}^{i..b})\ \beta(C_{y..j}^{i..x}) +$$
$$\sum_{B,C \in \mathcal{N}\ b \leq i \leq N, 0 \leq j \leq x} p(B \rightarrow \langle\ A\ C\ \rangle)\ \alpha(B_{j..y}^{x..i})\ \beta(C_{j..x}^{b..i}) +$$

The probability of a given string pair (having a specific label) is given by the product of corresponding inside and outside scores:

$$p(A_{x..y}^{a..b}) = \alpha(A_{x..y}^{a..b})\ \beta(A_{x..y}^{a..b})$$

A general constraint with stochastic ITGs (as with stochastic CFGs) is that rule probabilities have to sum up to one for any non-terminal symbol A:

$$\sum_{\phi} p(A \rightarrow \phi) = 1$$

For the EM algorithm, we need to compute expected values of rule observations $E(A \rightarrow \phi)$ to update grammar rule probabilities with the objective of maximizing the likelihood of seeing the training data according to our current model. Rule probabilities are then re-estimated using fractional counts:

$$\hat{p}(A \to \phi) = \frac{E(A \to \phi)}{\sum_{\psi} E(A \to \psi)}$$

Inside-outside probabilities can be used to compute expected counts for each applicable grammar rule in each sentence pair $(\mathbf{s}\|\mathbf{t})$ in the bitext B. Expectations of terminal rules are calculated as follows:[4]

$$E(A \to a) = \sum_{(\mathbf{s}\|\mathbf{t})\in B} \sum_{a,b,x,y} \begin{cases} \alpha(A_{x..y}^{a..b})\,\beta(A_{x..y}^{a..b}) & \text{if } s_{a..b}/t_{x..y} = a \\ 0 & \text{otherwise} \end{cases}$$

The computation of non-terminal rule expectations depends on the orientation of the rule. For straight rules:

$$E(A \to [\,B\ C\,]) = \sum_{(\mathbf{s}\|\mathbf{t})\in B} \sum_{a,b,x,y} \sum_{\substack{a \le i \le b \\ x \le j \le y}} \alpha(A_{x..y}^{a..b})\, p(A \to [\,B\ C\,])\beta(B_{x..j}^{a..i})\beta(C_{j..y}^{i..b})$$

For inverted rules:

$$E(A \to \langle\,B\ C\,\rangle) = \sum_{(\mathbf{s}\|\mathbf{t})\in B} \sum_{a,b,x,y} \sum_{\substack{a \le i \le b \\ x \le j \le y}} \alpha(A_{x..y}^{a..b})\, p(A \to [\,B\ C\,])\beta(B_{j..y}^{a..i})\beta(C_{x..j}^{a..i})$$

Finally, the denominator of the re-estimation formula can be computed as follows:

$$\sum_{\psi} E(A \to \psi) = E(A) = \sum_{(\mathbf{s}\|\mathbf{t})\in B} \sum_{a,b,x,y} \alpha(A_{x..y}^{a..b})\,\beta(A_{x..y}^{a..b})$$

With this, it is possible to induce a grammar purely from sentence aligned bitexts [Wu, 1995]. In such an unsupervised grammar induction, one usually assumes a generic grammar with only one non-terminal symbol (besides the start symbol). In other words, we ignore constituent labels (and, hence, structural dependencies that could be carried by additional non-terminals) and create a **bracketing inversion transduction grammar** (BITG). Even though the training algorithm is tractable, it is still quite expensive especially for long sentence pairs. Rough estimates of lexical rules and pruning strategies can help to improve efficiency [Saers, 2011, Saers et al., 2009]. Blunsom et al. [2009] propose a Bayesian model using inference based on a Gibbs sampler for efficient grammar induction. EM is also sensitive to initialization; therefore, it may be useful to bias the initial distribution according to some prior knowledge. It is possible to include a bias for straight rules to prefer identical word ordering which can be useful for many related language pairs. Furthermore, structural ambiguities

---

[4]In all formulas listed here, we require that $0 \le a \le b \le N$ and $0 \le x \le y \le M$ with $N = |\mathbf{s}|$ and $M = |\mathbf{t}|$.

in bracketing grammars that cannot be handled by probabilistic optimization may be avoided using some simple heuristics [Wu, 1997].

Another possibility is to integrate knowledge from existing grammars. The ITG training procedures can be constrained by patterns defined by another (linguistically motivated) grammar. For example, it can be useful to define a coarse grammar for frequent constituent patterns to guide the search procedures. This can be done for either one or for both languages [Wu, 1995]. Furthermore, it is also possible to integrate a detailed monolingual grammar for one side of the bitext. Monolingual rules can be converted to be part of the resulting bilingual ITG using some heuristics. In this way, the ITG is strongly biased towards the linguistic description of one language [Wu and Wong, 1998]. However, this often causes a degradation in parsing quality for the other language.

6.3   SUMMARY AND FURTHER READING

In this chapter, we considered hierarchical alignment algorithms that either try to align existing structures in both halves of the bitext or induce a common structure for aligned sentence pairs. Aligning existing trees is mainly useful for cross-linguistic research (for example, [Cyrus, 2006, Rios et al., 2009]) and bilingual transfer rule induction for approaches that are bound to certain grammar formalisms (see, for example, [Buch-Kromann, 2007, Graham and van Genabith, 2009, Lavoie et al., 2001]). The majority of such tree-to-tree alignment algorithms is based on association-based link heuristics or discriminative classifier-based approaches. The latter requires aligned training data. However, good results can be achieved with small amounts of training examples, simple features and appropriate search constraints. One problem with tree-to-tree alignment is the mismatch between independently designed grammars that lead to strong restriction of the search space. It is often difficult to harmonize two structures that have been designed without cross-lingual symmetries in mind. Nevertheless, aligning such structures can lead to a valuable partial mapping of linguistically motivated segments and sub-structures. Further ideas for the alignment of syntactic phrases are, for example, discussed in [Imamura, 2001, Watanabe et al., 2002]. Ding and Palmer [2004], Yamamoto and Matsumoto [2000], and Menezes and Quirk [2005] look at mappings between dependency structures.

Transduction grammars (or synchronous grammars), on the other hand, aim at a symmetric generative explanation of translated texts. The generation of sentence pairs is based on a common structure with permutations in one language allowed. Segmentation and alignment is integrated in the biparsing algorithm when applying a (usually stochastic) transduction grammar to parallel data. Inversion transduction grammars describe a sub-class of transduction grammars that allow tractable computation. They can be induced from plain bitexts without syntactic annotation. Linguistic annotation can be integrated as additional search bias to guide the optimization process. Furthermore, beside creating a hierarchical alignment structure, ITGs can also be used to induce symmetric word alignment [Saers and Wu, 2009] or to restrict the search space in other alignment models [Cherry and Lin, 2006a,b]. Zhang and Gildea [2004] present a comparison between various syntax-based alignment models for inducing word alignments. They compare purely generic

ITG models with models that incorporate linguistically motivated monolingual syntactic annotation. Their conclusion is that generic ITGs perform very well for this task, better than the ones with monolingual parsing constraints. Some improvements for the latter can be achieved with tree cloning operations that allow more flexibility in alignment decisions [Gildea, 2003].

Zhang and Gildea [2005] show how ITG rules can be lexicalized to improve the expressive power of the grammar and to achieve better alignments at least for shorter sentences. Dedicated pruning techniques need to be used to reduce parsing complexity. Zhang et al. [2008] show how ITGs can be extended to include multi-word terminals, which leads to further improvements in alignment and statistical machine translation. They use Bayesian learning techniques and sparse priors to avoid overfitting problems of the EM algorithm, which has a positive effect on alignment and end-to-end translation performance.

Training transduction grammars is still expensive. Another class with even stronger rule restriction called **linear transduction grammars** is presented in [Saers, 2011, Saers et al., 2010]. This formalism allows efficient computations even for large data sets at the expense of a reduced generative capacity. Another way of reducing run-time complexity for synchronous parsing is presented by Dyer [2010]. The author of this paper proposes a two-step-parse algorithm that combines monolingual parses to produce the final synchronous analysis.

CHAPTER 7

Concluding Remarks

The goal of this book was to provide an overview of various techniques for bitext alignment. We have seen the general concepts and strategies that can be applied to obtain a mapping between parallel documents. A large number of algorithms have been proposed to handle the alignment of bitexts on different levels of granularity. They have a common ground but often very different parametrization.

In general, we would like to see alignment as a process of making symmetric correspondences explicit in order to enable further processing of parallel resources. The connection between segmentation and alignment here is especially important. Finding corresponding units requires an identification of appropriate segments that can be linked. Many algorithms assume a fixed base segmentation and treat alignment as the identification of links between individual text elements (which may be paragraphs, sentences, words or whatever units need to be aligned). Other approaches treat alignment as a bisegmentation process in which source and target texts are divided such that pairs of segments correspond to each other one-by-one. The latter corresponds to the original definition of the term *alignment*, which refers to strictly monotonic mappings only. As this is usually not possible, especially not for sub-sentential structures in natural languages, the use of alignment has been extended to allow permutations as well. However, permutations increase complexity dramatically; therefore, search space restrictions have to be applied. We have discussed various ways of limiting alignment models to make optimization processes tractable. We have seen the importance of hierarchical refinement strategies (document alignment → sentence alignment → word/phrase alignment), functional constraints, reordering constraints, and other ways of biasing search and restricting model capacities. We have seen unsupervised and heuristic alignment approaches and classifier-based supervised alignment models. We did not discuss manual alignment which is, of course, another option.

Once again, it is important to stress that any alignment is meant to serve a specific purpose. Any bitext mapping is not useful in itself if it cannot be exploited in any way. Possible application areas are wide-spread. Statistical machine translation is only one of them. Bitexts can be exploited in various other ways including for cross-linguistic research, for the extraction of bilingual and monolingual knowledge, for the projection of tools and information from one language to another, for cross-lingual information retrieval and extraction, for the identification of language change and development. Bitexts have been discovered by many researchers due to the rich knowledge implicitly and explicitly stored within them. Their full potential becomes visible now as larger bitexts become more and more available, and, similarly important, due to the availability of robust alignment tools. One of the main challenges for the future is to handle noisy sources and to further develop techniques to identify parallel resources for more language pairs and more domains.

7.1   FINAL RECOMMENDATIONS

Building corpora is a time-consuming task, creating bitexts even more because of the additional alignment efforts that are necessary. Here are some general recommendations that might be useful when starting a new project:

- Look for available resources and tools before starting to develop them on your own.

- Define specific goals and requirements according to the application you have in mind.

- Locate data sources and study carefully what kind of data formats are available and how they can be handled.

- Spend time to optimize pre-processing.

    - proper conversion (text extraction, character encoding, etc.)

    - keep valuable information (markup, stylistic information, meta data)

    - think about the importance of segmentation (paragraph/sentence boundary detection, tokenization)

- Use available tools for alignment.

    - try different approaches

    - optimize parameters and combine different types of evidence

    - consider manual alignment efforts to improve automatic alignment quality by applying supervised / semi-supervised techniques; consider bootstrapping strategies; manual alignment is also important for evaluation

- Make data and tools **available** to others!

    - avoid restrictions and usage limits as much as possible

    - describe sources and processing steps that have been performed

    - mention possible shortcomings, errors and limitations

A lot of the techniques described in this book are implemented in freely available software packages. This has created a booming research on bitext alignment and related topics and lead to the availability of many data resources. A list of resources and tools is included in appendix A. Share your efforts and contribute to the growing community. Good luck with your projects!

APPENDIX A

Resources & Tools

Here is a selection of resources and tools. The list is neither complete nor guaranteed to be up-to-date (but, hopefully, still useful to start with).

PARALLEL CORPORA

Hansards: debates in the House and Senate of the 36th Canadian Parliament, French-English
http://www.isi.edu/natural-language/download/hansard/

Europarl: European Parliament Proceedings Parallel Corpus, 21 languages
http://www.statmt.org/europarl/

MultiUN: a Multilingual corpus from United Nation Documents, 7 languages [Eisele and Chen, 2010] http://www.euromatrixplus.net/multi-un/

JRC-Acquis: Acquis Communautaire (European Union law), 22 languages [Steinberger et al., 2006] http://langtech.jrc.it/JRC-Acquis.html

OPUS: a collection of freely available parallel corpora, many languages
http://opus.lingfil.uu.se/

Multext-East: multilingual resources for Eastern and Southeastern European languages
http://nl.ijs.si/ME/V4/

Apertium: multilingual data collections from the Official Journal of the European Union, currently 23 languages: http://apertium.eu/data

LDC: the Linguistic Data Consortium provides a large number of parallel corpora:
http://www.ldc.upenn.edu/

ELRA: European Language Resources Association, look for written parallel corpora
http://catalog.elra.info/

TOOLS FOR AQUIRING BITEXTS

Bitextor: an automatic bitext generator from websites: http://bitextor.sourceforge.net/

STRAND: A system for automatically acquiring pairs of translated documents from the Web:
http://www.umiacs.umd.edu/~resnik/strand/

TOOLS FOR AUTOMATIC SENTENCE ALIGNMENT

Gale&Church: the classical length-based sentence alignment approach.
Vanilla implementation of the approach: `http://nl.ijs.si/telri/Vanilla/`
A re-implementation in Perl is available at
`http://www.statmt.org/europarl/v6/tools.tgz` (together with the Europarl corpus)
or bundles as Perl module
`http://code.google.com/p/corpus-tools/downloads/list`
`http://search.cpan.org/~achimru/Text-GaleChurch-1.00/lib/Text/`
`GaleChurch.pm`

hunalign: a fast and accurate sentence aligner that combines length-based and lexical methods, available from: `http://mokk.bme.hu/resources/hunalign`

GMA: Dan Melamed's Geometric Mapping approach, available from
`http://nlp.cs.nyu.edu/GMA/`

Bob Moore's sentence aligner: a hybrid multi-step sentence aligner.
Search for "bilingual sentence aligner" at `http://research.microsoft.com`

Gargantua: another freely available sentence aligner
`http://sourceforge.net/projects/gargantua/`

Subtitle aligner: a time-overlap aligner for movie subtitles in .srt format, available from
`http://opus.lingfil.uu.se/tools.php`

Champollion: a sentence aligner that combines lexical information and length information. (Not to be confused with the multilingual term extraction tool by Smadja with the sama name [Smadja et al., 1996]; see below in the section on word alignment.)
`http://champollion.sourceforge.net/`

Alinea: a tool for automatic sentence alignment, evaluation and bilingual concordances.
`http://w3.u-grenoble3.fr/kraif/index.php?Itemid=43`

Align: a sentence alignment tools that looks for word-to-word translation anchors.
`http://www.cse.unt.edu/~rada/wa/tools/aberger/`

cwb-align: sentence aligner as part of the corpus work bench (CWB)
`http://cwb.sourceforge.net/`

LF aligner: an alignment tool for creating translation memories (based on hunalign)
`http://sourceforge.net/projects/aligner/`

TagAligner: a tool for segmentation and alginment of documents with markup for the use in computer-aided translation tools: `http://tag-aligner.sourceforge.net/`

TOOLS FOR AUTOMATIC WORD ALIGNMENT & LEXICON EXTRACTION

GIZA++: the standard implementation of the IBM alignment models and HMM alignment with several extensions: `http://code.google.com/p/giza-pp/`

MGIZA++: a multi-threaded version of GIZA++ to run in parallel on multi-core engines: `http://geek.kyloo.net/software/doku.php/mgiza:overview`

Chaski: a distributed toolkit for statistical machine translation including distributed word alignment and distributed phrase extraction
`http://geek.kyloo.net/software/doku.php/chaski:overview`

Berkeley Aligner: a tool for joint (agreement) training of IBM alignment models. Supports also a syntactic distortion model
`http://code.google.com/p/berkeleyaligner/`
`http://nlp.cs.berkeley.edu/Main.html#WordAligner`

PostCat: a posterior constrained alignment toolkit [Ganchev et al., 2008]
`http://www.seas.upenn.edu/~strctlrn/CAT/CAT.html`

anymalign: a multi-lingual word aligner based on string differences and sampling:
`http://users.info.unicaen.fr/~alardill/anymalign/`

MTTK: a multi-threaded alignment tool for word & chunk (phrase) alignment (only for academic use): `http://mi.eng.cam.ac.uk/~wjb31/distrib/mttkv1/`

cdec-aligner: unsupervised discriminative CRF-based word alignment, part of the cdec SMT decoder package
`http://cdec-decoder.org/index.php?title=Lexical_translation_/_Word_alignment`

NATools: a collection of toosl for parallel corpus processing
`http://linguateca.di.uminho.pt/natools/` (includes billingual lexicon extraction based on the Twente word alignment system, which is still available at
`http://wwwhome.cs.utwente.nl/~irgroup/align/download.html`)

K-vec: a re-implementation of the alignment approach presented by Fung and Church [1994]:
`http://www.d.umn.edu/~tpederse/parallel.html`

Champollion: a collocation translation tool (do not confuse with the sentence alignment tool listed above with the same name).
`http://definingterms.com/Champollion/`

Uplug: a toolbox for parallel text alignment including word alignment based on association clues:
`http://sourceforge.net/projects/uplug/`

TOOLS FOR MANUAL ALIGNMENT & VISUALIZATION

Alpaco: a Perl/Tk based tool for manual word alignment based on the Blinker project
http://www.d.umn.edu/~tpederse/parallel.html

UMIACS Word Aligner: an interface for manual word alignment
http://www.umiacs.umd.edu/~nmadnani/alignment/forclip.htm
http://www.clsp.jhu.edu/ws99/projects/mt/toolkit/

i*Link: a tool for interactive word alignment
http://www.ida.liu.se/~nlplab/ILink/

HandAlign: another tool for manual word/phrase alignment
http://www.umiacs.umd.edu/~hal/HandAlign/index.html

ISA/ICA: interactive sentence alignment (ISA) and interactive word alignment via web interfaces
(part of Uplug): http://sourceforge.net/projects/uplug/

Alignment Set Toolkit: Perl tools for word alignment visualization and evaluation
http://gps-tsc.upc.es/veu/personal/lambert/software/AlignmentSet.html

Cairo: word alignment visualization as part of the original Egypt toolkit for statistical machine
translation: http://www.clsp.jhu.edu/ws99/projects/mt/toolkit/

OTHER TOOLS & RESOURCES

Sub-Tree Aligner: automatic tree alignment
http://www.ventsislavzhechev.eu/Home/Software/Software.html

Lingua-Align: discriminative tree-to-tree alignment
http://stp.lingfil.uu.se/~joerg/Lingua/

TreeAligner: a tool for manual tree-to-tree alignment with search function
http://kitt.cl.uzh.ch/kitt/treealigner

Algraeph: a graph alignment tool
http://daeso.uvt.nl/algraeph/index.html

SMULTRON: the Stockholm MULtilingual TReebank (English, German, Swedish)
http://www.cl.uzh.ch/research/paralleltreebanks/smultron_en.html

PCEDT: the Prague Czech-English Dependency Treebank
http://ufal.mff.cuni.cz/pcedt/

CDT: Copenhagen Dependency Treebank, some parallel parts
http://code.google.com/p/copenhagen-dependency-treebank/

Bibliography

Alfred V. Aho and Jeffrey D. Ullman. Properties of syntax directed translations. *Journal of Computer and System Sciences*, 3(3):319 – 334, 1969. DOI: 10.1016/S0022-0000(69)80018-8 Cited on page(s) 113

Alfred V. Aho and Jeffrey D. Ullman. *The theory of parsing, translation, and compiling*. Prentice-Hall, Inc., Upper Saddle River, NJ, USA, 1972. Cited on page(s) 114

Lars Ahrenberg. LinES: An English-Swedish parallel treebank. In *Proceedings of the 16th Nordic Conference of Computational Linguistics*, 2007. Cited on page(s) 107

Lars Ahrenberg, Mikael Andersson, and Magnus Merkel. A simple hybrid aligner for generating lexical correspondences in parallel. In *Proceedings of the 36th Annual Meeting of the Association of Computational Linguistics (ACL)*, 1998. DOI: 10.3115/980845.980851 Cited on page(s) 6, 86, 103

Lars Ahrenberg, Magnus Merkel, Anna Sågvall Hein, and Jörg Tiedemann. Evaluation of word alignment systems. In *Proceedings of the 2nd International Conference on Language Resources and Evaluation, (LREC'2000)*, volume III, pages 1255–1261, Athens, Greece, 2000. Cited on page(s) 104

Stephen Armstrong, Colm Caffrey, Marian Flanagan, Dorothy Kenny, Minako O'Hagan, and Andy Way. Leading by example: Automatic translation of subtitles via EBMT. *Perspectives: Studies in Translatology*, 14(3):163 – 184, 2006. Cited on page(s) 53, 54

Necip Fazil Ayan and Bonnie J. Dorr. Going beyond AER: An extensive analysis of word alignments and their impact on MT. In *Proceedings of the 21st International Conference on Computational Linguistics and 44th Annual Meeting of the Association for Computational Linguistics*, pages 9–16, Sydney, Australia, 2006a. DOI: 10.3115/1220175.1220177 Cited on page(s) 77, 104

Necip Fazil Ayan and Bonnie J. Dorr. A maximum entropy approach to combining word alignments. In *Proceedings of the Human Language Technology Conference of the NAACL, Main Conference*, pages 96–103, New York City, USA, 2006b. DOI: 10.3115/1220835.1220848 Cited on page(s) 77, 90, 92

Necip Fazil Ayan, Bonnie J. Dorr, and Nizar Habash. Multi-align: combining linguistic and statistical techniques to improve alignments for adaptable MT. In *Proceedings of the 6th Conference of the Association for Machine Translation in the Americas (AMTA 2004)*, pages 17–26, 2004. DOI: 10.1007/978-3-540-30194-3_3 Cited on page(s) 104

Necip Fazil Ayan, Bonnie J. Dorr, and Christof Monz. NeurAlign: Combining word alignments using neural networks. In *Proceedings of the Human Language Technology Conference and the Conference on Empirical Methods in Natural Language Processing (HLT/EMNLP*, pages 65–72, Vancouver, British Columbia, Canada, 2005. DOI: 10.3115/1220575.1220584 Cited on page(s) 104

Colin Bannard and Chris Callison-Burch. Paraphrasing with bilingual parallel corpora. In *43rd Annual Meeting of the Association of Computational Linguistics (ACL)*, 2005. DOI: 10.3115/1219840.1219914 Cited on page(s) 6, 103

Leonard E. Baum, Ted Petrie, George Soules, and Norman Weiss. A maximization technique occurring in the statistical analysis of probabilistic functions of markov chains. *The Annals of Mathematical Statistics*, 41(1):164–171, 1970. DOI: 10.1214/aoms/1177697196 Cited on page(s) 73, 98

Alexandra Birch, Chris Callison-Burch, and Miles Osborne. Constraining the phrase-based, joint probability statistical translation model. In *5th Conference of the Association for Machine Translation in the Americas (AMTA)*, Boston, Massachusetts, 2006. Cited on page(s) 104

Phil Blunsom and Trevor Cohn. Discriminative word alignment with conditional random fields. In *Proceedings of the 21st International Conference on Computational Linguistics and 44th Annual Meeting of the Association for Computational Linguistics*, pages 65–72, Sydney, Australia, 2006. DOI: 10.3115/1220175.1220184 Cited on page(s) 97, 98, 99

Phil Blunsom, Trevor Cohn, Chris Dyer, and Miles Osborne. A Gibbs sampler for phrasal synchronous grammar induction. In *Proceedings of the Joint Conference of the 47th Annual Meeting of the ACL and the 4th International Joint Conference on Natural Language Processing of the AFNLP: Volume 2 - Volume 2*, pages 782–790, Stroudsburg, PA, USA, 2009. Cited on page(s) 120

Léon Bottou. *Une Approche théorique de l'Apprentissage Connexionniste: Applications à la Reconnaissance de la Parole*. PhD thesis, Université de Paris XI, Orsay, France, 1991. Cited on page(s) 83

Peter F. Brown, John Cocke, Stephen A. Della-Pietra, Vincent J. Della-Pietra, Frederick Jelinek, Robert L. Mercer, and Paul Rossin. A statistical approach to language translation. In *Proceedings of the International Conference on Computational Linguistics (COLING)*, 1988. DOI: 10.3115/991635.991651 Cited on page(s) 4, 61, 66

Peter F. Brown, John Cocke, Stephen A. Della-Pietra, Vincent J. Della-Pietra, Frederick Jelinek, John D. Lafferty, Robert L. Mercer, and Paul Rossin. A statistical approach to machine translation. *Computational Linguistics*, 16(2):76–85, 1990. DOI: 10.3115/991365.991407 Cited on page(s) 66

Peter F. Brown, Jennifer C. Lai, and Robert L. Mercer. Aligning sentences in parallel corpora. In *Proceedings of the 29th Annual Meeting of the Association of Computational Linguistics (ACL)*, 1991. DOI: 10.3115/981344.981366 Cited on page(s) 38, 56

Peter F. Brown, Stephen A. Della-Pietra, Vincent J. Della-Pietra, and Robert L. Mercer. The mathematics of statistical machine translation. *Computational Linguistics*, 19(2):263–313, 1993. Cited on page(s) 13, 61, 66, 67, 70, 71, 72, 103

Matthias Buch-Kromann. Computing translation units and quantifying parallelism in parallel dependency treebanks. In *Proceedings of the Linguistic Annotation Workshop*, pages 69–76, Prague, Czech Republic, 2007. DOI: 10.3115/1642059.1642071 Cited on page(s) 121

Chris Callison-Burch. Syntactic constraints on paraphrases extracted from parallel corpora. In *Proceedings of the Conference on Empirical Methods in Natural Language Processing (EMNLP)*, 2008. DOI: 10.3115/1613715.1613743 Cited on page(s) 6

Michael Carl and Sisay Fissaha. Phrase-based evaluation of word-to-word alignments. In *HLT-NAACL 2003 Workshop: Building and Using Parallel Texts: Data Driven Machine Translation and Beyond*, Edmonton, Alberta, Canada, 2003. DOI: 10.3115/1118905.1118912 Cited on page(s) 104

Jason S. Chang and Mathis H. Chen. An alignment method for noisy parallel corpora based on image processing techniques. In *Proceedings of the 35th Annual Meeting of the Association for Computational Linguistics (ACL)*, 1997. DOI: 10.3115/979617.979655 Cited on page(s) 57

Jiang Chen and Jian-Yun Nie. Automatic construction of parallel english-chinese corpus for cross-language information retrieval. In *Proceedings of the sixth conference on Applied natural language processing*, pages 21–28. Association for Computational Linguistics, 2000. DOI: 10.3115/974147.974151 Cited on page(s) 32

Colin Cherry and Dekang Lin. A probability model to improve word alignment. In Erhard Hinrichs and Dan Roth, editors, *Proceedings of the 41st Annual Meeting of the Association for Computational Linguistics*, pages 88–95, 2003. Cited on page(s) 104

Colin Cherry and Dekang Lin. A comparison of syntactically motivated word alignment spaces. In *Proceedings of the 11th Conference of the European Chapter of the Association for Computational Linguistics*, Trento, Italy, 2006a. Cited on page(s) 12, 25, 79, 81, 121

Colin Cherry and Dekang Lin. Soft syntactic constraints for word alignment through discriminative training. In *Proceedings of the 21st International Conference on Computational Linguistics and 44th Annual Meeting of the Association for Computational Linguistics; Main Conference Poster Sessions*, pages 105–112, Sydney, Australia, 2006b. Cited on page(s) 103, 121

David Chiang. A hierarchical phrase-based model for statistical machine translation. In *Proceedings of the 43rd Annual Meeting of the Association for Computational Linguistics (ACL'05)*, pages 263–270, Ann Arbor, Michigan, 2005. DOI: 10.3115/1219840.1219873 Cited on page(s) 115

Yun-Chuang Chiao and Pierre Zweigenbaum. Looking for candidate translational equivalents in specialized, comparable corpora. In *Proceedings of the International Conference on Computational Linguistics (COLING)*, 2002. DOI: 10.3115/1071884.1071904 Cited on page(s) 34

Thomas C. Chuang and Jason S. Chang. Adaptive sentence alignment based on length and lexical information. In *Proceedings of the ACL-02 Demonstration Session*, 2002. Cited on page(s) 57

Kenneth Ward Church. Char align: A program for aligning parallel texts at the character level. In *Proceedings of the 31st Annual Meeting of the Association for Computational Linguistics (ACL)*, 1993. Cited on page(s) 48, 53, 57

Kenneth Ward Church and Patrick Hanks. Word association norms, mutual information, and lexicography. *Computational Linguistics*, 16:22–29, 1990. DOI: 10.3115/981623.981633 Cited on page(s) 86

Kenneth Ward Church and Jonathan Isaac Helfman. Dotplot: A program for exploring self-similarity in millions of lines of text and code. *Journal of Computational and Graphical Statistics*, 2 (2):pp. 153–174, 1993. DOI: 10.2307/1390697 Cited on page(s) 52

John Cocke and Jacob T. Schwartz. Programming languages and their compilers: Preliminary notes. Technical report, Courant Institute of Mathematical Sciences, New York University, 1970. Cited on page(s) 117

Michael Collins. Discriminative training methods for hidden markov models: Theory and experiments with perceptron algorithms. In *Proceedings of the Conference on Empirical Methods in Natural Language Processing (EMNLP)*, pages 1–8, Stroudsburg, PA, USA, 2002. DOI: 10.3115/1118693.1118694 Cited on page(s) 92

Josep M. Crego and Nizar Habash. Using shallow syntax information to improve word alignment and reordering for SMT. In *Proceedings of the Third Workshop on Statistical Machine Translation*, pages 53–61, Columbus, Ohio, 2008. DOI: 10.3115/1626394.1626401 Cited on page(s) 103

Lea Cyrus. Building a resource for studying translation shifts. In *Proceedings of LREC*, 2006. Cited on page(s) 121

Ido Dagan. Lexical disambiguation: Sources of information and their statistical realization. In *In Meeting of the Association for Computational Linguistics*, pages 341–342, 1991. DOI: 10.3115/981344.981393 Cited on page(s) 6

Ido Dagan and Kenneth W. Church. Termight: Identifying and translating technical terminology. In *Proceedings of the 4th Conference on Applied Natural Language Processing*, pages 34–40, Stuttgart, Germany, 1994. DOI: 10.3115/974358.974367 Cited on page(s) 100, 103

Ido Dagan, Kenneth Ward Church, and William A. Gale. Robust bilingual word alignment for machine aided translation. In *Proceedings of the Workshop on Very Large Corpora (VLC)*, 1993. Cited on page(s) 104

Hal Daumé III. *Practical Structured Learning Techniques for Natural Language Processing*. PhD thesis, University of Southern California, Los Angeles, CA, 2006. Cited on page(s) 83

Mark W. Davis, Ted E. Dunning, and William C. Ogden. Text alignment in the real world: Improving alignments of noisy translations using common lexical features, string matching strategies and n-gram comparisons. In *Proceedings of the Meeting of the European Chapter of the Association of Computational Linguistics (EACL)*, 1995. DOI: 10.3115/976973.976984 Cited on page(s) 57

Herve Dejean, Eric Gaussier, Cyril Goutte, and Kenji Yamada. Reducing parameter space for word alignment. In *HLT-NAACL 2003 Workshop: Building and Using Parallel Texts: Data Driven Machine Translation and Beyond*, Edmonton, Alberta, Canada, 2003. DOI: 10.3115/1118905.1118910 Cited on page(s) 103

Arthur P. Dempster, Nan M. Laird, and Donald B. Rubin. Maximum likelihood from incomplete data via the em algorithm. *Journal of the Royal Statistical Society. Series B (Methodological)*, 39(1): pp. 1–38, 1977. Cited on page(s) 64

John DeNero and Dan Klein. Discriminative modeling of extraction sets for machine translation. In *Proceedings of the 48th Annual Meeting of the Association for Computational Linguistics*, pages 1453–1463, 2010. Cited on page(s) 103

Y. Deng, S. Kumar, and W. Byrne. Segmentation and alignment of parallel text for statistical machine translation. *Journal of Natural Language Engineering*, 13(3):235–260, 2006. DOI: 10.1017/S1351324906004293 Cited on page(s) 57

Yonggang Deng and William Byrne. HMM word and phrase alignment for statistical machine translation. In *Proceedings of the Human Language Technology Conference and Conference on Empirical Methods in Natural Language Processing (HLT/EMNLP)*, pages 169–176, Vancouver, British Columbia, Canada, 2005. DOI: 10.3115/1220575.1220597 Cited on page(s) 103

Yonggang Deng and Yuqing Gao. Guiding statistical word alignment models with prior knowledge. In *Proceedings of the 45th Annual Meeting of the Association of Computational Linguistics*, pages 1–8, Prague, Czech Republic, 2007. Cited on page(s) 103

Mona Diab and Steve Finch. A statistical word-level translation model for comparable corpora. In *Proceedings of the Conference on Content-based multimedia information access (RIAO)*, 2000. Cited on page(s) 34

Mona Diab and Philip Resnik. An unsupervised method for word sense tagging using parallel corpora. In *Proceedings of the 40th Annual Meeting on Association for Computational Linguistics*, pages 255–262, Stroudsburg, PA, USA, 2002. DOI: 10.3115/1073083.1073126 Cited on page(s) 6

Lee R. Dice. Measures of the amount of ecologic association between species. *Ecology*, 26(3): 297–302, 1945. DOI: 10.2307/1932409 Cited on page(s) 50

Thomas G. Dietterich. Machine learning for sequential data: A review. In T. Caelli, editor, *Structural, Syntactic, and Statistical Pattern Recognition*, volume 2396 of *Lecture Notes in Computer Science*, pages 15–30. Springer Verlag, 2002. Cited on page(s) 83

Yuan Ding and Martha Palmer. Automatic learning of parallel dependency treelet pairs. In *Proceedings of the Internation Joint Conference on Natural Language Processing (IJCNLP)*, 2004. Cited on page(s) 121

Elżbieta Dura and Barbara Gawronska. Novelty extraction from special and parallel corpora. In Zygmunt Vetulani and Hans Uszkoreit, editors, *Human Language Technology. Challenges of the Information Society*, volume 5603 of *Lecture Notes in Computer Science*, pages 291–302. Springer Berlin / Heidelberg, 2009. Cited on page(s) 5

Chris Dyer. Two monolingual parses are better than one (synchronous parse). In *Proceedings of the Annual Conference of the North American Chapter of the Association for Computational Linguistics (NAACL)*, pages 263–266, 2010. Cited on page(s) 122

Chris Dyer, Jonathan H. Clark, Alon Lavie, and Noah A. Smith. Unsupervised word alignment with arbitrary features. In *Proceedings of the 49nd Meeting of the Association for Computational Linguistics (ACL'11)*, 2011. Cited on page(s) 103

Helge Dyvik. Translations as semantic mirrors: From parallel corpus to wordnet. In *Proceedings of ICAME 2002*, Gothenburg, Sweden, 2002. Cited on page(s) 6

Macklovitch E., Simard M., and Langlais Ph. Transsearch: A free translation memory on the world wide web. In *Second International Conference On Language Resources and Evaluation (LREC)*, volume 3, pages 1201–1208, Athens Greece, 2000. Cited on page(s) 6

Andreas Eisele and Yu Chen. MultUN: A multilingual corpus from united nation documents. In *Proceedings of the 7th International Conference on Language Resources and Evaluation (LREC)*, 2010. Cited on page(s) 125

Jessica Enright and Grzegorz Kondrak. A fast method for parallel document identification. In *Human Language Technologies 2007: The Conference of the North American Chapter of the Association for Computational Linguistics; Companion Volume, Short Papers*, pages 29–32, 2007. Cited on page(s) 17, 31

Miquel Esplá-Gomis. Bitextor, a free/open-source software to harvest translation memories from multilingual websites. In *Beyond Translation Memories Workshop (MT Summit*, Ottawa, Canada, 2009. Cited on page(s) 33, 36

Luis Serrano Fernandez. Translation, censorship and cinema: Translated film material from english into spanish in the late francoist regime. *Studos de Tradução*, 2003. Cited on page(s) 5

G. David Forney Jr. The Viterbi algorithm. *Proceedings of the IEEE*, 61(3):268 – 278, 1973. Cited on page(s) 73

George Foster, Simona Gandrabur, Philippe Langlais, Graham Russell, Michel Simard, and Pierre Plamondon. Statistical machine translation: Rapid development with limited resources. In *Proceedings of the MT Summit IX*, 2003. Cited on page(s) 103

Heidi Fox. Phrasal cohesion and statistical machine translation. In *Proceedings of the Conference on Empirical Methods in Natural Language Processing (EMNLP)*, pages 304–311, Philadelphia, 2002. DOI: 10.3115/1118693.1118732 Cited on page(s) 81

Alexander Fraser and Daniel Marcu. Measuring word alignment quality for statistical machine translation. *Computational Linguistics*, 33(3), 2007a. DOI: 10.1162/coli.2007.33.3.293 Cited on page(s) 23, 104

Alexander Fraser and Daniel Marcu. Getting the structure right for word alignment: LEAF. In *Proceedings of the Joint Conference on Empirical Methods in Natural Language Processing and Computational Natural Language Learning (EMNLP/CoNLL)*, pages 51–60, 2007b. Cited on page(s) 104

Ken'ichi Fukushima, Kenjiro Taura, and Takashi Chikayama. A fast and accurate method for detecting English-Japanese parallel texts. In *Proceedings of the Workshop on Multilingual Language Resources and Interoperability*, pages 60–67, Sydney, Australia, 2006. DOI: 10.3115/1613162.1613170 Cited on page(s) 36

Pascale Fung and Percy Cheung. Multi-level bootstrapping for extracting parallel sentences from a quasi-comparable corpus. In *Proceedings of the 20th International Conference on Computational Linguistics (COLING)*, pages 1051–1057, Geneva, Switzerland, 2004a. DOI: 10.3115/1220355.1220506 Cited on page(s) 28

Pascale Fung and Percy Cheung. Mining very-non-parallel corpora: Parallel sentence and lexicon extraction via bootstrapping and EM. In *Proceedings of the Conference on Empirical Methods in Natural Language Processing (EMNLP)*, pages 57–63, Barcelona, Spain, 2004b. Cited on page(s) 34, 35

Pascale Fung and Kenneth W. Church. K-vec: A new approach for aligning parallel texts. In *Proceedings 15th International Conference on Computational Linguistics (COLING)*, pages 1096–1102, Kyoto, Japan, 1994. DOI: 10.3115/991250.991328 Cited on page(s) 127

Pascale Fung and Kathleen R. McKeown. Aligning noisy parallel corpora across language groups: Word pair feature matching by dynamic time warping. In *1st Conference of the Association for Machine Translation in the Americas (AMTA)*, 1994. Cited on page(s) 57

Pascale Fung and Lo Yuen Yee. An IR approach for translating new words from nonparallel, comparable texts. In *Proceedings of the 36th Annual Meeting of the Association of Computational Linguistics (ACL)*, 1998. DOI: 10.3115/980845.980916 Cited on page(s) 34

Pascale Fung, Pierre Zweigenbaum, and Reinhard Rapp, editors. *Proceedings of the 2nd Workshop on Building and Using Comparable Corpora: from Parallel to Non-parallel Corpora*. Association for Computational Linguistics, Singapore, August 2009. Cited on page(s) 36

William A. Gale and Kenneth W. Church. Identifying word correspondence in parallel texts. In *Proceedings of the workshop on Speech and Natural Language*, pages 152–157, Stroudsburg, PA, USA, 1991a. DOI: 10.3115/112405.112428 Cited on page(s) 103

William A. Gale and Kenneth Ward Church. A program for aligning sentences in bilingual corpora. In *Proceedings of the 29th Annual Meeting of the Association of Computational Linguistics (ACL)*, 1991b. DOI: 10.3115/981344.981367 Cited on page(s) 38, 39, 41, 47, 56

William A. Gale and Kenneth Ward Church. A program for aligning sentences in bilingual corpora. *Computational Linguistics*, 19(1), 1993. DOI: 10.3115/981344.981367 Cited on page(s) 38, 45

Kuzman Ganchev, João V. Graça, and Ben Taskar. Better alignments = better translations? In *Proceedings of ACL-08: HLT*, pages 986–993, Columbus, Ohio, 2008. Cited on page(s) 104, 127

Ismael García Varea, Daniel Ortiz, Francisco Nevado, Pedro A. Gomez, and Francisco Casacuberta. Automatic segmentation of bilingual corpora: A comparison of different techniques. In Jorge S. Marques, Nicolás Pérez de la Blanca, and Pedro Pina, editors, *Pattern Recognition and Image Analysis*, volume 3523 of *Lecture Notes in Computer Science*, pages 614–621. Springer Berlin / Heidelberg, 2005. Cited on page(s) 3

Éric Gaussier. Flow network models for word alignment and terminology extraction from bilingual corpora. In *Proceedings of the 17th International Conference on Computational Linguistics (COLING)*, pages 444–450, Stroudsburg, PA, USA, 1998. DOI: 10.3115/980451.980921 Cited on page(s) 104

Eric Gaussier, J.M. Renders, I. Matveeva, Cyril Goutte, and Herve Dejean. A geometric view on bilingual lexicon extraction from comparable corpora. In *Proceedings of the 42nd Meeting of the Association for Computational Linguistics (ACL'04), Main Volume*, pages 526–533, Barcelona, Spain, 2004. DOI: 10.3115/1218955.1219022 Cited on page(s) 34

Daniel Gildea. Loosly tree-based alignment for machine translation. In *Proceedings of the 41st Annual Meeting of the Association of Computational Linguistics (ACL)*, 2003. DOI: 10.3115/1075096.1075107 Cited on page(s) 122

Annette Rios Gonzales, Anne Göhring, and Martin Volk. A Quechua-Spanish parallel treebank. In *Proceedings of TLT7*, pages 53–64, 2009. Cited on page(s) 107

Cyril Goutte, Kenji Yamada, and Eric Gaussier. Aligning words using matrix factorisation. In *Proceedings of the 42nd Meeting of the Association for Computational Linguistics (ACL'04), Main Volume*, pages 502–509, Barcelona, Spain, 2004. DOI: 10.3115/1218955.1219019 Cited on page(s) 104

Yvette Graham and Josef van Genabith. An open source rule indution tool for transfer-based smt. *The Prague Bulletin of Mathematical Linguistics, Special Issue: Open Source Tools for Machine Translation*, 91, 2009. DOI: 10.2478/v10108-009-0014-6 Cited on page(s) 121

Ralph Grishman. Iterative alignment of syntactic structures in a bilingual corpus. In *Proceedings Second Annual Workshop on Very Large Corpora*, Kyoto, Japan, 1994. Cited on page(s) 108

Declan Groves, Mary Hearne, and Andy Way. Robust sub-sentential alignment of phrase-structure trees. In *Proceedings of the 20th International Conference on Computational Linguistics (COLING)*, pages 1072–1078, Geneva, Switzerland, 2004. DOI: 10.3115/1220355.1220509 Cited on page(s) 108, 110

Sofia Gustafson-Čapková, Yvonne Samuelsson, and Martin Volk. SMULTRON (version 1.0) - The Stockholm MULtilingual parallel TReebank. http://www.ling.su.se/dali/research/smultron/index.htm, 2007. Cited on page(s) 10, 107

Brian Harris. Bi-Text, a new concept in translation theory. *Language Monthly*, 54:8–10, 1988. Cited on page(s) 1

Masahiko Haruno and Takefumi Yamazaki. High-performance bilingual text alignment using statistical and dictionary information. In *Proceedings of the 34th Annual Meeting of the Association for Computational Linguistics (ACL)*, 1996. DOI: 10.3115/981863.981881 Cited on page(s) 51, 57

Martin Hassel and Hercules Dalianis. Identification of Parallel Text Pairs Using Fingerprints. In *Proceedings of Recent Advances in Natural Language Processing 2009*, Borovets, Bulgaria, 2009. Cited on page(s) 36

Monika Henzinger. Finding near-duplicate web pages: a large-scale evaluation of algorithms. In *Proceedings of the 29th annual international ACM SIGIR conference on Research and development in information retrieval*, pages 284–291, 2006. DOI: 10.1145/1148170.1148222 Cited on page(s) 33

Djoerd Hiemstra. Multilingual domain modeling in Twenty-One: Automatic creation of a bi-directional translation lexicon from a parallel corpus. In *Proceedings of the 8th Meeting of Computational Linguistics in the Netherlands (CLIN)*, volume 25, pages 41–58, Nijmegen, The Netherlands, 1998. Rodopi, Amsterdam, Atlanta. Cited on page(s) 103

Kenji Imamura. Hierarchical phrase alignment harmonized with parsing. In *Proceedings of the 6th Natural Language Processing Pacific Rim Symbopium (NLPRS-2001)*, pages 377–384, 2001. Cited on page(s) 121

Einav Itamar and Alon Itai. Using movie subtitles for creating a large-scale bilingual corpora. In *Proceedings of the 6th International Language Resources and Evaluation (LREC'08)*, Marrakech, Morocco, 2008. Cited on page(s) 56

Abraham Ittycheriah and Salim Roukos. A maximum entropy word aligner for Arabic-English machine translation. In *Proceedings of the Human Language Technology Conference and the Conference on Empirical Methods in Natural Language Processing (HLT/EMNLP*, pages 89–96, Vancouver, British Columbia, Canada, 2005. DOI: 10.3115/1220575.1220587 Cited on page(s) 89, 91

Hiroyuki Kaji and Toshiko Aizono. Extracting word correspondences from bilingual corpora based on word co-occurrence information. In *Proceedings of the 16th International Conference on Computational Linguistics (COLING)*, 1996. DOI: 10.3115/992628.992636 Cited on page(s) 103

Hiroyuki Kaji, Yuuko Kida, and Yasutsugu Morimoto. Learning translation templates from bilingual text. In *Proceedings of the 14th international conference on Computational linguistics (COLING)*, pages 672–678, Stroudsburg, PA, USA, 1992. DOI: 10.3115/992133.992174 Cited on page(s) 107, 109

Tadao Kasami. An efficient recognition and syntax-analysis algorithm for context-free languages. Scientific report afcrl-65-758, Air Force Cambridge Research Lab, Bedford, MA, 1965. Cited on page(s) 117

Martin Kay and Martin Röscheisen. Text-translation alignment. *Computational Linguistics*, 19(1), 1993. Cited on page(s) 48, 49, 50, 51

Martin Kay and Martin Röscheisen. Text-translation alignment. Technical report, Xerox Palo Alto Research Center, 1988. Cited on page(s) 48, 49

Sue Ker and Jason S. Chang. A class-based approach to word alignment. *Computational Linguistics*, 23:313–343, 1997. Cited on page(s) 86

Kevin Knight. Automating knowledge acquisition for machine translation. *AI Magazine*, 18(4), 1997. Cited on page(s) 103

Kevin Knight. A statistical MT tutorial workbook. available at http://www.isi.edu/~knight/, 1999. Cited on page(s) 67, 103

Philipp Koehn. Europarl: A parallel corpus for statistical machine translation. In *Proceedings of the 10th Machine Translation Summit (MT Summit X)*, Phuket, Thailand, 2005. Cited on page(s) 2

Philipp Koehn. *Statistical Machine Translation*. Cambridge University Press, 2010. Cited on page(s) 67, 70, 103

Philipp Koehn, Franz Josef Och, and Daniel Marcu. Statistical phrase based translation. In *Proceedings of the Joint Conference on Human Language Technologies and the Annual Meeting of the North American Chapter of the Association of Computational Linguistics (HLT-NAACL)*, 2003. DOI: 10.3115/1073445.1073462 Cited on page(s) 74, 77

Philipp Koehn, Joel Martin, Rada Mihalcea, Christif Monz, and Ted Pedersen, editors. *ACL 2005 Workshop: Building and Using Parallel Texts: Data Driven Machine Translation and Beyond*, University of Michigan, Ann Arbor, 2005. Cited on page(s) 36

Lambros Kranias, Nicoletta Calzolari, Gregor Thurmair, Yorick Wilks, Eduard Hovy, Gudrun Magnusdottir, Anna Samiotou, and Khalid Choukri, editors. *The Amazing Utility of Parallel and Comparable Corpora*, 2004. Cited on page(s) 36

Harold W. Kuhn. The hungarian method for the assignment problem. *Naval Research Logistics Quarterly*, 2:83–97, 1955. DOI: 10.1002/nav.3800020109 Cited on page(s) 93

Akira Kumano and Hideki Hirakawa. Building an MT dictionary from parallel texts based on linguistic and statistical information. In *Proceedings of the 15th International Conference on Computational Linguistics (COLING)*, 1994. DOI: 10.3115/991886.991896 Cited on page(s) 103

Simon Lacoste-Julien, Ben Taskar, Dan Klein, and Michael I. Jordan. Word alignment via quadratic assignment. In *Proceedings of the Human Language Technology Conference of the NAACL, Main Conference*, pages 112–119, New York City, USA, 2006. DOI: 10.3115/1220835.1220850 Cited on page(s) 89, 94, 95, 96, 97

John D. Lafferty, Andrew McCallum, and Fernando C. N. Pereira. Conditional random fields: Probabilistic models for segmenting and labeling sequence data. In *Proceedings of the 18th International Conference on Machine Learning*, pages 282–289, San Francisco, CA, USA, 2001. Morgan Kaufmann Publishers Inc. Cited on page(s) 83, 97

Patrik Lambert, Adrià De Gispert, Rafael Banchs, and José Mariño. Guidelines for word alignment evaluation and manual alignment. *Language Resources and Evaluation*, 39:267–285, 2005. DOI: 10.1007/s10579-005-4822-5 Cited on page(s) 104

Philippe Langlais. A System to Align Complex Bilingual Corpora. Technical report, CTT, KTH, Stockholm, Sweden, 1998. TMH-QPSR 4/1997. Cited on page(s) 51

Philippe Langlais, Michel Simard, and Jean Véronis. Methods and practical issues in evaluating alignment techniques. In *Proceedings of the 36th Annual Meeting of the Association of Computational Linguistics (ACL)*, 1998. DOI: 10.3115/980845.980964 Cited on page(s) 104

Adrien Lardilleux and Yves Lepage. The contribution of the notion of hapax legomena to word alignment. In *Proceedings of 3rd Language & Technology Conference The 3rd Language and Technology Conference (LTC'07)*, pages 458–462, Poznań Poland, 2007. Cited on page(s) 102

Adrien Lardilleux and Yves Lepage. A truly multilingual, high coverage, accurate, yet simple, sub-sentential alignment method. In *Proceedings of the 8th conference of the Association for Machine Translation in the Americas (AMTA 2008)*, pages 125–132, Waikiki, Hawai'i, USA, October 2008a. Cited on page(s) 102

Adrien Lardilleux and Yves Lepage. Multilingual alignments by monolingual string differences. In *Proceedings of the 22nd International Conference on Computational Linguistics (COLING); Companion volume: Posters and Demonstrations*, pages 53–56, Manchester, UK, 2008b. Cited on page(s) 101

Adrien Lardilleux and Yves Lepage. Sampling-based multilingual alignment. In *Proceedings of Recent Advances in Natural Language Processing (RANLP)*, 2009. Cited on page(s) 102

Adrien Lardilleux, Jonathan Chevelu, Yves Lepage, Ghislain Putois, and Julien Gosme. Lexicons or phrase tables? an investigation in sampling-based multilingual alignment. In *3rd International Workshop on Example-Based Machine Translation*, pages 45–52, Dublin, Ireland, 2009. Cited on page(s) 102

Caroline Lavecchia, Kamel Smaili, and David Langlois. Building parallel corpora from movies. In *Proceedings of the 4th International Workshop on Natural Language Processing and Cognitive Science - NLPCS 2007*, Funchal, Madeira, 2007. Cited on page(s) 53

Alon Lavie, Alok Parlikar, and Vamshi Ambati. Syntax-driven learning of sub-sentential translation equivalents and translation rules from parsed parallel corpora. In *Proceedings of the ACL-08: HLT Second Workshop on Syntax and Structure in Statistical Translation (SSST-2)*, pages 87–95, Columbus, Ohio, 2008. DOI: 10.3115/1626269.1626280 Cited on page(s) 107, 108, 110

Benoit Lavoie, Michael White, and Tanya Korelsky. Inducing lexico-structural transfer rules from parsed bi-texts. In *Workshop on Data-Driven Machine Translation at 39th Annual Meeting of the Association of Computational Linguistics (ACL)*, 2001. DOI: 10.3115/1118037.1118040 Cited on page(s) 121

Vladimir Levenshtein. Binary codes capable of correcting deletions, insertions and reversals. *Soviet Physics Doklady*, 10(8):707–710, 1966. Cited on page(s) 32

P. M. Lewis, II and R. E. Stearns. Syntax-directed transduction. *J. ACM*, 15:465–488, 1968. DOI: 10.1145/321466.321477 Cited on page(s) 113

Bo Li and Juan Liu. Mining Chinese-English parallel corpora from the web. In *Proceedings of the 3rd International Joint Conference on Natural Language Processing (IJCNLP)*, 2008. Cited on page(s) 36

Percy Liang, Ben Taskar, and Dan Klein. Alignment by agreement. In *Proceedings of the Human Language Technology Conference of the NAACL, Main Conference*, pages 104–111, New York City, USA, 2006. DOI: 10.3115/1220835.1220849 Cited on page(s) 73, 77, 78, 79

Yang Liu, Qun Liu, and Shouxun Lin. Log-linear models for word alignment. In *Proceedings of the 43rd Annual Meeting of the Association for Computational Linguistics (ACL'05)*, pages 459–466, Ann Arbor, Michigan, 2005. DOI: 10.3115/1219840.1219897 Cited on page(s) 89, 90, 92, 104

Yang Liu, Qun Liu, and Shouxun Lin. Discriminative word alignment by linear modeling. *Computational Linguistics*, 36:303–339, 2010. DOI: 10.1162/coli_a_00001 Cited on page(s) 103

Adam Lopez and Philip Resnik. Word-based alignment, phrase-based translation: What's the link? In *5th Conference of the Association for Machine Translation in the Americas (AMTA)*, Boston, Massachusetts, 2006. Cited on page(s) 104

Xiaoyi Ma. Champollion: A robust parallel text sentence aligner. In *Proceedings of the 5th International Conference on Language Resources and Evaluation (LREC)*, Genova, Italy, 2006. Cited on page(s) 57

Xiaoyi Ma and Mark Y. Liberman. Bits: a method for bilingual text search over the web. In *Machine translation summit VII*, Kent Ridge Digital Labs, National University of Singapore, 1999. Cited on page(s) 32, 33

Wesley Mackay and Grzegorz Kondrak. Computing word similarity and identifying cognates with pair hidden markov models. In *Proceedings of the 9th Conference on Computational Natural Language Learning (CoNLL 2005)*, pages 40–47, Ann Arbor, Michigan, 2005. DOI: 10.3115/1706543.1706551 Cited on page(s) 88

Lieve Macken, Julia Trushkina, and Lidia Rura. Dutch parallel corpus: MT corpus and translator's aid. In *Proceedings of the MT Summit XI*, 2007. Cited on page(s) 6

Lieve Macken, Els Lefever, and Veronique Hoste. Linguistically-based sub-sentential alignment for terminology extraction from a bilingual automotive corpus. In *Proceedings of the 22nd International Conference on Computational Linguistics (COLING)*, pages 529–536, Manchester, UK, 2008. DOI: 10.3115/1599081.1599148 Cited on page(s) 103

Daniel Marcu and Daniel Wong. A phrase-based, joint probability model for statistical machine translation. In *Proceedings of the Conference on Empirical Methods in Natural Language Processing (EMNLP)*, pages 133–139, Philadelphia, 2002. DOI: 10.3115/1118693.1118711 Cited on page(s) 104

Erwin Marsi and Emiel Krahmer. Automatic analysis of semantic similarity in comparable text through syntactic tree matching. In *Proceedings of the 23rd International Conference on Computational Linguistics (COLING)*, pages 752–760, Beijing, China, 2010. Cited on page(s) 5

Joel Martin, Rada Mihalcea, and Ted Pedersen. Word alignment for languages with scarce resources. In *Proceedings of the ACL Workshop on Building and Using Parallel Texts*, pages 65–74, Ann Arbor, Michigan, 2005. DOI: 10.3115/1654449.1654460 Cited on page(s) 104

Raquel Martínez, Joseba Abaitua, and Arantza Casillas. Bitext correspondences through rich mark-up. In *Proceedings of the 36th Annual Meeting of the Association for Computational Linguistics (ACL) and 17th International Conference on Computational Linguistics (COLING)*, ACL '98, pages 812–818, 1998. DOI: 10.3115/980691.980703 Cited on page(s) 53

Yuji Matsumoto, Takehito Utsuro, and Hiroyuki Ishimoto. Structural matching of parallel texts. In *Proceedings of the 31st Annual Meeting of the Association for Computational Linguistics (ACL)*, 1993. DOI: 10.3115/981574.981578 Cited on page(s) 108, 109

Evgeny Matusov, Richard Zens, and Hermann Ney. Symmetric word alignments for statistical machine translation. In *Proceedings of the 20th International Conference on Computational Linguistics (COLING)*, pages 219–225, Geneva, Switzerland, 2004. DOI: 10.3115/1220355.1220387 Cited on page(s) 78, 80, 81

Beáta Megyesi, Bengt Dahlqvist, Eva Pettersson, and Joakim Nivre. Swedish-turkish parallel tree-bank. In *In Proceedings of Language Resources and Evaluation (LREC08)*, 2008. Cited on page(s) 107

I. Dan Melamed. Automatic evaluation and uniform filter cascades for inducing n-best translation lexicons. In *Proceedings of the Third Workshop on Very Large Corpora (VLC)*, 1995. Cited on page(s) 88, 103

I. Dan Melamed. A geometric approach to mapping bitext correspondence. In *Proceedings of the Conference on Empirical Methods in Natural Language Processing (EMNLP)*, 1996a. Cited on page(s) 48, 49, 51, 57

I. Dan Melamed. Automatic construction of clean broad-coverage translation lexicons. In *Proceedings of the Conference of the Association for Machine Translation in the Americas*, 1996b. Cited on page(s) 6, 103

I. Dan Melamed. A word-to-word model of translational equivalence. In *Proceedings of the 35th Annual Meeting of the Association for Computational Linguistics (ACL)*, 1997. DOI: 10.3115/979617.979680 Cited on page(s) 103

I. Dan Melamed. Manual annotation of translational equivalence: The Blinker project. Technical report, University of Pennsylvania – Institute for Research in Cognitive Science, 1998. Cited on page(s) 104

I. Dan Melamed. Models of translational equivalence among words. *Computational Linguistics*, 26: 221–249, 2000. DOI: 10.1162/089120100561683 Cited on page(s) 12, 80, 86

I. Dan Melamed. *Empirical Methods for Exploiting Parallel Texts*. MIT Press, 2001. Cited on page(s) 6, 24, 86

Arul Menezes and Chris Quirk. Dependency treelet translation: The convergence of statistical and example-based machine-translation? In *Proceedings of the Workshop on Example-based Machine Translation at MT Summit X*, Phuket, Thailand, 2005. Cited on page(s) 121

Arul Menezes and Stephen D. Richardson. A best-first alignment algorithm for automatic extraction of transfer mappings from bilingual corpora. In *Workshop on Data-Driven Machine Translation at 39th Annual Meeting of the Association of Computational Linguistics (ACL)*, 2001. DOI: 10.3115/1118037.1118043 Cited on page(s) 108, 110

Magnus Merkel. *Understanding and enhancing translation by parallel text processing*. PhD thesis, Linköping University, The Institute of Technology, NLPLAB - Natural Language Processing Laboratory, 1999. Cited on page(s) 6, 24

Rada Mihalcea and Ted Pedersen, editors. *HLT-NAACL 2003 Workshop: Building and Using Parallel Texts: Data Driven Machine Translation and Beyond*, Edmonton, Alberta, Canada, 2003a. Cited on page(s) 36

Rada Mihalcea and Ted Pedersen. An evaluation exercise for word alignment. In *Proceedings of the HLT-NAACL 2003 Workshop on Building and Using Parallel Texts: Data Driven Machine Translation and Beyond*, 2003b. DOI: 10.3115/1118905.1118906 Cited on page(s) 104

Rada Mihalcea and Ted Pedersen. *Guidelines for the Shared Task on Word Alignment*, 2003c. http://www.cse.unt.edu/~rada/wpt/WordAlignment.Guidelines.txt. Cited on page(s) 104

Robert C. Moore. Fast and accurate sentence alignment of bilingual corpora. In Stephen D. Richardson, editor, *Machine Translation: From Research to Real Users, 5th Conference of the Association for Machine Translation in the Americas, AMTA 2002 Tiburon, CA, USA, October 6-12, 2002, Proceedings*, volume 2499 of *Lecture Notes in Computer Science*. Springer, 2002. Cited on page(s) 53, 57

Robert C. Moore. Improving ibm word alignment model 1. In *Proceedings of the 42nd Meeting of the Association for Computational Linguistics (ACL'04), Main Volume*, pages 518–525, Barcelona, Spain, 2004. DOI: 10.3115/1218955.1219021 Cited on page(s) 75, 79

Robert C. Moore. A discriminative framework for bilingual word alignment. In *Proceedings of the Human Language Technology Conference and the Conference on Empirical Methods in Natural Language Processing (HLT/EMNLP*, pages 81–88, Vancouver, British Columbia, Canada, 2005. DOI: 10.3115/1220575.1220586 Cited on page(s) 89, 91

Robert C. Moore, Wen-tau Yih, and Andreas Bode. Improved discriminative bilingual word alignment. In *Proceedings of the 21st International Conference on Computational Linguistics and 44th Annual Meeting of the Association for Computational Linguistics*, pages 513–520, Sydney, Australia, 2006. DOI: 10.3115/1220175.1220240 Cited on page(s) 89, 91, 92

James Munkres. Algorithms for the assignment and transportation problems. *Journal of the Society for Industrial and Applied Mathematics*, 5(1):32–38, 1957. DOI: 10.1137/0105003   Cited on page(s) 93

Dragos Stefan Munteanu, Alexander Fraser, and Daniel Marcu. Improved machine translation performance via parallel sentence extraction from comparable corpora. In *Proceedings of the Joint Conference on Human Language Technologies and the Annual Meeting of the North American Chapter of the Association of Computational Linguistics (HLT-NAACL)*, 2004. Cited on page(s) 34, 35

Peter Nabende, Jörg Tiedemann, and John Nerbonne. Pair hidden markov model for named entity matching. In *Innovations and Advances in Computer Science and Engineering*, pages 497–502. Springer Heidelberg, 2010. DOI: 10.1007/978-90-481-3658-2_87   Cited on page(s) 88

David Nadeau and George Foster. Real-time identification of parallel texts from bilingual news feed. In *In: CLINE 2004, Computational Linguistics in the North East*, pages 21–36, 2004. Cited on page(s) 36

Makoto Nagao. A framework of a mechanical translation between japanese and english by analogy principle. In *Proceedings of the international NATO symposium on Artificial and human intelligence*, pages 173–180, New York, NY, USA, 1984. Elsevier North-Holland, Inc. Cited on page(s) 106

Jian-Yun Nie and Jian Cai. Filtering noisy parallel corpora of web pages. In *Proceedings of IEEE symposium on NLP and knowledge engineering*, pages 453–458, Tucson AZ, 2001. DOI: 10.1109/ICSMC.2001.969854   Cited on page(s) 33

Jian-Yun Nie, Michel Simard, Pierre Isabelle, and Richard Durand. Cross-language information retrieval based on parallel texts and automatic mining of parallel texts from the web. In *Proceedings of the 22nd annual international ACM SIGIR conference on Research and development in information retrieval*, pages 74–81, New York, NY, USA, 1999. ACM. DOI: 10.1145/312624.312656   Cited on page(s) 36

Doug Oard and Franz Josef Och. Rapid response machine translation for unexpected languages. In *Proceedings of the MT Summit IX*, 2003. Cited on page(s) 103

Franz Josef Och and Hermann Ney. A comparison of alignment models for statistical machine translation. In *Proceedings of the 19th International Conference on Computational Linguistics (COLING)*, pages 1086–1090, 2000. DOI: 10.3115/992730.992810   Cited on page(s) 74

Franz Josef Och and Hermann Ney. A systematic comparison of various statistical alignment models. *Computational Linguistics*, 29(1):19–52, 2003. DOI: 10.1162/089120103321337421   Cited on page(s) 70, 73, 74, 90

Franz Josef Och, Christoph Tillmann, and Hermann Ney. Improved alignment models for statistical machine translation. In *Proceedings of the Joint Conference on Empirical Methods in Natural Language Processing and Very Large Corpora (EMNLP/VLC)*, pages 20–28, 1999. Cited on page(s) 77

Pablo Gamallo Otero. Learning bilingual lexicons from comparable English and Spanish corpora. In *Proceedings of the MT Summit XI*, 2007. Cited on page(s) 34

Alexandre Patry and Philippe Langlais. Automatic identification of parallel documents with light or without linguistic resources. In *18th Annual Conference on Artificial Intelligence (AI)*, pages 354–365, Victoria, British-Columbia, Canada, jan 2005. Cited on page(s) 17, 30, 31, 35

Emanuele Pianta and Luisa Bentivogli. Knowledge intensive word alignment with KNOWA. In *Proceedings of the 20th International Conference on Computational Linguistics (COLING)*, pages 1086–1092, Geneva, Switzerland, 2004. DOI: 10.3115/1220355.1220511 Cited on page(s) 103

Jessie Pinkham, Kevin Knight, and Franz Josef Och, editors. *DMMT '01: Proceedings of the workshop on Data-driven methods in machine translation - Volume 14*, Stroudsburg, PA, USA, 2001. Cited on page(s) 36

Maja Popovic and Hermann Ney. Improving word alignment quality using morpho-syntactic information. In *Proceedings of the 20th International Conference on Computational Linguistics (COLING)*, pages 310–314, Geneva, Switzerland, 2004. DOI: 10.3115/1220355.1220400 Cited on page(s) 103

Vasin Punyakanok and Dan Roth. Inference with classifiers: The phrase identification problem. *UIUC Technical Report*, 2005. Cited on page(s) 83

Reinhard Rapp. Identifying word translations in non-parallel texts. In *Proceedings of the 33rd Annual Meeting of the Association for Computational Linguistics (ACL)*, 1995. DOI: 10.3115/981658.981709 Cited on page(s) 1, 34

Reinhard Rapp, Eric Gaussier, and Pascale Fung, editors. *Proceedings of the 3rd Workshop on Building and Using Comparable Corpora: from Parallel to Non-parallel Corpora*. ELRA, Valetta, Malta, 2010. Cited on page(s) 36

Philip Resnik. Mining the web for bilingual text. In *Proceedings of the 37th Annual Meeting of the Association of Computational Linguistics (ACL)*, 1999. DOI: 10.3115/1034678.1034757 Cited on page(s) 32

Philip Resnik and Noah A. Smith. The web as a parallel corpus. *Comput. Linguist.*, 29:349–380, September 2003. DOI: 10.1162/089120103322711578 Cited on page(s) 17, 30, 32, 33

Philip Resnik, Mari Olsen, and Mona Diab. The bible as a parallel corpus: Annotating the 'book of 2000 tongues'. *Computers and the Humanities*, 33:129–153, 1999. ISSN 0010-4817. DOI: 10.1023/A:1001798929185 Cited on page(s) 56

Annette Rios, Anne Göhring, and Martin Volk. A quechua-spanish parallel treebank. In *Proceedings of 7th Conference on Treebanks and Linguistic Theories (TLT)*, Groningen, The Netherlands, 2009. Cited on page(s) 121

Markus Saers. *Translation as Linear Transduction : Models and Algorithms for Efficient Learning in Statistical Machine Translation.* PhD thesis, Uppsala University, Department of Linguistics and Philology, 2011. Cited on page(s) 118, 120, 122

Markus Saers and Dekai Wu. Improving phrase-based translation via word alignments from stochastic inversion transduction grammars. In *Proceedings of the Third Workshop on Syntax and Structure in Statistical Translation (SSST-3)*, pages 28–36, Boulder, Colorado, 2009. DOI: 10.3115/1626344.1626348 Cited on page(s) 104, 116, 118, 121

Markus Saers, Joakim Nivre, and Dekai Wu. Learning stochastic bracketing inversion transduction grammars with a cubic time biparsing algorithm. In *Proceedings of the 11th Internationa Conference on Parsing Technology (IWPT)*, pages 29–32, Paris, 2009. DOI: 10.3115/1697236.1697242 Cited on page(s) 120

Markus Saers, Joakim Nivre, and Dekai Wu. A systematic comparison between inversion transduction grammar and linear transduction grammar for word alignment. In *Proceedings of SSST-4, 4th Workshop on Syntax and Structure in Statistical Translation*, pages 10–18, Beijing, China, 2010. Cited on page(s) 104, 122

Erik F. Tjong Kim Sang. Converting the scania framemaker documents to tei sgml. Technical report, Department of Linguistics, Uppsala University, 1996. Cited on page(s) 30

Alexander Schrijver. *Combinatorial Optimization - Polyhedra and Efficiency*, volume 24 of *Algorithms and Combinatoric*. Springer-Verlag, Berlin, 2003. Cited on page(s) 94

Nasredine Semmar and Christian Fluhr. Arabic to french sentence alignment: exploration of a cross-language information retrieval approach. In *Proceedings of the 2007 Workshop on Computational Approaches to Semitic Languages: Common Issues and Resources*, pages 73–80, 2007. DOI: 10.3115/1654576.1654589 Cited on page(s) 57

Michel Simard. Text-translation alignment: Three languages are better than two. In *Proceedings of the Joint Conference on Empirical Methods in Natural Language Processing and Very Large Corpora (EMNLP/VLC)*, 1999. Cited on page(s) 53

Michel Simard and Philippe Langlais. Statistical translation alignment with compositionality constraints. In *HLT-NAACL 2003 Workshop: Building and Using Parallel Texts: Data Driven Machine Translation and Beyond*, Edmonton, Alberta, Canada, 2003. DOI: 10.3115/1118905.1118909 Cited on page(s) 103

Michel Simard and Pierre Plamondon. Bilingual sentence alignment: Balancing robustness and accuracy. In *Proceedings of the Conference of the Association for Machine Translation in the Americas*, 1996. DOI: 10.1023/A:1008010319408 Cited on page(s) 3, 48, 49, 51, 53

Michel Simard, George F. Foster, and Pierre Isabelle. Using cognates to align sentences in bilingual corpora. In *CASCON '93: Proceedings of the 1993 conference of the Centre for Advanced Studies on Collaborative research*, pages 1071–1082, 1993. Cited on page(s) 51, 56

Anil Kumar Singh and Samar Husain. Comparison, selection and use of sentence alignment algorithms for new language pairs. In *Proceedings of the ACL Workshop on Building and Using Parallel Texts*, pages 99–106, Ann Arbor, Michigan, 2005. DOI: 10.3115/1654449.1654469   Cited on page(s) 57

Frank Smadja, Vasileios Hatzivassiloglou, and Kathleen R. McKeown. Translating collocations for bilingual lexicons: A statistical approach. *Computational Linguistics*, 22(1), 1996. Cited on page(s) 6, 86, 103, 126

Richard Sproat, Tao Tao, and ChengXiang Zhai. Named entity transliteration with comparable corpora. In *Proceedings of the 21st International Conference on Computational Linguistics and 44th Annual Meeting of the Association for Computational Linguistics*, pages 73–80, Sydney, Australia, 2006. DOI: 10.3115/1220175.1220185   Cited on page(s) 34

Ralf Steinberger, Bruno Pouliquen, and Johan Hagman. Cross-lingual document similarity calculation using the multilingual thesaurus eurovoc. In *In CICLing*, page 415, 2002. Cited on page(s) 31

Ralf Steinberger, Bruno Pouliquen, Anna Widiger, Camelia Ignat, Tomaž Erjavec, Dan Tufiş, and Dániel Varga. The jrc-acquis: A multilingual aligned parallel corpus with 20+ languages. In *Proceedings of the 5th International Conference on Language Resources and Evaluation (LREC)*, Genoa, Italy, 2006. DOI: 10.1007/3-540-45715-1_44   Cited on page(s) 125

Ben Taskar, Lacoste-Julien Simon, and Dan Klein. A discriminative matching approach to word alignment. In *Proceedings of the Human Language Technology Conference and the Conference on Empirical Methods in Natural Language Processing (HLT/EMNLP*, pages 73–80, Vancouver, British Columbia, Canada, 2005. DOI: 10.3115/1220575.1220585   Cited on page(s) 12, 87, 89, 92, 93, 94, 95

Jörg Tiedemann. Combining clues for word alignment. In *Proceedings of the Meeting of the European Chapter of the Association of Computational Linguistics (EACL)*, 2003a. DOI: 10.3115/1067807.1067852   Cited on page(s) 80, 81, 103

Jörg Tiedemann. Word to word alignment strategies. In *Proceedings of the 20th International Conference on Computational Linguistics (COLING)*, pages 212–218, Geneva, Switzerland, 2004. DOI: 10.3115/1220355.1220386   Cited on page(s) 81

Jörg Tiedemann. News from OPUS - A collection of multilingual parallel corpora with tools and interfaces. In N. Nicolov, K. Bontcheva, G. Angelova, and R. Mitkov, editors, *Recent Advances in Nat-*

ural Language Processing, volume V, pages 237–248. John Benjamins, Amsterdam/Philadelphia, Borovets, Bulgaria, 2009a. Cited on page(s) 2, 56

Jörg Tiedemann. Automatic construction of weighted string similarity measures. In *Proceedings of the Joint Conference on Empirical Methods in Natural Language Processing and Very Large Corpora (EMNLP/VLC)*, pages 213–219, University of Maryland, MD, 1999a. Cited on page(s) 88

Jörg Tiedemann. Word alignment - step by step. In *Proceedings of the 12th Nordic Conference on Computational Linguistics (NODALIDA)*, pages 216–227, University of Trondheim, Norway, 1999b. Cited on page(s) 100, 101

Jörg Tiedemann. *Recycling Translations – Extraction of Lexical Data from Parallel Corpora and their Application in Natural Language Processing*. PhD thesis, Uppsala University, Uppsala, Sweden, 2003b. Cited on page(s) 101

Jörg Tiedemann. Optimisation of word alignment clues. *Natural Language Engineering*, 11(03): 279–293, 2005. Special Issue on Parallel Texts. DOI: 10.1017/S1351324905003864 Cited on page(s) 87, 103

Jörg Tiedemann. Improved sentence alignment for movie subtitles. In *Proceedings of the Conference on Recent Advances in Natural Language Processing (RANLP'07)*, pages 582–588, Borovets, Bulgaria, 2007. Cited on page(s) 9, 47, 54, 55

Jörg Tiedemann. Synchronizing translated movie subtitles. In *Proceedings of the 6th International Language Resources and Evaluation (LREC'08)*, Marrakech, Morocco, 2008. Cited on page(s) 54, 55, 56

Jörg Tiedemann. Evidence-based word alignment. In *Proceedings of the RANLP Workshop on Natural Language Processing Methods and Corpora in Translation, Lexicography, and Language Learning*, pages 28–32, Borovets, Bulgaria, 2009b. Cited on page(s) 87, 89, 103

Jörg Tiedemann. Lingua-align: An experimental toolbox for automatic tree-to-tree alignment. In *Proceedings of the 7th International Conference on Language Resources and Evaluation (LREC'2010)*, Valetta, Malta, 2010. Cited on page(s) 109, 111

Jörg Tiedemann and Gideon Kotzé. A discriminative approach to tree alignment. In *Proceedings of the RANLP Workshop on Natural Language Processing Methods and Corpora in Translation, Lexicography, and Language Learning*, pages 33 – 39, Borovets, Bulgaria, 2009a. Cited on page(s) 110, 111

Jörg Tiedemann and Gideon Kotzé. Building a large machine-aligned parallel treebank. In Marco Passarotti, Adam Przepiórkowski, Savina Raynaud, and Frank Van Eynde, editors, *Proceedings of the 8th International Workshop on Treebanks and Linguistic Theories (TLT'08)*, pages 197–208. EDUCatt, Milano/Italy, 2009b. Cited on page(s) 110, 111

John Tinsley, Ventsislav Zhechev, Mary Hearne, and Andy Way. Robust language pair-independent sub-tree alignment. In *Proceedings of the MT Summit XI*, 2007. Cited on page(s) 107, 108

Kristina Toutanova, H. Tolga Ilhan, and Christopher D. Manning. Extentions to HMM-based statistical word alignment models. In *Proceedings of the Conference on Empirical Methods in Natural Language Processing (EMNLP)*, pages 87–94, Philadelphia, 2002. DOI: 10.3115/1118693.1118705 Cited on page(s) 73, 103

Dan Tufiş. A cheap and dast way to build useful translation lexicons. In *Proceedings of the International Conference on Computational Linguistics (COLING)*, 2002. DOI: 10.3115/1072228.1072230 Cited on page(s) 6, 103

Dan Tufiş, Radu Ion, and Nancy Ide. Fine-grained word sense disambiguation based on parallel corpora, word alignment, word clustering and aligned wordnets. In *Proceedings of the 20th International Conference on Computational Linguistics (COLING)*, Stroudsburg, PA, USA, 2004. DOI: 10.3115/1220355.1220547 Cited on page(s) 6

Dan Tufiş, Radu Ion, Alexandru Ceauşu, and Dan Ştefănescu. Improved lexical alignment by combining multiple reified alignments. In *Proceedings of the 11th Conference of the European Chapter of the Association for Computational Linguistics*, Trento, Italy, 2006. Cited on page(s) 104

Jakob Uszkoreit, Jay M. Ponte, Ashok C. Popat, and Moshe Dubiner. Large scale parallel document mining for machine translation. In *Proceedings of the 23rd International Conference on Computational Linguistics*, pages 1101–1109, 2010. Cited on page(s) 33, 34

Masao Utiyama and Hitoshi Isahara. Reliable measures for aligning Japanese-English news articles and sentences. In Erhard Hinrichs and Dan Roth, editors, *Proceedings of the 41st Annual Meeting of the Association for Computational Linguistics*, pages 72–79, 2003. DOI: 10.3115/1075096.1075106 Cited on page(s) 36

Antal van den Bosch. *Learning to pronounce written words: A study in inductive language learning*. PhD thesis, Maastricht University, 1997. Cited on page(s) 83

Pim van der Eijk. Automating the acquisition of bilingual terminology. In *Proceedings of the Meeting of the European Chapter of the Association of Computational Linguistics (EACL)*, 1993. DOI: 10.3115/976744.976759 Cited on page(s) 103

Lonneke van der Plas and Jörg Tiedemann. Finding medical term variations using parallel corpora and distributional similarity. In *Proceedings of the 6th Workshop on Ontologies and Lexical Resources (OntoLex 2010*, pages 28–37, Beijing, China, 2010. Cited on page(s) 103

Lonneke van der Plas and Jörg Tiedemann. Finding synonyms using automatic word alignment and measures of distributional similarity. In *Proceedings of the 21st International Conference on Computational Linguistics and 44th Annual Meeting of the Association for Computational Linguistics; Main Conference Poster Sessions*, pages 866–873, Sydney, Australia, 2006. Cited on page(s) 6

Gertjan van Noord. Textcat – implementation of the algorithm presented in Cavnar, W. B. and J. M. Trenkle, "N-Gram-Based Text Categorization" In Proceedings of Third Annual Symposium on Document Analysis and Information Retrieval, Las Vegas, NV, UNLV Publications/Reprographics, pp. 161-175, 1994. `http://www.let.rug.nl/~vannoord/TextCat/`, 2006. Cited on page(s) 29

Jean Véronis and Philippe Langlais. Evaluation of parallel text alignment systems: The arcade project. In *Parallel Text Processing, Kluwer Academic Publishers, Text, Speech and Language Technology Series*, pages 369–388, 2000. Cited on page(s) 19, 100

David Vilar, Maja Popovic, and Hermann Ney. AER: do we need to "improve" our alignments? In *Proceedings of the International Workshop on Spoken Language Translation*, Kyoto, Japan, 2006. Cited on page(s) 104

Begoña Villada Moirón and Jörg Tiedemann. Identifying idiomatic expressions using automatic word-alignment. In *Proceedings of the EACL Workshop on Multiword Expressions in a Multilingual Context*, Trento, Italy, 2006. Cited on page(s) 6

Andrew Viterbi. Error bounds for convolutional codes and an asymptotically optimum decoding algorithm. *IEEE Transactions on Information Theory*, 1967. DOI: 10.1109/TIT.1967.1054010 Cited on page(s) 73

Stephan Vogel. Pesa: Phrase pair extraction as sentence splitting. In *in Proceedings: the tenth Machine Translation*, 2005. Cited on page(s) 104

Stephan Vogel, Hermann Ney, and Christoph Tillmann. Hmm-based word alignment in statistical translation. In *Proceedings of the 16th International Conference on Computational Linguistics (COLING)*, 1996. DOI: 10.3115/993268.993313 Cited on page(s) 72, 73

Martin Volk and Søren Harder. Evaluating MT with translations or translators. What is the difference? In *Machine Translation Summit XI Proceedings*, Copenhagen, 2007. Cited on page(s) 53

Thuy Vu, Ai Ti Aw, and Min Zhang. Feature-based method for document alignment in comparable news corpora. In *Proceedings of the 12th Conference of the European Chapter of the Association for Computational Linguistics*, pages 843–851, 2009. Cited on page(s) 36

Jean Véronis, editor. *Parallel Text Processing: Alignment and use of translation corpora*. Dordrecht: Kluwer Academic Publishers, 2000. Cited on page(s) 1, 6, 25, 60, 86

Jean Véronis and Philippe Langlais. *Evaluation of parallel text alignment systems – The ARCADE project*, chapter 19. Dordrecht: Kluwer Academic Publishers, 2000. Cited on page(s) 104

Taro Watanabe, Kenji Imamura, and Eiichiro Sumita. Statistical machine translation based on hierarchical phrase alignment. In *Proceedings of the 9th International Conference on Theoretical and Methodological Issues in Machine Translation (TMI)*, 2002. Cited on page(s) 121

Dekai Wu. Aligning a parallel english-chinese corpus statistically with lexical criteria. In *Proceedings of the 32nd Annual Meeting of the Association for Computational Linguistics (ACL)*, 1994. DOI: 10.3115/981732.981744 Cited on page(s) 53, 56, 57

Dekai Wu. Trainable coarse bilingual grammars for parallel text bracketing. In *Proceedings of the Third Workshop on Very Large Corpora (VLC)*, 1995. Cited on page(s) 104, 114, 120, 121

Dekai Wu. A polynomial-time algorithm for statistical machine translation. In *Proceedings of the 34th Annual Meeting of the Association for Computational Linguistics (ACL)*, pages 152–158, 1996. DOI: 10.3115/981863.981884 Cited on page(s) 117

Dekai Wu. Stochastic inversion transduction grammars and bilingual parsing of parallel corpora. *Computational Linguistics*, 23(3), 1997. Cited on page(s) 81, 107, 114, 115, 116, 117, 118, 121

Dekai Wu. *CRC Handbook of Natural Language Processing*, chapter Alignment, pages 367–408. CRC Press, second edition, 2010. Cited on page(s) 3, 12, 24, 111

Dekai Wu and Hongsing Wong. Machine translation with a stochastic grammatical channel. In *Proceedings of the 36th Annual Meeting of the Association of Computational Linguistics (ACL)*, 1998. DOI: 10.3115/980691.980799 Cited on page(s) 121

Dekai Wu and Xuanyin Xia. Learning an English-Chinese lexicon from a parallel corpus. In *Proceedings of the Conference of the Association for Machine Translation in the Americas*, 1994. Cited on page(s) 103

Jia Xu, Richard Zens, and Hermann Ney. Partitioning parallel documents using binary segmentation. In *Proceedings on the Workshop on Statistical Machine Translation*, pages 78–85, New York City, 2006. DOI: 10.3115/1654650.1654662 Cited on page(s) 57

Kaoru Yamamoto and Yuji Matsumoto. Acquisition of phrase-level bilingual correspondence using dependency structure. In *Proceedings of the International Conference on Computational Linguistics (COLING)*, 2000. DOI: 10.3115/992730.992781 Cited on page(s) 121

Christopher C. Yang and Kar Wing Li. Building parallel corpora by automatic title alignment using length-based and text-based approaches. *Information Processing and Management.*, 40:939–955, November 2004. DOI: 10.1016/j.ipm.2003.11.002 Cited on page(s) 36

Daniel H. Younger. Recognition and parsing of context-free languages in time n^3. *Information and Control*, 10(2):189 – 208, 1967. DOI: 10.1016/S0019-9958(67)80007-X Cited on page(s) 117

Hao Zhang and Daniel Gildea. Syntax-based alignment: Supervised or unsupervised? In *Proceedings of the 20th International Conference on Computational Linguistics (COLING)*, pages 418–424, Geneva, Switzerland, 2004. DOI: 10.3115/1220355.1220415 Cited on page(s) 121

Hao Zhang and Daniel Gildea. Stochastic lexicalized inversion transduction grammar for alignment. In *Proceedings of the 43rd Annual Meeting of the Association for Computational Linguistics (ACL'05)*, pages 475–482, Ann Arbor, Michigan, 2005. DOI: 10.3115/1219840.1219899 Cited on page(s) 122

Hao Zhang, Liang Huang, Daniel Gildea, and Kevin Knight. Synchronous binarization for machine translation. In *Proceedings of the Human Language Technology Conference of the NAACL, Main Conference*, pages 256–263, New York City, USA, 2006. DOI: 10.3115/1220835.1220868 Cited on page(s) 115

Hao Zhang, Chris Quirk, Robert C. Moore, and Daniel Gildea. Bayesian learning of non-compositional phrases with synchronous parsing. In *Proceedings of ACL-08: HLT*, pages 97–105, Columbus, Ohio, 2008. Cited on page(s) 122

Bing Zhao and Stephan Vogel. Adaptive parallel sentences mining from web bilingual news collection. In *Proceeding of the IEEE International Conference on Data Mining (ICDM 2002)*, 2002. DOI: 10.1109/ICDM.2002.1184044 Cited on page(s) 34

Bing Zhao and Stephan Vogel. Word alignment based on bilingual bracketing. In *HLT-NAACL 2003 Workshop: Building and Using Parallel Texts: Data Driven Machine Translation and Beyond*, pages 15–18, Edmonton, Alberta, Canada, 2003. DOI: 10.3115/1118905.1118908 Cited on page(s) 104

Ventsislav Zhechev and Andy Way. Automatic generation of parallel treebanks. In *Proceedings of the 22nd International Conference on Computational Linguistics (COLING)*, pages 1105–1112, Manchester, UK, 2008. DOI: 10.3115/1599081.1599220 Cited on page(s) 108, 109, 110

Pierre Zweigenbaum, Eric Gaussier, and Pascale Fung, editors. *Proceedings of the 1st Workshop on Building and Using Comparable Corpora: from Parallel to Non-parallel Corpora*. ELRA, Marrakech, Marocco, 2008. URL http://comparable.limsi.fr/bucc-workshop.html. Cited on page(s) 36

Author's Biography

JÖRG TIEDEMANN

Jörg Tiedemann is currently employed as a visiting professor of computational linguistics at the Department of Linguistics and Philology at Uppsala University, Sweden. He got his Ph.D. from the same department in 2003. His work is mainly focused on machine translation, question answering and data mining from multilingual resources. He has initiated and still maintains a freely available collection of parallel corpora (OPUS), which is widely used and appreciated.

Printed in the United States
by Baker & Taylor Publisher Services